"Let it be said of this symposium and of this conference,
that this is where the movement began in America's third century
to build a better life for future generations
of American families, not only American individuals."

Hubert H. Humphrey, June 14, 1977

KIN AND COMMUNITIES
Families in America

Edited by
ALLAN J. LICHTMAN
and
JOAN R. CHALLINOR

Foreword by S. Dillon Ripley
Introduction by Wilton S. Dillon

Smithsonian Institution Press, Washington, D.C., 1979

Cover: *Family Group*, 1944. Henry Moore (British, born 1898); bronze (edition of nine); 14.9 x 10.6 x 7.3 cm (5 7/8 x 4 1/4 x 2 7/8 in.); Hirshhorn Museum and Sculpture Garden, Smithsonian Institution; photograph by John Tennant

Frontispiece: Courtesy Family Folklore Program, Office of American and Folklife Studies, Smithsonian Institution

Designed by Elizabeth Sur

Library of Congress Cataloging in Publication Data
Main entry under title:
Kin and Communities: Families in America
(Smithsonian International Symposia Series)
Proceedings of a Smithsonian Institution symposium
held in Washington, D.C., June 14–17, 1977.
Bibliographies included.
Includes index.
1. Family—United States—Congresses. I. Lichtman, Allan J. II. Challinor, Joan R. III. Series.
HQ536.K48 301.42'0973 78-24246
ISBN 0-87474-608-6
ISBN 0-87474-609-4 pbk.

Other books in this series:

Simon and Schuster:
Knowledge Among Men (1966)

Smithsonian Institution Press:
The Fitness of Man's Environment (1968)
Man and Beast: Comparative Social Behavior (1971)
The Cultural Drama: Modern Identities and Social Ferment (1974)
The Nature of Scientific Discovery (1974)

DEDICATIONS

To those whose love and caring have made my work possible:
my parents, Emanuel and Gertrude Lichtman
my sister, Ronnie
my brother, Steven
and my daughter, Kara

A.J.L.

To my dearest kin
Julia, Mary, Sarah and Tom
and especially to
David Challinor
loyal husband, expert editor
and unfailing supporter of his wife's career

J.R.C.

The Smithsonian Institution gratefully acknowledges contributions in support of the symposium.

American Security and Trust Company

Bendix Corporation

James R. Bird

Bucyrus-Erie Company

Bunge Corporation

Champion Spark Plug Company

Eaton Corporation

Ellis L. Phillips Foundation

Exxon Corporation

Flour Corporation

Ford Motor Company Fund

Harcourt Brace Jovanovich, Inc.

Hoffmann-LaRoche Foundation

I U International

Marriott Corporation

Massey-Ferguson, Inc.

McDonald's Corporation

National Institute of Child Health and Human Development, U.S. Department of Health, Education, and Welfare

National Savings and Trust Company

Pet Incorporated

Ralston Purina Trust Fund

Riggs National Bank

Rockefeller Brothers Fund

Rockefeller Foundation

Roots Foundation

Ruder & Finn

Sperry Rand Corporation

G. Violet Sturgeon

Wenner-Gren Foundation

Weyerhaeuser Company

Contents

Acknowledgments

The editors of this book wish first to pay tribute to Wilton S. Dillon, from whose lively imagination the subject of this symposium sprang in 1970. This was several years before the search for roots became a national pastime, and the study of the family became a dynamic historic discipline. We attribute Wilton's prescience to his extraordinary sensitivity as well as to the wide view of the world he enjoys from his office high up in the Smithsonian's tower.

The symposium itself would have been far less successful had it not been for Carla Borden, Jane Wallace, and Dorothy Richardson who looked to the day-to-day details. Their steady hands and unfailing good humor immeasurably aided those of us whose humor was not always of the best and whose demands were sometimes admittedly excessive.

Due to a series of extraordinary coincidences at a most crucial time, the editors of this book received the help of Priscilla M. Roberts, graduate student from King's College, Cambridge. Her typing was swift and accurate. Her editorial skills embolden us to believe that somewhere on this globe well-written English is alive and well.

Finally, we wish to thank the Challinor family, one and all, who suffered a broken summer vacation so that this book might meet its deadline.

Preface

S. DILLON RIPLEY
Secretary, Smithsonian Institution,
Washington, D.C.

The Smithsonian's academic interests in families and communities lie deep in our institutional past. Almost since its founding, the Smithsonian has been involved in scholarly pursuits to add new knowledge about how human settlements are composed, from ancient sites to modern ecological studies. Our scholars also have had a long interest in the care of the young, a central question in the life sciences. Moreover, increased awareness of museums as vital parts of the world's educational system make us more attentive to families as our first centers of learning. What happens to children in their early nurturing shapes the style and character of institutions as different in scale as the nuclear family and the state. Thus it is appropriate that the publication of *Kin and Communities: Families in America* coincides with the International Year of the Child. Proclaimed for 1979 by the United Nations and member governments, the observance focuses attention on the needs and contributions of children. These contemporary issues can be understood better from the biological, cultural, and historical perspectives of *Kin and Communities* now assembled under the editorship of Allan J. Lichtman and Joan R. Challinor of The American University.

This volume is the major publication to emerge from a two-year Bicentennial education program of which the Smithsonian international symposium of June 14–17, 1977, was the climax. The theme was the inspiration of Wilton S. Dillon, director of Smithsonian symposia and seminars, an anthropologist, who drew upon unanswered questions posed during such symposia now published as *Man and Beast: Comparative Social Behavior* and *The Cultural Drama*. He and Carla M. Borden, sociologist, consulted many colleagues and enlisted their cooperation in organizing a program which remains central to a Smithsonian tradition: studying the ideas and artifacts which accompany the movement of people and the transmission of the cultural dowry of the human family.

A distinguished national advisory panel and an unusual cooperation between the Smithsonian and The American University Department of History helped prepare the gathering of scholars and other interested citizenry in Washington over the two-year period. An audio-cassette of the opening ceremony, June 14, 1977, containing the keynote address by the late Senator Hubert H. Humphrey, is part of the legacy of the "Kin and Communities" program along with this book and other publications to follow.

In addition to hearing essays, participants in the program could find Smithsonian museums filled with reminders of various family inheritances—from nomadic hunters to settled farmers. We had a special exhibition, designed by Richard Ahlborn and assistants from Catholic University, on "Family Reunions." Visitors interested in pursuing the concepts of family and community in natural history could witness, for example, the prairie dog habitat at the National Zoological Park, or the changing flora of the Chesapeake Bay Center. Our art galleries preserve not only family portraits and photographs, but celebrate in other forms of painting and sculpture the basic relationships of parents and children, friends and lovers, as witness the work of Henry Moore and Auguste Rodin. Our festivals of American folklife for years to come will reflect variations on the theme of the 1977 symposium. Our scholars interested in the technology and politics of space exploration also are speculating on what kind of laws and social rules will govern family life in space colonies, and what those space families will know of their earth ancestors when we celebrate the American Tricentennial in 2076.

Alex Haley and Margaret Mead contributed to the "Kin and Communities" symposium, encouraging all people to find their roots and discover their kinship with each other. Mrs. Rosalynn

Carter, just returning from Latin America, urged us to take notice of the warmth and depth of family feelings elsewhere in this hemisphere. Their words reminded me again that I never saw either set of my grandparents face to face, always having to depend on my parents and others for impressions of them, to fill in for myself my own mental pictures of personal links with the larger human family.

In 1871, the Smithsonian contributed to intellectual history by publishing Lewis Henry Morgan's classic, *Systems of Consanguinity and Affinity in the Human Family*. In between that event and today, Smithsonian studies of kinship continue to take biological and cultural forms, and Morgan's theories of cultural evolution—read by Karl Marx and Friedrich Engels—continue to generate debate. In 1977, as part of the "Kin and Communities" symposium, the Wenner-Gren Foundation and Columbia University helped us to arrange a centennial observance of the publication of another Morgan classic, *Ancient Society*, held in the Smithsonian's Dibner Library. The increase of knowledge is dependent upon such legacies, the stimuli of commemorative events, and the support of foundations, corporations, and taxpaying citizens.

The Smithsonian is proud, therefore, to contribute on many levels—personal and scholarly—to knowledge of the families and communities of which we are all a part.

Foreword

WILTON S. DILLON
Director, Office of Smithsonian Symposia and Seminars,
Smithsonian Institution, Washington, D.C.

What have human families in common with those of other creatures who care for their offspring after birth? Where did Americans come from and why did they leave their places of origin? Were they chasing game across the Bering Straits? Were they escaping war, famine, conscription, jail, poverty, or just seeing what was on the other side? Did the new arrivals travel as singles or in family groups, or as whole communities, Pilgrim style? What kinds of linkages or networks evolved to create new communities out of isolated individuals and families? Does a sense of kinship vary from region to region? Do families help in hard times? What are the burdens of membership in dynastic families? Do work, racism, and technology combine to explain how internal family migrations were set into motion? What can individuals today learn of these processes or patterns from their own families? What does the future hold for family institutions, or kin-type social inventions? Do public policies make any difference to strengthening the bonds of families and communities? Who should be responsible for children, the sick, and elderly dependents?

Many other questions could have been asked of the scholars and other citizens who participated in the "Kin and Communities" programs from 1975 to 1977. Out of all the questions and investigations, Dr. Margaret Mead,* who chaired the Smithsonian's two-year program and symposium manifest in this volume, believes that a new time perspective may be one of the most lasting benefits of learning to examine American history through tracing the lives of one's kith and kin as well as neighbors and strangers. A young person today, discovering something about grandparents to tell unborn grandchildren, can quickly understand a span of five generations; discover how close we still are to the formation of this republic out of our Old World roots; and by learning to count in biological generations—twenty-five-year units of time—can realize that the American Tricentennial is not far away.

"Whoever our actual forebears were—the original Americans who met the first European settlers or the newest arrivals—the Bicentennial is for them as well as for us," Dr. Mead wrote in 1975. "And whatever their origin—whether they came from the British Isles, the steppes of Russia, the Great Plains of North America, from the cathedral cities or the little villages of Europe, the rain forests of Africa or the sunny Mediterranean coast, from farms or fishing hamlets or the back streets of ancient cities—they have made our history rich and variegated. Through their lives, the life of our country as a free and independent nation has become our common heritage, and the celebration is a way of binding together the past, the present, and the future for every one of us."

The 1976 celebration may be over, but the curiosity and questions generated during this republic's birthday party are still with us and deserving of attention by citizens at large and especially by teachers in high schools, colleges, and universities. In the United States, the National Archives is preparing for this wave of personal and scholarly interest in family matters to last through the turn of the century. (And in Japan, for example—thanks to Alex Haley's inspiration—young city-dwellers are returning to villages to seek their antecedents.) The educational opportunities are enormous.

This collection of essays is not designed as a didactic textbook, but as a set of readings on which teachers in various disciplines can draw. Whether a curriculum is offered as "general education" or a "core" approach to learning, *Kin and Communities: Families in America* demonstrates the interdependence of various specialties, and the useful interplay of "objective" and "subjective" components of knowledge. The essays of this volume are liberating in the sense that liberal arts education is supposed to excite the mind to find some new connections between "old facts" and propositions from both the humanities and the sciences. This is an enduring aim of the Smithsonian symposia series.

One proposition worth discussing in college or high school seminars, as well as in centers of continuing education, is an observation made by Alexis de Tocqueville in *Democracy in America* (1835): "Democracy loosens social ties, but tightens natural ones; it brings kindred more closely together, while it throws citizens more apart."

Does this proposition still hold today? And if so, what does it mean? What is the importance of kinship in a modern nation-state facing its third century? How do we compare with our mega-state peers, the Chinese and the Soviets, from the perspective of family solidarity versus social and political solidarity? Does participation in a larger political community necessarily mean that kinship ties are loosened, or does a strong family arrangement contribute to strong national or international allegiances? What have families to contribute to creating a sense of community and the responsibilities of citizenship? How do our ethnic heritages help bring both kindred and the larger society more closely together? How do families help preserve and transmit the cultural "dowry" the United States has received from its diverse background?

Such questions will find partial responses in the essays which follow. None can be answered from within the confines of a department of anthropology, history, sociology, economics, or geography. Our times require the holism of Alfred North Whitehead's *Aims of Education* if citizens, including scholars, are to make sense of their personal, vocational, and professional lives, and to understand more fully how the smallest units of society relate to larger communities. In the intellectual and social fragmentation which marks late twentieth century America, nothing seems to me more positive than the growing realization that we all have roots in the same human family—one species with many cultures. Different "blood lines" do not prevent our potential for developing a sense of kindred with each other.

Wars and rumors of wars indeed are still with us. But a new

personalism—some might use the word humanism—has begun to develop as a corollary to the revival of interest in our ethnic and cultural repertories. Witness the civic delight citizens of Baltimore take in their festive flaunting of their multi-cultural neighborhoods when neighborhood flags fly over booths at the city's annual fair. The Bicentennial observance, in a manner more subliminal than the highly visible appeal of the Tall Ships, prompted many Americans to focus on the advantages of being a part of a political experiment—the continuing creating and growth of a community fashioned out of more diversity than perhaps any nation-state or empire has ever attempted. Each of us has multiple identities. Life is more richly textured when we recognize, in ourselves and in others, that we are carriers of culture traits which historically have origins on all the continents.

As Secretary Ripley pointed out in the preface, families are our first centers of learning. Not all parents as teachers, however, are aware of their families as microcosms of historical experience or of their households as living museums. Nor have all professional teachers escaped this country's preoccupation with governance and economics. They, along with the media, have dulled the attention students have given to families as the primal institutions out of which the nation is still evolving. We still tend to blame almost every social ill on the person temporarily occupying the White House. It will take far more than the inspiration in these essays to shift the attention of our citizenry away from the federal cockpit, and to realize that the central government is not synonymous with society. The genesis of *Kin and Communities* can be found in the Watergate and Vietnam traumas. A number of us were prompted to wonder how we could fill in some dangerous gaps in knowledge about the enduring place of families and communities as building blocks in this and other societies, to find some balance in our understanding of the biological, historical, and social processes which spin a web between our smallest social units and the largest institutions. This book is one offering in this direction.

In inviting Allan J. Lichtman and Joan R. Challinor to serve as editors of this volume, I welcomed their Old World roots and their experience as parents, scholars, and concerned citizens in delivering a book which happily falls into a natural sequence with the earlier volumes of this series. For example, the biological and pre-history chapters are links to our *Man and Beast* inquiries of 1969, and several others would have fitted nicely into *The Cultural Drama*, published in 1974. In 1981, we will build upon all the previous symposia in yet another effort at synthesis with a volume to focus on how humans adapt—the biological and cultural factors which determine or influence how we cope with disease, malnutrition, and population.

In welcoming scholars to the 1970 symposium on protest and change, Secretary Ripley's words deserve remembering today: "Here, in the midst of the massive temples of the world's most powerful democracy, we exist as a tiny enclave of encounter, a community of learning, a company of scholars accessible to everyone, a recipient of the nation's treasure, custodian of its past, and guardian . . . of a legacy for its future."

*Dr. Mead died on November 15, 1978, as this volume was going to press.

Introduction

ALLAN J. LICHTMAN
Associate Professor, History Department,
The American University, Washington, D.C.

Rarely has a single theme like the family simultaneously elicited the concern of policy makers, the regard of scholars, and the attention of ordinary Americans. The essays and colloquia chosen for this collection from The Smithsonian Institution's Sixth International Symposium illustrate these multiple levels of interest in family studies. Drawing on disciplines such as biology, anthropology, psychiatry, sociology, and history, the formal articles included in Part I contribute to an understanding of American families and to current debates over family policy. These essays eloquently address some of the most controversial issues of our own time, including, for example, the influences of heredity, environment and historical experience on values and social structure, the effectiveness of intervention in family life, the cultural meanings of kin and community, and the differences between contemporary and past families. The panel sessions included in Part II on family photographs, documents, and oral traditions offer guidance both to scholars of family life and to individuals interested in their own family heritage. The final session, entitled "Whither Families?," analyzes the forces buffeting families today and suggests ways of strengthening the bonds of kinship and community in the United States.

People naturally seek refuge from a troubled present in the nostalgic vision of a more congenial past. Although a few bold social critics proclaim the need to transform the family, more familiar is the assertion that America's social ills are intimately connected with the declining health and vitality of family life. In the keynote address for the Smithsonian Symposium, the late Senator Hubert H. Humphrey admonished that "we are seeing what appears to be . . . a growing disintegration of the family. . . . It is my judgment that the social disintegration that is taking place is the major problem that confronts our society."[1]

As historian John Demos has perceptively noted, a sense of dread and foreboding about changes in American family life unites both conservatives and liberals.[2] Conservatives lament the loss of parental authority, the high rate of divorce, the experiments with new forms of living arrangements, and the disregard of traditional standards of morality. Liberals bemoan the loss of support and security provided by an "extended family" of parents, children, and other relatives, or by close relationships with neighbors and kinfolk. Critics of family life in contemporary America cite cold-blooded statistics on divorce, single-parent families, infant mortality, and juvenile delinquency, as well as more impressionistic evidence of malaise within the family. Along with the "energy crisis," the "pollution crisis," and the "crime crisis," Americans are urged to heed the "family crisis." According to Margaret Mead, "it is time for us to look squarely at the problems that beset families and to ask what must be done to make family life more viable, not only for ourselves now, but also in prospect for all the children growing up who will have to take responsibility for the next generation."[3]

However, while commentators warn of a disintegrating family, millions of Americans are affirming the importance of their family heritage. People are seeking to answer questions about their own identity by reconstructing their family's past. Family history, many Americans are coming to recognize, is a unifying theme that integrates the individual with a continuing process that transcends the limitations of a single life. In the essay selected for this volume, the anthropologist David M. Schneider writes that "the most rootless yearn for roots; the most mobile bemoan their placeless fate; the most isolated yearn for kin and community, for these represent the basic things that for many Americans make life worth living."[4]

Genealogy, the study of a person's lines of familial descent (often presented in the form of a "family tree") has recently flourished in the United States. Once dominated by those seeking membership in hereditary societies such as the Daughters of the American Revolution, genealogy has now become the province of all Americans. But the recovery of a family's heritage means more than filling in the branches of a family tree. The study of personal family history can combine genealogy's emphasis on the background of one's own family and the emphasis of academic history on a broad knowledge of family life and the relationship between the family and the outside world. In this volume's colloquium on family documents, Allen F. Davis noted that a family historian "can reconstruct in written form a family history that goes beyond the mere listing of births, deaths, [and] marriages." By using their imaginations, he stated, people can "breathe life" into the facts of genealogy and perhaps "appreciate and understand what it must have been like to have lived in 1880, 1840, or 1810."[5] Historians of their own family can explore such themes as the structure and dynamics of family life, the attitudes of family members, geographic and social mobility within a family, and the influence on family life of such developments as depression, war, and social change.[6]

Interest in the quest for personal family history has followed an earlier awakening of scholarly interest in studies of the family. In virtually every society, past and present, the family has been the most fundamental and durable of institutions. The family has had the primary responsibility for replacing the population and for protecting, nurturing, and socializing children. It offers love and emotional support to both children and adults and arranges the daily activities of its members. Interactions within the family shape values and attitudes and may determine the opportunities open to individuals during the course of their lives.

This new emphasis on the family is most evident in the discipline of history. Historical studies of the family are part of a general redirection of historical scholarship that began in the 1960s. Traditionally, historians have bypassed the family, focusing instead on prominent individuals and momentous events. "No great man lives in vain," wrote the British historian Thomas Carlyle. "The history of the world is but the biography of great men." Textbooks on American history, for example, usually include illuminating discussions of imposing figures such as George Washington and Andrew Carnegie and of such pivotal episodes as the signing of the Declaration of Independence and the decision to enter World War I. However inspirational and important, such history has little to say about the experiences of most Americans.

Since the 1960s, a self-proclaimed group of "new" historians has sought to understand the experiences of ordinary people. Practitioners of the new history, such as Maris A. Vinovskis, Glen H. Elder, Jr., and John Modell, among the scholars represented in this collection, reject the "old" history's preoccupation with society's elite as well as its concern with the description of particular episodes. These historians concentrate on reconstructing the day-to-day realities that confronted the vast majority of men and women in past times. In the works of the new historians, ordinary people become the main protagonists of a rewritten historical script. No longer just the "biography of great men," or the narrative of epic events, history becomes the story of how most people lived and worked, and of the values and expectations that they shared. Reversing the usual interpretation of causation in history, many of the new historians also argue that history proceeds from the "bottom up" rather than from the "top down."[7]

The new history relies heavily on quantitative procedures and theories drawn from the social sciences. Statistical methods are necessary to form collective profiles of groups of inarticulate people whose lives survive only as entries in vital records or perhaps in the reports of census takers and tax collectors. Even in verbal form, statements about large groups are necessarily quantitative and can be verified reliably only by systematic forms of analysis. Students of family history try to use tested methods of statistical analysis and to study entire groups by means of random samples of individuals drawn from the group. Unlike traditional historians, they avoid dependence upon the "representative" individual. Maris A. Vinovskis and Barbara G. Rosenkrantz, for instance, apply techniques of multivariate analysis (a form of analysis that indicates how several different variables influence behavior) to information on care of the insane from a Massachusetts census of 1850. Like many of the new historians, however, they do not rely exclusively on quantifiable data, but integrate this material with evidence taken from such written sources as letters, diaries, and government reports. Only through the integration of quantitative and traditional forms of historical research can the historian grasp the meaning of results obtained in numerical form. The ultimate task of the historian is to make such quantitative data available and comprehensible to those interested in family history.

Social science theory supplements the common sense of historians by offering guidelines for organizing and unifying data on families. Many of the central themes of family history—family structure, sex roles, family life-cycles, and social control—arise from the theoretical work of psychologists and sociologists. Theories taken from social science help to explain what happened in the past. Knowledge of theory also expands the imagination of the historian, helping him to make the inferential leap from information about the circumstances of life (for example, age at marriage, number of children, wealth, age at death) to conclusions about the emotional texture of life in the past. What, for example, were the implications of lack of privacy in seventeenth century Plymouth, or the difficulties faced by women on the frontier? Some historians have even sought to test the application of social science theories to different historical conditions. History thus becomes a laboratory for testing and refining generalizations about the behavior of individuals and groups.

Social scientists too are becoming increasingly sensitive to the importance of considering temporal change in their work. Writing about his own discipline, sociologist Michael Gordon noted that, "Until fairly recently American sociology had been remarkably ahistorical, but now a concern with long-term trends is increasingly evident in many areas, especially the family. . . . In fact, the degree of similarity between social-historical work and some historical sociology is so great that it is often difficult to tell if the author of an article in some interdisciplinary journal is a sociologist or a historian."[8] As Gordon's comments indicate, recent scholarship on the family demonstrates a remarkable convergence in the approaches of traditionally separate disciplines. Not only are many studies avowedly interdisciplinary in intent, but the perspectives of different disciplines are also becoming difficult to distinguish. Irrespective of their disciplinary affiliation, most of the authors represented in this volume integrate historical study with theory taken from the social sciences.

In his commentary on several of the papers in this collection, the historian Bernard Bailyn observed that the combination of history and social science has turned the attention of scholars away from the "manifest, palpable, and hence headline" events of an era and toward "latent events" that "did not lie in the consciousness of the people of the time." These latent events are actually "discovered by historians" using concepts derived from social science; they are not events "that participants themselves were aware of and hence that spring out of the self-conscious documentation of the past." People of the eighteenth century, for instance, may not have been aware of changes in the ages of marriage or declining respect for traditional social statuses. Yet these are major issues that scholars "are now discussing in great detail."[9]

The melding of history, quantification, and social science theory also influences the capacity of scholars to communicate with a wide audience. At the same time that scholars are urging increased cooperation across disciplines, they are in danger of isolating one another through technical language that is incomprehensible to all but the trained specialist. Problems of communication create yet a wider gulf between the scholar and the public. Often filled with statistics and the jargon of social science, recent work on the family may be impenetrable to most readers. Non-scholars interested in the substance of family studies may not even be able to grasp the issues that are being addressed. Despite the complexity of their work, scholars should strive to write in clear and graceful prose and, when appropriate, to explain technical matters in ordinary language. A major objective of this collection is to communicate the results of sophisticated research to a general audience, not necessarily equipped with a specialized vocabulary.

The first two articles included in Part I, Devra G. Kleiman, "Lessons from Nature? Monogamy Among Humans and Other Mammals," and T. Dale Stewart, "The First Americans: Migrations to a New World," take a broad approach to the study of families. Although works on the family often integrate history and social science, they rarely include contributions from the science of biology. A major exception to this generalization is Edward Osborne Wilson, *Sociobiology: The New Synthesis.* Wilson argues in this important and controversial book that the course of human affairs from prehistoric times to the present can best be explained by a biological analysis of man and his environment.

Although Kleiman does not embrace Wilson's biological determinism she demonstrates the relevance of biology to the analysis of the forms assumed by human as well as by animal families. Kleiman's essay refutes naive views of what constitute *natural* arrangements of parents and offspring and of what social relations are most compatible with the maintenance of monogamy. Kleiman notes that mammalian methods of reproduction and nurture favor polygyny, the mating of a single male with many females. Monogamous mating strategies are, in fact, very rare, and associated with conditions peculiar to certain species. Types of monogamy also vary according to factors such as the structure of mammalian groups, male contributions to nurture, the quality of relationships between bonded pairs, and the timing of the eventual dispersal of offspring. Kleiman finds similar variations in human monogamy linked to these same factors. Most striking is her conclusion that monogamy has evolved in human societies under conditions "inconsistent with what is known of monogamy in other mammals." Kleiman's analysis implicitly challenges the assertions both of those who maintain that equality for women is inconsistent with traditional family life and of those who claim that equality can be achieved only with the abolition of marriage and the family. Rather, she argues that greater equity between sexes in the social and economic spheres and increased parental care by fathers are features of life that actually sustain monogamy among other mammals. Male dominance and sex role differentiation, in contrast, are characteristics more suitable to polygyny than monogamy.

In broad strokes, covering many thousands of years, Stewart chronicles the migrations of peoples to North America prior to the first landing of Christopher Columbus in 1492. Stewart dates the first peopling of America at least twelve thousand years ago. He notes that a relatively homogeneous group of Asians crossed a land bridge into Alaska and spread rapidly to the southern tip of South America. Interactions with European migrants after 1492 led to a drastic decline in the population of these First Americans, making possible the vast migrations of the Second Americans in the nineteenth and twentieth centuries. This historical process, Stewart concludes, explains why "the remaining First Americans find themselves a minority group striving for identity in the vast lands which they were the first to discover and settle."

In contrast to the broad perspective of the two previous works, David F. Musto, "Continuity Across Generations: The Adams Family Myth," considers the detailed analysis of individual families. In this important article, Musto argues that families pass on from one generation to the next a common view of the world and of the family's place in it. In his view, this "family myth" becomes an interpretation of the "myriad events" of daily life that "is as natural and imperceptible as breathing." Musto aptly notes that study of how such continuity is "achieved or missed" and of whether new identities can be shaped through changes in family structure or outside intervention, has profound implications for policy in such realms as penology, mental health, childcare, and welfare. Musto specifically applies the notion of the family myth to four generations of the illustrious Adams family of New England. He concludes that the family imposed on each generation of Adams men the conviction that their destiny was to become leaders of the nation's foreign and domestic affairs; anything less would be regarded as failure. Moreover, the "merited reward" of national prominence "should never be sought by political maneuvers, but rather should be awaited patiently and confidently." Few family members, Musto concludes, could withstand the pressures of this family myth. Musto's work thus suggests that to understand how an individual confronts the world, it may be necessary to study several generations of a family's history.

The next three articles, Glen H. Elder, Jr., and Richard C. Rockwell, "The Depression Experience in Men's Lives"; John Modell, "Changing Risks, Changing Adaptations: American Families in the Nineteenth and Twentieth Centuries"; and Jacquelyne Johnson Jackson and Bertram Emmanuel Walls, "Aging Patterns in Black Families," all focus on the theme of "life cycles." Scholars now recognize that families as well as individuals have a life cycle of their own. Families are now regarded not as static entities that can neatly be pigeonholed into such categories as "nuclear family" or "extended family," but as arrangements for coping with life that change and evolve over time.

The first of these three papers continues Elder's seminal work on how economic deprivation during the Great Depression affected family life and individual development. In their essay Elder and Rockwell caution against global generalizations on how historical change affects the values and life chances of individuals. They note that what happens during the full course of a person's life mediates the effects of earlier episodes, that individuals encounter events at different stages in their lives, and that people experience events in different ways. Not all families, for instance, suffered economic distress during the 1930s. The burdens of economic deprivation were also greater for those who were children rather than adolescents during the Great Depression. Yet many of the children from deprived households were able to adopt strategies for occupational advancement that led to success in their worklife. Occupational success, in turn, mitigated the effects of the depression years on men's values and attitudes. Elder and Rockwell discovered that a pronounced emphasis on materialism and security primarily characterized only those who failed to achieve a relatively successful worklife. Values such as income and job security, the authors observe, "were subordinated to life quality matters in the social world of men who rose above the limitations of family deprivation through worklife advancement."

Whereas Elder and Rockwell explore the effects of an economic crisis that occurred at a specific stage in the family cycle, Modell examines changes in family life from the nineteenth to the twentieth century. Greater uncertainty and risk in the earlier period, Modell contends, produced distinct patterns of economic cooperation within the family and introduced variations in family life "not reflected in ideal statements about modal families under average conditions." Modell's study exposes the fallacy of glorifying the past as a golden age of family harmony and stability. If families today are more likely to be disrupted voluntarily by divorce, families of the past, he demonstrates, were more likely to be disrupted involuntarily by death, disease, and economic distress. Modell challenges the supposition that modernization has undermined the traditional form of the "ideal" family and thus led to greater variation and spontaneity within families. He suggests instead that declining uncertainty in the twentieth century has actually "led to diminished variety in family life."

Jackson and Walls examine the Black family in the latter stages of its life cycle, considering whether the kinship networks of aged blacks in contemporary America differ significantly from those of aged whites. The authors contribute to recent efforts to replace conjecture and guesswork about black families with the careful analysis of available evidence. Their study draws an important distinction between the effects on behavior of a distinctive black culture and of "institutionalized racism," a sustained and systematic pattern of discrimination. Contrary to the conventional wisdom, their review of the evidence reveals more "similarity than dissimiliarity" between the kinship networks of aged blacks and whites. The "few differences" which do emerge, they argue, "can best be explicated not by race, but by institutionalized racism."

The next three articles, David M. Schneider, "Kinship, Community, and Locality in American Culture"; Seena B. Kohl, "The Making of a Community: The Role of Women in an Agricultural Setting"; and Barbara G. Rosenkrantz and Maris A. Vinovskis, "Caring for the Insane in Ante-Bellum Massachusetts: Family, Community, and State Participation," also center on a common theme, the interactions between families and communities. Schneider's paper, the most theoretical of the contributions to this collection, examines neither "real" nor "ideal" behavior, but rather the systems of symbols that are part of the notions of kinship and community in American culture. According to Schneider, culture gives meaning to all forms of social action. In his view, elements of culture like kinship and community have a "material or substantive element" as well as a "code for conduct." Although the substance of kinship is blood and the substance of community is locality, they have a common code, termed "diffuse, enduring solidarity," colloquially translated as "love." This common code for conduct means that both kinship and community are symbols of unity and part of the same "galaxy of American culture." In contrast, the galaxy of work and commerce is marked by a code for conduct that includes the pursuit of self-interest and the rational calculation of costs and benefits. Further analysis of this rift within American culture would help explain both the stresses experienced by American families and our current yearning to discover the people and places of our family's past.

Kohl's paper chronicles the contribution of women to stages in the settlement of a frontier community in Saskatchewan, Canada. Since the region had been settled fairly recently, she was able to supplement written sources with the oral recollections of actual settlers. Her work demonstrates the crucial role of women in maintaining the settlement and in forging a community life in which people were bound together, not only by shared tasks and activities, but also by shared sentiment. In addition to performing traditional household jobs, women "were full participants . . . in the development of an economic enterprise which laid the base for contemporary agriculture." Women also became carriers of culture within the community as well as "household managers and quartermasters," setting "the style and substance of consumption."

Rosenkrantz and Vinovskis address in their essay one of the most notable trends in the modernization of American society: the assumption of responsibility for family welfare by organizations outside the family. Since the era of the American Revolution, families have become increasingly dependent upon the judgment and authority of experts such as doctors, lawyers, and social workers. And families have become more and more reliant on the services of institutions such as hospitals and asylums. The authors document the shift away from family care for the insane in ante-bellum Massachusetts, showing that the government both assumed financial responsibility for the insane and established asylums for their treatment. Using sophisticated methods of multivariate analysis, Rosenkrantz and Vinovskis further demonstrate that the "elderly insane were much less likely to be in an asylum than their younger counterparts." Elderly people had become the "invisible insane" of ante-bellum Massachusetts, excluded from asylums because superintendents incorrectly regarded them as incurable.

Rosenkrantz and Vinovskis further discuss the dreary history of the asylum in nineteenth century Massachusetts. Asylums were originally founded by optimistic, humane reformers intent upon offering the best available therapy to the mentally ill. For the government supporting these asylums, however, the goals of controlling costs and finding convenient custody for those deemed dangerous to society displaced the goal of treating the insane. The reformers themselves also found that curing the insane was far more difficult than they had initially anticipated. By the late nineteenth century the asylum had been transformed from a place of refuge and therapy to an institution for the cheap custody of people forgotten and ignored by the rest of society.

The final essay in Part I, Francis L. K. Hsu, "Roots of the American Family: From Noah to Now," presents an unconventional etiology of the ills besetting American families. Like many other commentators, Hsu diagnoses a family crisis in contemporary America. But he denies that there has been a recent decline in the quality of family life that can be attributed to industrialization, urbanization, or any other trend of the past few centuries. Rather, he argues that our short-sighted analysis of modernization has blinded us to the essential continuity of families in America. Despite significant variation across time and space, Hsu contends that family life in the Western world primarily reflects an individualism that has been part of the Western tradition for thousands of years. In contrast to Chinese society, Hsu maintains, Western society has always been "centrifugal or outward looking" and thus characterized by "an atomistic situation in which humans become emotional islands." He contends that all the ingredients of Western family life, including mobility, lack of reverence for parents, struggles for authority, and fragmentation of the kin group, which "social scientists claim to be the results of industrialization," can be identified in the biblical myth of Noah and the great flood. None of these elements, however, are to be found in the Chinese counterpart of the flood myth. If his analysis is correct, Hsu concludes, then none of the currently proposed remedies for the family crisis (for example, increased availability of childcare, stricter treatment of juvenile delinquents, flexible working hours for parents, welfare reform) will be effective. We must achieve, Hsu insists, a revolution of human sentiment in our society by incorporating elements of the Eastern tradition so as to moderate the individualism of our own culture.

Materials collected in Part II of this volume are not essays by individuals, but edited transcripts of colloquia held at the Kin and Communities symposium. Participants in the first three sessions, on "Family Photo Interpretation" (created by my co-editor Joan R. Challinor), "Collecting Oral History," and "Family Documents," discuss the use of these sources in studying the experiences of families and communities. Their comments should be of interest both to scholars and to individuals seeking to discover and preserve the history of their own family.

Photographs have recently become a major source for recovering family history. Although many families may possess few documents that illuminate their past, almost every American family has photographs that may be of interest both to family members and professional historians. Photographs can disclose people's dress and appearance, the kinds of objects they owned, the types of houses in which they lived, the rituals they followed, the places they visited, and the changes that occurred during the course of their lives. Participants in the session on family photographs stressed the need for devising a vocabulary and methodology for analyzing visual images. What conclusions, for example, can be drawn from observations of the ways in which families arranged themselves before the camera? How does the study of snapshots differ from the analysis of formal portraits? Panelists discussed recent trends in photographic work, including the use of professionally-made movies about families as rites of passage for young movie-makers. Participants also considered the study of photograph albums, as well as the use of photographs for teaching history and for releasing memories of family life.

Oral history is the effort to elicit and record people's recollections of their experiences, their beliefs and attitudes, their skills and accomplishments. All of us carry traditions that are passed on by word of mouth and never written. Locked in our memories, as well, are fascinating details of personal and family history that are invariably lost to posterity. Both historians and folklorists are now aware that the oral histories of individuals and groups offer information and insights that can be obtained from no other source. Folklorists are using oral interviews to preserve elements of our traditions such as occupational skills, home remedies, religious beliefs, family legends, and immigrant perceptions of their adopted country. Historians are drawing upon oral accounts to understand the biographies of notable people, to clarify events hidden from public view, and to trace the life histories of ordinary families and individuals. After introductory remarks presenting their approaches to oral history, participants in the session on oral history discuss the ethics and morality of recording people's histories, as well as techniques for conducting and taping interviews.

The inspection of written documents can uncover a family's history for a past time when the taking of oral history is impossible. The marshalling of independent sources of evidence is often necessary for the reliable verification of information about a family's past. Written materials available to family members may not be as richly detailed as oral testimony; but they may include data about names, dates, and places that family members cannot accurately supply. Information unknown to surviving relatives may also be inserted in documents. Written sources relevant to family history include Bibles, letters, and diaries found in the home; deeds, wills, and birth certificates located in county courthouses; census returns, and passenger arrival lists stored in the National Archives and Records Service. Participants in the colloquia on family documents consider, in turn, the use of personal papers collected from a member of one's own family; the location and use of key state and local documents; the types of records available from the federal government; and the translation of documents into written history.

The final selection, "Whither Families?," includes reflections by some of the nation's most distinguished students of the family. These panelists explore such key issues as whether geographic mobility and patterns of residence are weakening family ties and whether we can strengthen the sentiment that unites members of families and communities. In her concluding remarks, Margaret Mead, leader of the colloquium, touched upon fundamental themes guiding the entire symposium. "The panel . . . has recognized," Mead stated, "that the family today is in no great danger. We will still have some kind of families, and children will be reared in them. The problem is, what are we doing to the people in families today; how many of them are suffering; how many of them break up; how many of them are unable to sustain the relationships they want?" Summarizing the symposium, Mead said, "We have attempted to emphasize the relationships between genealogy, interest in one's past, and respect for one's ancestors. All of these should contribute to a sense of identity in the present and to community planning for the future."

Notes

1. Keynote Address, The Smithsonian Institution's Sixth International Symposium, Washington, D. C., June 14, 1977.

2. John Demos, "The American Family in Past Time," *The American Scholar* 43 (Summer, 1974), p. 422.

3. Margaret Mead, "Can the American Family Survive," *Redbook*, February 1977, p. 154.

4. See pp. 165 *infra.*

5. See pp. 302 *infra.*

6. For further discussion, see Allan J. Lichtman, *Your Family History: How To Use Oral History, Personal Family Archives, And Public Documents To Discover Your Heritage* (New York, 1978), pp. 14–47.

7. For an analysis of the "new" history, see Allan J. Lichtman and Valerie French, *Historians And The Living Past: The Theory and Practice of Historical Study* (Arlington Heights, Ill., 1978), pp. 122–52.

8. Michael Gordon, "Introduction," *The American Family in Social-Historical Perspective*, 2nd ed., ed. Michael Gordon (New York, 1978), p. 2.

9. Comments presented at The Smithsonian Institution's Sixth International Symposium, Washington, D. C., June 15, 1977.

Part 1

ESSAYS ON THE FAMILY

Lessons from Nature? Monogamy Among Humans and Other Mammals

DEVRA G. KLEIMAN
Reproduction Zoologist, National Zoological Park,
Smithsonian Institution, Washington D.C.

The fitness of an individual, in genetic terms, depends upon the number of surviving offspring (or amount of genetic material) that the individual contributes to future generations, relative to other conspecifics. Among vertebrates, the sex that invests most in future offspring will be in greatest demand. This results in high levels of competition for mates of the limiting sex and intense sexual selection (Wilson, 1975). The degree of sexual selection strongly influences the social and mating system of a species.

Among mammals, females gestate young internally and after birth feed them with milk, a product of the mammary glands. This greater female output in reproduction results in intense male competition for females in most mammals, and polygyny (one male mates with many females) is the most common mating strategy. Monogamy is very rare (Eisenberg, 1966; Kleiman, 1977).

By contrast, among birds and fish, males can perform the same parental duties as females, except for egg production. And males can theoretically invest more than the females in child-rearing if they assume all responsibility for protection of eggs, incubation, and food provisioning after hatching. Thus, mating systems such as monogamy (one male and one female mate exclusively with each other) and polyandry (one female mates with many males) are more commonly found in these vertebrates.

As with other reproductive and social systems, definitions of monogamy are derived from several sources, including the mating strategy, the rearing strategy, and an emotional or social bond, with the emphasis differing depending upon the animal group being considered. The following definition for mammals encompasses several variables. Monogamy is a reproductive strategy in which a single male and female mate with each other and continue to interact during the rearing of offspring, while maintaining an exclusive and highly specific pattern of social and sexual interaction.

Variation in Monogamy

Among mammals, there is variability in the expression of this reproductive strategy. Such variability arises from (a) the social structure, that is, group size and composition, (b) the amount of parental investment by males, (c) the quality of the relationship in bonded pairs, and (d) the mechanism and timing of dispersal of maturing offspring. In birds, but less so in mammals, an additional factor promoting variability is the duration of the monogamous relationship. Birds may have seasonal or "lifetime" bonds; few monogamous mammals appear to have short-term bonds, lasting only for a single reproductive effort.

Elephant shrews—Rathbun's (1976; in press) pioneering field study was the first to show that elephant shrews (Macroscelididae) are monogamous. Elephant shrews are small insectivorous mammals which have radiated into deserts, bushland, and tropical rain forests on the continent of Africa. They subsist mainly on invertebrates, are cursorial, and rarely use nests, but instead rely on flight and crypticity for protection from predation.

The maintenance of a territory from which other adults are excluded is a joint effort by an adult female and male, although they do not cooperate or act synchronously. Aggression between adults tends to be sex specific, that is, a paired male chases away other males while the female partner keeps the territory free of transient females. Such sex specific aggression results in there being little opportunity for sexual interactions outside the context of the pair bond. That is, sexual infidelity is prevented by limiting the potential for its practice.

What, then, are the characteristics of the elephant shrew pair bond? They are not as we would imagine them. A pair of rufous elephant shrews (*Elephantulus rufescens*) are rarely in the same place at the same time. They neither sleep nor rest together, nor do they forage for food as a pair. Unless the female is in heat, their relations are best described as neutral or antagonistic, and the female rufous elephant shrew often appears dominant. Females may chase the male away when they meet, and may defend a rich food source, such as a termite concentration, from the male. Such social activities as mutual grooming, complex courtship rituals, or the sharing of food, are simply not part of the elephant shrew repertoire. Females are also usually the same size as or larger than males.

Female rufous shrews can breed continuously, and young are born every two or three months. The female comes into heat shortly after giving birth and thus is gestating while lactating and rearing an earlier litter. The mating is short and without complex courtship rituals, probably an evolutionary adaptation to the elephant shrew's susceptibility to predation.

One or two young are born in an advanced stage of development (precocial), and the female keeps them hidden either in a nest (golden-rumped elephant shrew) or some other sheltered site (rufous elephant shrew). However, she spends little time with them other than for suckling. The young develop rapidly and are often driven off by the parents or leave the parental territory before the next litter is born. The male elephant shrew interacts little with his offspring although he may check on them occasionally. His main function appears to be the maintenance of the resources within the joint territory which permits the female successfully to rear the young. Parental investment by the male is therefore indirect; the father does not feed, directly protect, or socialize with his young.

Monogamy in the elephant shrew, therefore, involves exclusivity in mating, little direct parental care by males, and social interactions in which the female is dominant within the pair, but both are aggressive to same-sexed intruders. Bonded pairs are not socially cohesive in that they do not act synchronously or indulge in behaviors promoting cohesion such as mutual grooming or courtship. I have previously referred to this system as *facultative* monogamy (Kleiman, 1977). It is the least recognized form of monogamy in mammals in nature because the pair are rarely together during routine daily activities and casual observations might suggest instead, a solitary and polygynous social and reproductive strategy.

Canids—More socially "advanced" than facultative monogamy is the simplest form of *obligate* monogamy, the major change being the direct incorporation of the male into child-rearing activities, mainly from the time of weaning. Many species of smaller wild dogs and foxes (Canidae) fit this mold. The smaller canids are primarily omnivorous in diet, feeding on invertebrates and small vertebrates, but also on carrion and vegetable matter when available (Kleiman and Eisenberg, 1973). A male and female pair (for example, the crab eating fox, *Cerdocyon thous*, of South America) jointly hold a territory and are usually seen with each other. Typically, males are more involved in territorial maintenance and defense. For example, they scent-mark at higher frequencies than females. Yet, aggression toward strangers is usually sex specific, as in elephant shrews, although occasionally a pair may jointly attack an outsider.

A major departure from the elephant shrew form of monogamy is in the social interaction of the bonded pair. Crab eating fox partners often hunt or forage close together (although they do not show cooperative hunting) and if separated for short periods, will reunite with a greeting ceremony consisting of a raised tail, mutual sniffing and licking of the face. During resting, they may sleep in physical contact, and they periodically groom each other by licking and nibbling. When traveling together, sites within the home range may be alternately scent-marked with urine; both sexes lift the leg for urine-marking using a posture which is similar, but with a slightly different orientation. Thus, bonded pairs leave a joint sign of their presence within their mutual territory.

Aggression within pairs is rarely seen, except during the early stages of pair formation. Males seem slightly more aggressive than females, and are also just slightly larger. Within an established pair, however, conflicts are minimal (Kleiman and Brady, 1978).

Most small wild dogs and foxes only breed annually although some can breed twice a year in the tropics. Mating itself occurs over several days, and during each copulation the pair remains locked together for an average of fifteen to twenty minutes. The two-month-long pregnancy is terminated by the birth of from three to six young in a relatively altricial condition. Young are maintained in a burrow, or nest, which is constructed mainly by the female. The male appears to remain in the territory but to visit the young irregularly during the first few weeks.

At some point, the male begins to bring food back to the den area, initially for the female and only later for the young. Small mammals, birds, or reptiles may be killed and deposited at the burrow entrance or cached by the male. Larger quantities of food which cannot be carried in the mouth are eaten and later regurgitated to the female or young if they exhibit the appropriate begging response—licking the corner of the lips on the muzzle. The young are initially weaned onto partly digested food provided by both parents (the mother also regurgitates food to the offspring and carries dead prey to the den) and then begin to feed on dead prey material. As weaning progresses, the male becomes directly involved with the young, and the family group may begin foraging together. The parents gradually become less tolerant of interactions, and by five months of age the offspring of most canid species are able to forage independently. Eventually the family unit breaks up, and by the time the female is pregnant again, only the pair remains together.

This variant of monogamy is characterized both by direct and indirect forms of male parental investment and by a more clearly manifested social bond between the breeding pair. Although males may be slightly more dominant than females, equality within a pair is the norm. A nuclear family exists only on a temporary seasonal basis.

Other canid species have elaborated on this schema, the main differences being not only the increased male parental care but also the use of older juveniles from previous litters in the child-rearing phase. Jackals and coyotes (*Canis* spp.) commonly show this trait; yearlings remain with their parents and act as helpers for their younger siblings (Moehlmann, 1976). In certain other canid species, this form of obligate monogamy has been carried even further.

African wild dogs (*Lycaon pictus*) range widely over the African savannahs in large packs which cooperatively hunt large game such as zebra, gazelle, and antelope. Typically, only one pair in a pack breeds (Frame and Frame, 1976), and thus more than one litter is rarely born or survives. A pack is an extended family composed of related males and related females, but, except for young littermates, adult males and adult females are unrelated. Nonbreeding females may be littermates of the reproductive female, that is, they may be sisters or daughters. Males are brothers, sons and fathers, nephews and uncles. In a stable pack, one pair is bonded, and only one female becomes pregnant.

The inhibition of reproduction in adults of both sexes is accomplished by aggression of the dominant male or female towards same-sexed relatives. Females tend to be more intensely aggressive than males and may attack if a female relative tries to mate, or may even kill the offspring of a sister, should pregnancy and birth occur (Van Lawick, 1973). Moreover, the pack as a group is loyal to the dominant female and, if another female gives birth, will feed neither her nor her young (Van Lawick, 1973).

When young are born, the mother takes initial responsibility for nursing and protecting them; however, other pack members, both males and females, become involved in guarding the young at an early age. The relative contribution of the father is not known. All pack members bring food back to the mother and her litter. The principal means of food transmission is by regurgitation, since the hunting dog preys primarily on large game which cannot be carried by mouth. Food sharing with the mother begins shortly after birth; the litter size is unusually large[1] so that nursing must create a considerable energetic drain. As the young develop, they are weaned onto regurgitated meat and eventually join the pack in hunting forays.

Within a pack, although regurgitation of food is primarily an adaptation for feeding weanlings and the nursing mother, any adult that begs is likely to be fed. Thus, if an adult other than the mother remains to protect the litter while the remainder of the pack is hunting, it too will be fed. In the wild dog reproductive strategy, there are many nonreproductive animals. However, they contribute genetic material to future generations by aiding in the survival of nephews and nieces. The distribution of food to all pack members, and not just young, is of major importance in promoting cohesion within a pack; the stereotyped food-begging response is derived from a juvenile behavior and undoubtedly functions to decrease aggression within the adults.

One other point concerning the hunting dog is of interest. Both in newborn litters and in adults the sex ratio is skewed in favor of males (Kleiman and Eisenberg, 1973); thus not only are more males born than females, but more survive the adulthood. Aggression among females and female emigration are probably major causes of mortality in females, Thus, the most intensely competitive sex is female. Such a sex ratio is mainly found in species exhibiting polyandry (Jenni, 1974).

Marmosets and tamarins—The marmosets and tamarins (Callitrichidae) are a family of primates endemic to Central and South America. All of the species are small and highly arboreal. They feed on a relatively omnivorous diet, including fruits, insects, and small vertebrates such as lizards. One of the species, the pygmy marmoset (*Cebuella pygmaea*) is highly specialized for feeding on exudates from trees, that is, on sap or gum (Ramirez *et al.*, 1977). All of these monkeys have multiple young in a litter, and since they do not build nests, must carry their offspring, which results in a major energetic drain on the mother. Monogamy, therefore, involves considerable parental investment by males through the aid they provide in carrying young.

The social group may be either a nuclear or an extended family. There are insufficient data from the wild to indicate (a) whether there are species differences in group structure, or (b) the degree to which nonreproductive adults in social groups are kin to the main breeding pair. Certainly, some reproductive-age animals are matured offspring.

In established family groups in captivity, little aggression is seen (Epple, 1975), yet breeding is restricted to one pair. Hearn (1977) has noted that young common marmoset (*Callithrix jacchus*) females will not begin to exhibit estrous cycling as long as they remain in the presence of their parents. Thus, reproductive inhibition is of a physiological nature and not through direct aggression. Adults are, however, extremely aggressive to strangers and, as in the hunting dog, aggression appears to be more intense among females.

Pair bonds are strong, and are mainly characterized by social behaviors, such as resting in contact and mutual grooming. In family groups in, for example, the lion tamarin (*Leontopithecus rosalia*), sexual behavior is rarely observed and is usually restricted to periods of estrus. The pair bond is evident in other ways. Pairs produce a "Long Call" as a duet (McLanahan and Green, 1977) and commonly scent-mark in alternation at the same site (Mack and Kleiman, in press). This synchrony of behavior is similar to that observed in pair-bonded dogs and foxes, and seems only to occur in obligate monogamy where males provide direct help to the female in child-rearing.

Among all marmosets and tamarins, the father and older juveniles become involved in child-rearing within two weeks of a birth. The timing of the involvement appears to depend on the number and size of the offspring (Kleiman, 1977), and this varies not only between species but from birth to birth within individual pairs. In many marmoset species, males and older juveniles begin carrying newborn infants on the day of birth. In large family groups, a considerable portion of child-rearing falls on older siblings, and the father's role is not predominant. This resembles the wild dog pattern.

Carrying young is one major burden in which all family members are involved. A second is feeding the young. Between five and six weeks of age, when lion tamarin infants begin eating solid foods, all members of the family begin to provide food to the infants (Hoage, 1977), and this food sharing is associated with special signals by the donor. The tendency to protect and defend food, which is more typical of mammals, is suspended within the family group situation.

To summarize, there is, in several families of mammals, a form of monogamy termed obligate, in which pair bonds are strong, and sexual infidelity is rare. Such species live in either nuclear or extended family groups, and not only does the father exhibit considerable parental investment, but other kin, such as siblings, uncles, and aunts, also contribute significantly to child-rearing. Kin are, however, usually non-reproductive, either through direct aggression by the breeding pair or via more subtle inhibitory influences. The family as a unit defends its territory (although the reproductive pair are often more synchronous in such activities) and cooperates in food acquisition and distribution. Young animals are the preferred recipients of food, but all family members profit.

The most intense aggression occurs among females, and they tend to be dominant within the family group and to their mate. A breeding female can count on the loyalty of family members and appears to need this loyalty to increase the likelihood of the survival of her offspring. This contrasts significantly with the monogamous strategy exhibited by the elephant shrews, where the female's major need appears to be the maintenance of resources in the territory with which successfully to rear her young.

The lack of direct paternal care by males of species exhibiting facultatitive monogamy suggests that parental investment by males, as we normally view it, is not the major selective force dictating the evolution of this reproductive strategy in mammals. Within facultatitive monogamy, several forces seem to come into play, which derive from the ecological specializations of mammals like elephant shrews (Rathbun 1976, in press). Firstly, the species is of relatively small size and, due to predation pressure, not highly mobile. Secondly, it is territorial but can only defend a territory of a limited size. Thirdly, some essential resources such as food and shelter are clumped, but scattered in time and space. Such resources are rich, but relatively scarce. Under these conditions, a female cannot share a territory with another reproductive female, but cannot defend the necessary resources alone. A male cannot defend a territory big enough to hold more than one female and still be safe from predators. Thus, the male's major investment comes from his indirect participation in parental care through the defense of a common territory, belonging jointly to him and one female.

Among species showing obligate monogamy, some of these conditions may also hold, but the female reproductive burden is great enough to make direct parental investment by a male or older young necessary. This results in the strong pair bond and the maintenance of a family unit.

Human Monogamy

Monogamy in humans seems to include all forms of monogamy as seen in other mammals, yet the behavioral characteristic associated with monogamy in humans differ from what I have described above. Moreover, monogamy in many human societies is culturally imposed and is often not, in fact, the true reproductive strategy. More commonly, men mate with more than a single woman, either successively or simultaneously, thus exhibiting polygyny. Fewer women than men produce children by more than one mate, in part because the reproductive life of a woman is shorter than that of a man. However, monogamy has been described in numerous human cultures, which suggests that it is an adaptive reproductive strategy for humans (West and Konner, 1976).

The factors promoting the evolution of monogamy in humans are unclear, especially since early humans were probably highly social, and lived in tribes or bands (Tanner and Zihlman, 1967; Wilson, 1975). It may be that the need for direct paternal care was the major force promoting monogamy. Such a necessity could have been a result of the increasing dependence of the human infant and its slower maturation rate, which derived from other simultaneously occurring changes, such as increasing brain size. At some point, the child-rearing burden on the female may have increased to the point at which a female needed the involvement of a single male, and other female helpers may not have been available to help since they were also reproducing continuously. The involvement of older offspring would have been minimal, especially for the first eight to ten years of a woman's reproductive life. Humans may, at this stage in their evolution, have been exhibiting contradictory evolutionary tendencies. With a larger brain size, a slower maturation rate of young, and a longer life, they were exhibiting characteristics typical of species adapted to stable environments. Yet, increasing dominance by humans over other sympatric species was leading to a major expansion both of human geographic range and of population numbers. With all breeding females reproducing, humans were also exhibiting characteristics typically associated with opportunistic species adapted to unstable conditions, in which population increases and crashes are common.

Such a unique situation may have allowed humans to evolve monogamy within the confines of a highly social and originally polygynous condition. Thus, bonded pairs had to exist within a larger social system which, because of the greater temptation to sexual infidelity, was an inherently unstable situation. Many culturally-imposed sexual taboos may have derived from this instability, and the more frequent sexual activity observed in humans when compared with non-human primates may have evolved as a major method of reducing sexual infidelity. Whereas, in mammals, monogamy is always associated with intra-sexual competition and aggression, especially among females, such behavior would have been strongly selected against in early human societies, where cooperation between all group or troop members was required, especially within each sex. Also, a nuclear family alone could probably not have survived in the ecological conditions in which humans evolved. Both food acquisition and defense, and protection from predation, still required a larger social group.

As already mentioned, the major variations within human monogamy are the same as in other mammals, and depend on the degree of parental investment by males, the age at which offspring disperse, and the degree to which offspring and other non-reproductive kin aid in child-rearing efforts. In the American suburban-middle-class family, monogamy is typically of the facultative or simple obligate form, depending upon the degree of male investment. Some women rear their children essentially alone, the male being responsible for protecting the home and indirectly providing food through wages received from a job, but having little interaction with the young and a weak emotional bond with both wife and children. Sexual infidelity by the male may be common, since his relationship to his family is so indirect. Under these same external conditions, some men are bonded strongly to their wife and family; it would be interesting to determine whether there is an inverse relationship between the strength of the pair bond and the degree of paternal care, on the one hand, and sexual infidelity, on the other hand. West and Konner (1976) have shown that fathers tend to be closer to their offspring in non-industrial monogamous cultures, but that such factors as the subsistence adaptation and degree of warfare influence the paternal investment.

In Western society today, we rarely see the occurrence of an extended family which includes non-reproductive mature offspring and non-reproductive kin, such as parents, uncles and aunts. This variant of obligate monogamy has developed mainly in societies where population expansion was impossible and territories (or land holdings) limited.

The peculiar ecological and evolutionary conditions in which monogamy may have evolved in humans resulted in the retention of behavioral characteristics more suitable to polygyny. Male dominance is common in social spheres. Men are larger than women, and there is also more male-male competition and greater male aggression. Moreover, sexual differentiation of roles is typical, and males rarely become involved in child care to the degree we observe in other mammals exhibiting obligate monogamy. These characteristics are inconsistent with much that is known of monogamy in other mammals (Kleiman, 1977).

Clearly, humans are extremely flexible and adaptable, both in their social structure and in their social behavior. Currently, numerous alternative social, reproductive, and rearing strategies are being attempted, including "serial" monogamy, and all-female groupings, with males being peripheral in the rearing process. Women are also demanding greater equality in the economic and social sphere, both characteristics which are common to other monogamous mammals. It is certainly too early to determine whether such alternative life styles will be successful. Since the major measure of biological success is the amount of genetic material passed on to future generations (that is, the number of offspring which breed and rear young), and since humans cannot continue expanding in population size at the same rate as they have, it may ultimately be impossible to predict or even judge whether humans would do better to maintain a monogamous reproductive strategy, but make their social behavior more consistent with it (greater paternal care, equality of opportunity, and decreased differentiation of sex roles), or to maintain heterosexual social and economic relationships more consistent with polygyny or polygamy while females rear young either alone or in all-female groups.

Acknowledgments

The research on canids and tamarins was supported by the Smithsonian Research Foundation and the National Institute of Mental Health (MH 25242 and MH 27241). I would like to thank J. F. Eisenberg and K. Ralls for comments on the manuscript.

Note

1. It is worth noting that the hunting dog has the largest litter of any of the canid species—nine to ten pups are not unusual—but it also has the most help in child-rearing.

References

Eisenberg, J. F., 1966. "The Social Organization of Mammals." *Handb. Zool.*, VIII (10/7), Leiferung 39:1–92.

Epple, G., 1975. "The Behavior of Marmoset Monkeys (Callithricidae)." *Primate Behavior*, Vol. 4 (L. A. Rosenblum, ed.), Academic Press, New York, pp. 195–239.

Frame, L. H. and Frame, G. W., 1976. "Female African Wild Dogs Emigrate." *Nature*, 263:227–29.

Hearn, J. P., 1977. "The Endocrinology of Reproduction in the Common Marmoset, *Callithrix jacchus.*" *The Biology and Conservation of the Callithrichidae* (D. G. Kleiman, ed.), Smithsonian Institution Press, Washington, D. C.

Hoage, R. (1978). "Biosocial Development in the Golden Lion Tamarin, *Leontopithecus rosalia rosalia.*" Ph.D. Dissertation, University of Pittsburgh.

Jenni, D. A., 1974. "Evolution of Polyandry in Birds." *Am. Zoologist,* 14:129–44.

Kleiman, D. G., 1977. "Monogamy in Mammals." *Quart. Rev. Biol.,* 52:36–69.

Kleiman, D. G. and Brady, C., 1978. "Coyote Behavior in the Context of Recent Canid Research: Problems and Perspectives, pp. 163–88. *Coyote Biology* (M. Bekoff, ed.), Academic Press, New York.

Kleiman, D. G. and Eisenberg, J. F., 1973. "Comparisons of Canid and Felid Social Systems from an Evolutionary Perspective." *Anim. Behav.* 21:637–59.

Van Lawick, H., 1973. *Solo.* Houghton-Mifflin Co., Boston.

Mack, D. S. and Kleiman, D. G. (in press). "Distribution of Scent Marks in Different Contexts in Captive Lion Tamarins, *Leontopithecus rosalia* (Primates)." *Biology of the Callitrichidae* (H. Rothe, ed.), University of Göttingen.

McLanahan, E. B. and Green, K. M., 1977. "The Vocal Repertoire and an Analysis of the Contexts of Vocalizations in *Leontopithecus rosalia.*" *The Biology and Conservation of the Callitrichidae* (D. G. Kleiman, ed.), Smithsonian Institution Press, Washington, D. C.

Moehlman, P. D., 1976. "Developmental Behavior and Social Organization of Black-backed Jackals (*Canis mesomelas*)." Paper presented at Animal Behavior Society Annual Meetings, University of Colorado, Boulder, June 20–25, 1976.

Ramirez, M. F., C. H. Freese, and J. Revilla, 1977. "Feeding Ecology of the Pygmy Marmoset, *Cebuella pygmaea,* in Northeastern Peru." *The Biology and Conservation of the Callitrichidae* (D. G. Kleiman, ed.), Smithsonian Institution Press, Washington, D. C.

Rathbun, G., 1976. "The Ecology and Social Structure of the Elephant-shrews, *Rhynchocyon chrysopygus* Gunter and *Elephantulus rufescens* Peters." Ph.D. Thesis, University of Nairobi, Kenya.

Rathbun, G. B. (in press). "Ecology and Social Structure of Elephant-shrews." *Z. Tierpsychol.*

Rothe, H., 1975. "Some Aspects of Sexuality and Reproduction in Groups of Captive Marmosets *(Callithrix jacchus)*." *Z. Tierpsychol.* 37:255–73.

Tanner, N. and A. Zihlman, 1976. "*Women in Evolution. Part I: Innovation and Selection in Human Origins.*" *Signs*, 1:585–608.

West, M. M. and Konner, M. J., 1976. "The Role of the Father: An Anthropological Perspective, pp. 185–216. *The Role of the Father in Child Development* (M. E. Lamb, ed.), John Wiley and Sons, Inc., New York.

Wilson, E. O., 1975. *Sociobiology: The New Synthesis.* Harvard University Press, Cambridge.

The First Americans: Migrations to a New World

T. DALE STEWART
Anthropologist Emeritus, National Museum of Natural History, Smithsonian Institution, Washington, D.C.

Evidence of a meager but persuasive nature has led scholars to believe that some time around the tenth century A.D. Vikings from northwestern Europe, who had voyaged to, and set up colonies in, western Greenland, voyaged still farther westward and reached the coast of North America. The remains of one lone occupation area on the coast of Labrador, scanty enough to suggest a brief sojourn, mark the farthest extent of the earliest-known European thrust into this part of the Western Hemisphere. The uncharacteristic failure of the Vikings to follow up on their remarkable navigational achievement and to lay claim to the whole North American continent must rank as one of the greatest missed opportunities of all times; they even failed to maintain their Greenland colonies.

One likely explanation for the Vikings' rapid retreat from Labrador is suggested by the recent archaeological work in that part of North America by William Fitzhugh of the Smithsonian's Department of Anthropology. He found that the Indians there had reached a higher population density in pre-Columbian times than previously suspected. This could mean that these Indians put up stouter opposition to the Vikings than did the Greenland Eskimos. In any case, so far as Europe was concerned, knowledge of the exciting prospects that lay over the western horizon of the Atlantic Ocean existed for the next few centuries as little more than rumors among scholars and as gossip among sailors.

Europeans were not much better informed as to what lay to the east of them. The few intrepid travelers who made their way to

Asia and back, usually taking years to do so, recounted their adventures for a price to recoup their finances. Not all of these accounts were recorded, and those spoken to audiences were often exaggerated in the retelling. One such traveler's account which has become famous is that of Marco Polo of Venice who returned from a long sojourn in Asia late in the thirteenth century. We are indebted for the recording of his colorful account to a scribe who happened to be imprisoned with him shortly after his return. From one copy of Marco Polo's travels that Columbus read in Sevilla, the latter learned of the riches of the Indies and Cathay, and of a land to the east of Asia said to be separated therefrom by a strait called "Anian."

Whether or not the Strait of Anian was anything more than the body of water between Asia and Japan is now anyone's guess. But one thing is sure: Marco Polo was not above embroidering his account of what he had seen. This is evident, particularly as regards the wealth of a place called "Chepangu." He described a palace there as "entirely roofed with fine gold, just as our churches are roofed with lead. . . . Moreover, all the pavement of the Palace, and the floors, of its chambers, are entirely of gold, etc." Very likely the prospect of a place with so much gold formed one of the inducements that led Columbus to undertake his voyage of exploration westward over the Atlantic.

Scholars now believe that Columbus combined the maritime gossip and scholarly rumors from the North with Marco Polo's account of his travels to the East and concluded that the quickest and most direct route to the fabulous East would be by ship straight westward from southern Europe. If he had any inkling of the actual circumference of the earth, he might not have undertaken his famous voyage of 1492, but in this case ignorance paid off handsomely. As we now know, Columbus brought back the first sure evidence of the existence of a "New World," the full vast extent of which would not be fully delimited until the eighteenth century. Also, he brought back from the lands he visited, soon to be called "America," some of the people he met there, for these lands were inhabited: America had already been discovered. Although today we call the inhabitants of Columbus' New World "Indians," and thereby perpetuate his mistaken belief that he had reached the Eastern Indies, more and more we are recognizing the right of these inhabitants to be called "First Americans." By this token we must call all the people whose ancestors reached America in 1492 and thereafter "Second Americans."

Columbus recorded in his Journal his initial impression of the First Americans. It is rather flattering: "[They are] all of good stature," he said, "fine looking; their hair not crisped but straight and coarse like horse hair, head and forehead broader than I have ever seen in any other people; eyes fine and large; none [is] dark hued, but of the color of the Canaries. . . . Their limbs are stai[gh]t, and . . . well formed . . ."

From the beginning the relations between the First and Second Americans seldom were smooth, and rapidly went from bad to worse. The fact that America had already been discovered and peopled meant nothing to Columbus and the explorers who followed him; these Europeans felt they had the right to any lands they could take by force, and especially if the inhabitants were heathen, as the Indians gave evidence of being through their worship of strange gods. Besides, whatever scruples the Europeans may have had in the beginning as regards the treatment of Indians evaporated when gold was discovered, mainly in the Greater Antilles, in Central America and in western South America. With this discovery, the fate of the Indians was sealed. It took less than a half century for the Europeans to find and begin exploiting the main American gold-yielding areas. And as gold began flowing to Europe the size of the Indian population in the regions being exploited plunged downward. To the many Indians slain by sword and gun were added many, many more who succumbed to smallpox and other disease plagues which had slipped in from the Old World to become allies of the Europeans in their conquest.

The effect of European invasion upon the size of the Indian

population is best documented for Mexico. Bernal Diaz del Castillo, one of the foot soldiers who entered that country with Cortez in 1519, recalled many years later that a Negro with smallpox had arrived with Narvaez. Appraising this event, he said: ". . . and a very black dose it was for New Spain, for it was because of him that the whole country was stricken, with a great many deaths." According to one estimate, the Indian population of Mexico dropped about fifteen millions in the first ten years after the conquest.

The full dimension of the great tragedy that befell the Indians in this way was not appreciated for a long time. And by then it was too late to do more than pick up the pieces and try to grasp the extent of lost glories. In my last trip to Mexico City I saw some of those pieces, only recently discovered during the construction of the newly-opened subway. From these and from many other examples we realize now that in 1492 the high cultures of Mexico and Peru—areas often spoken of as "Nuclear America"—held a promise of being able to reach heights comparable to those of such Old World cultural centers as Egypt, Mesopotamia and China.

The contacts of the Europeans with the culturally less-developed Indians outside Nuclear America progressed more slowly, but here too were accompanied by the steady decimation of the inhabitants. As the Indians died off or retreated ahead of European advance, the few that remained would not submit to enslavement. The Europeans were forced, therefore, to introduce blacks from Africa to serve as laborers.

Negro slaves were introduced first into the areas around the Caribbean dominated by Spain and soon afterwards into the Portuguese part of South America. In both these areas the remaining Indians often found themselves in the company of run-away Negro slaves, who like the Indians were trying to hide from the Europeans. Inevitably this association led to miscegenation. Much later when Negro slaves were introduced into the southeastern United States, most of the Indians there had disappeared or were being moved westward. The result is that Indian-Negro miscegenation was less in the United States. Scarcely any Indian-Negro miscegenation occurred on the western side of either North or South America.

European explorations by ship kept pace with those by land and quickly pushed beyond America into the vast reaches of the Pacific Ocean. These European exploratory thrusts revealed that the New World included not only a continuous land mass extending great distances north and south of the places visited by Columbus, but also innumerable islands and archipelagoes scattered throughout the Pacific Ocean. And with few exceptions the widely-spaced specks of land in the ocean, like America, were already inhabited. Furthermore, the Pacific explorations by Bering and Cook made in the eighteenth century continued to reveal new lands, notably a great projecting land mass to the northwest that narrowed the distance between America and Asia to a few miles, and a great continent—Australia—in the southwestern Pacific.

When, toward the end of the eighteenth century, cartographers fitted these latest pieces of discovered land into their jigsaw map of the world, a surprising fact about the New World became apparent: it is widely separated from the Old World everywhere except at two points in Asia. One of these points is, of course, Bering Strait; the other is the sequence of narrow straits separating a chain of islands between Australia and the Malay Peninsula. Seeing this, scholars began to realize that man could not have reached any part of the New World before 1492, except by moving out of Asia at these two widely-separated points.

This broad concept of the New World, which includes in addition to America the lands in the Pacific discovered by Europeans, is not the one held by most Americans. Until I visited Australia a few years ago I, too, was one of those who thought of the New World in the narrow sense. Australian scholars convinced me that my view of this matter was parochial and that from the historical and anthropological standpoints the broad concept is fully justified. Moreover, it brings the peopling of America into better perspective.

The peopling of the Pacific part of the New World is a separate story requiring only two comments: firstly, the people who came out of Asia in that direction were very different in appearance and physical make-up from those who crossed into America at the Arctic Circle; and secondly, the innovativeness of the southeasterly-moving people was not challenged by a climate as rigorous as that experienced by the First Americans.

Since the program in which we are participating was planned as a part of the Smithsonian's celebration of the two hundredth anniversary of the founding of our nation, it is pertinent to mention that one of the wisest of our nation's founding fathers—Thomas Jefferson—was among the relatively few who at that time perceived the source of the First Americans. In his *Notes on the State of Virginia*, written around 1781, he said, in part:

> . . . the late discoveries of Captain Cook coasting from Kamschatka to California, have proved that if the two continents of Asia and America be separated at all, it is only by a narrow straight. So that from this side [of Asia] . . . , inhabitants may have passed into America; and the resemblance between the Indians of America and the eastern inhabitants of Asia would induce us to conjecture, that the former are the descendants of the latter . . .

The route by which the Eskimos reached the northeastern part of America, particularly Greenland, remained a mystery to Jefferson. This was because it would be many more years yet before the continuous distribution of the Eskimos from Greenland westward to Bering Strait and across into northeastern Asia would be established. However, Jefferson conjectured that they, too, came from some northern part of the Old World.

Considering Jefferson's interest in the First Americans and in the lands they had peopled, as further evidenced by the detailed set of observations which he had asked Lewis and Clark to make when he sent them off across country in 1804 to explore a route to the Pacific coast, he must have pondered questions like: When did the First Americans enter the Western Hemisphere? What induced them to make the long journey? What did they bring with them in the way of culture? How different were the American fauna and flora then?

Answers to all such questions had to await the slow progress of the respective sciences. For example, anthropology—the science primarily concerned with these matters—did not become formally organized in the United States until late in the last century, nearly four hundred years after Columbus had brought America to European attention. And by that time most of the remaining Indians of the United States had been relocated, most of their tribal lands expropriated, and their traditional ways of life left largely in disarray. More recently a similar fate has befallen the more remote Eskimos and closely related Aleuts.

In spite of the late start in looking for answers, the remarkable history of the First Americans can now be reliably outlined, thanks especially to the ability of archaeologists, assisted by specialists in other branches of science, to read the signs left in the ground by these immigrants from Asia.

What is the time scale of the peopling of America by the First Americans? A few decades ago Ales Hrdlicka, then the Smithsonian's authority on early man, maintained that the First Americans had been here no more than about five thousand years. Today, thanks to radiometric dating, no one seriously questions that they were here at least twelve thousand years ago. Beyond this, ages in the range of between twenty and fifty thousand years are being advanced, but on the basis either of less convincing evidence, or of questionable dating methods, or both.

The difficulty in finding convincing evidence of man's presence in America prior to twelve thousand years ago is illustrated by the late Louis Leakey's work in California on the alluvial fans which in Pleistocene times spread out into the Mohave Desert from the Calico Hills. Having identified therein some chipped stones which he regarded as primitive human tools, Leakey set about proving that they occurred in "significant assemblages," to use his expression. In the end, after digging deeply into the fans at several points and recovering an assemblage of flaked stones that satisfied him, he failed to convince most archaeologists that the flaking on the stones was anything but natural.

Interestingly, the date of man's first entrance into Australia has been equally difficult to establish. There, too, dates of some twenty to thirty thousand years or more for man's presence have been put forth with much the same variations in persuasiveness. This parallelism rests primarily on the phenomenon of continental glaciation. For over a century it has been known that cyclical changes in climate over long periods of time resulted in the periodic accumulation of ice and snow on the high-latitude portions of the continents during the coldest times. The source of the water represented in the immense quantities of continental ice and snow was the oceans, the world-wide level of which was lowered thereby. Through this sea-level lowering, the shallowest parts of the oceanbeds, most of which border the land masses, were exposed.

Of special significance in the present connection was the emergence of land in the north around Bering Strait and in the south along the island chain between the Malay Peninsula and Australia. At each of these places the emerged inter-continental land is referred to as a "landbridge." The Bering landbridge is now viewed as having provided the First Americans with an easy access from northern Asia to America. And likewise the Australian landbridge, incomplete though it was, provided the First Australians with relatively easy access from southern Asia to Australia and eventually pointed their followers to the other parts of the Pacific portion of the New World.

Geologists have determined that, through some climatic quirk, the Bering landbridge and large continental areas on either side were not glaciated. They call this unglaciated area, which on the

American side included the central part of Alaska, "Beringia." Bordering Beringia on the east was the immense continental ice sheet extending all the way to the Atlantic coast and southward into the upper tier of the United States. These geographical features made the Alaskan end of Beringia a *cul-de-sac* so far as human and animal migrations in that direction were concerned. Therefore, the people of America beyond this point had to await the recession of the continental glaciers.

Although the approximate dates of the opening and closing of the Bering landbridge over the past fifty thousand years are known, only now is attention being focused on man's route southward from Beringia. From all indications, the first route to become available was just east of the Canadian Rockies. That the first route southward was probably in this location is suggested not only by the evidence of glacial recession here, constituting a "corridor," but by a concentration of poleo-Indian sites satisfactorily dated to around twelve thousand years ago in the part of the United States just south of the corridor exit. Whether or not this corridor was available and used by man prior to twelve thousand years ago, seemingly a real possibility, is currently under intensive investigation.

Man was not the only animal to cross from Asia over the Bering landbridge into Alaska in ancient times and then to follow the Canadian corridor into the heart of North America. The remains of many species of the Pleistocene fauna, now extinct, have been found all along this route. They include such large animals as the mammoth, mastodon, horse, bison, and so on—the so-called "megafauna." A mural by the noted biological artist, Jay Matternes, in the Hall of Pleistocene Paleontology in the National Museum of Natural History, shows an assemblage of this fauna in an Alaskan setting with a newly-arrived group of men looking on. Proof of the early association of man and megafauna in Beringia and elsewhere has been found by paleontologists in the form of bands of these animals bearing signs of butchering.

Finds of this sort have led to the hypothesis that man was not just wandering aimlessly, but was being led on by these animals in his search for food. During the greater part of his existence man was a hunter, and at the same time, of course, a gatherer of whatever else was edible. In the Far North his continued existence depended primarily upon hunting. For this purpose he used, among other things, spears tipped with stone blades. A few of the blades have been found with animal bones along the ancient route into America.

Owing to the fact that this migratory process was so slow, perhaps advancing only a short distance in a generation or so, Nature had ample opportunities to obliterate the evidence, either by washing it away or by covering it with wind-blown or water-laid deposits. This means that so far mainly the covered evidence, in the age range of ten to twelve thousand years, has come to light. I saw evidence of this at three Alaskan archaeological sites I was privileged to visit in 1975.

At the first of these sites, actually a complex of sites occupying the whole of Cape Kruzenstern north of Bering Strait, I looked down from a helicopter upon a series of over one hundred parallel beach lines extending back from the coast for up to three miles to a palisade-like cliff. The late Louis Giddings found that the present beach contained the cultural remains of recent Eskimos, and that behind this the former beaches contained evidence of successively older occupations, until on top of the palisade the remains gave evidence of being some ten thousand years old. Unlike many archaeological sites that exhibit vertical stratigraphy indicating the passage of time, Cape Kruzenstern presents a horizontal stratigraphy. This is reminiscent also of tree-ring chronology.

The second site, known as Trail Creek, is located in the heart of the Alaskan Peninsula, some one hundred and twenty miles to the south of Cape Kruzenstern. It consists of several caves in a limestone cliff—among the few caves in Alaska known to be suitable for human occupancy. In one of these caves Helge Larsen, the Danish archaeologist, dug through a succession of occupation levels to discover at the bottom some cultural objects in association with the bones of Pleistocene animals, including horses. Again the maximum date is around ten thousand years ago. Clearly, hunters in this remote region had sought shelter in these caves from time to time in the past, perhaps during blizzards.

The third site I visited was just off the highway near Mount McKinley National Park on the unglaciated north side of the Alaskan Range. I reached this site by walking down the rocky bed of a tributary of the Nenana River, appropriately called Dry Creek, and then climbing up the steep side of an ancient terrace. On top, under several feet of win-deposited loess, are two occupation strata containing microblades, the cores from which the blades were struck, hearths, faunal remains, and so on, dating back ten to twelve thousand years. When A. P. Okladnikov, the Russian archaeologist, visited this site just ahead of me, he is reported to have characterized it as very like some he had seen in Siberia. Subsequently the excavations at the Dry Creek site were carried to completion by Roger Powers of the University of Alaska under a joint program of the National Park Service and the National Geographic Society. This program, coordinated with a similar one in northwestern Canada, is attempting to find the earliest evidence of man in this part of the world.

Note that everything I have been relating about the finds at these three prehistoric sites relates to the culture of the occupants and not to the occupants themselves. No early human skeletons were discovered there. However, the indirect clues to human activities, when fitted into the overall picture, make it possible to draw some important deductions about what kind of people were involved. Theirs was a cold-adapted culture, probably indicating previous long residence in northern Asia. The moderate time scale represented—short by evolutionary standards—gives strong support to the idea that they did not differ much in appearance from their descendents of historic times, nor, on the other hand, from their distant relatives presently living in Asia. Back in 1913 Hrdlicka called attention to the strong resemblance between particular inhabitants of Inner Mongolia and American Indians. The continued existence of Eskimoid peoples in northeastern Asia has already been mentioned. Whatever their earlier physiognomies, certainly these First Americans were able to control fire, make warm clothing and warm shelters, and provide themselves with food, all of which imply effective means of communication—language. To comprehend fully what this means we should contemplate the question, could any of us survive even a single Arctic winter without matches and metal tools? Evidently the capabilities of the First Americans, both physical and mental, were such that they maintained orderly family relationships and slowly multiplied.

In one respect at least Nature was on the side of the First Americans during their sojourn in the Far North. Cold climates are known to be unfavorable for the persistence of disease germs. This led me some years ago to theorize that Arctic cold served to filter out whatever disease germs the First Americans may have had with them when they entered the Arctic. Be this as it may, something of the sort probably explains why in 1492, as already mentioned, their descendants had no immunity to Old World diseases.

With this background let us turn to the period ten to twelve thousand years ago, when the First Americans had certainly exited from the glaciated part of North America. At this stage it is customary to refer to them as paleo-Indians, a name that emphasizes their migratory progress. This name serves also as a reminder that the ancestors of the present Aleuts and Eskimos never followed the paleo-Indians southward from Alaska; instead they either continued in, or became adapted to, an Arctic seafaring way of life. By occupying the Arctic coasts of Alaska they effectively filled the role of the cork in the neck of the bottle so far as further large-scale immigration across Bering Strait was concerned.

A thing to remember is that the paleo-Indians, like their forebears in Alaska, had no concept that they were in a geographical cul-de-sac—no longer as small as Alaska, but instead continental in size, becoming constricted farther south and then opening out into a second continent even less accessible from the Old World than the first. Imagine a healthy, cold-adapted people in a hunting and gathering stage of culture moving into the wide-open spaces of what is now the western United States, where the summers were hot, the winters cold, and where the vast herds of animals had never seen such a vicious predator. How long would it take these people and their descendants to reach all parts of this vast cul-de-sac that is America?

In recent years archaeologists—among them Dennis Stamford of the Smithsonian—have found further evidence in our western States that the paleo-Indians preyed upon the Pleistocene megafauna. Some zoologists have linked these finds to the rapid extinction of this fauna by around ten thousand years ago and attributed to man a major role in this process, on the grounds that the paleo-Indians tended to resort to needless overkill. Opponents of this idea cite the fact that other species not hunted by man were disappearing simultaneously. Whatever caused such widespread and rapid extinction, the argument about overkill has led to speculations about the rate of human population growth in paleo-Indian times and of the accompanying movement southward of this expanding population. According to one calculation, the paleo-Indians could have reached the southern tip of South America from the northern part of the United States in as little as one thousand, two hundred and fifty years. Implausible as this seems in view of the great distance to be covered, interspersed here and there with inhospitable terrain, the estimate is supported by finds of man's presence in South America almost as early as in North America. Only better dated finds in both areas will settle this matter.

Our concern here is not so much with the rate of the paleo-

Indians' initial spread over the American continents as with their rate of population growth. Archaeologists were unable to get at this growth until they began studying the succession of baked-clay pottery types leading back in time from those the Indians were making when the Europeans arrived. Since pottery retains its characteristics even when broken into bits, and is relatively indestructible, the type succession was found to go back some four thousand years, to a time that American archaeologists refer to as "Archaic." Whether the seemingly rather sudden appearance on the coast of Ecuador of well-made pottery at that early date is an illusion resulting from incomplete investigation, or is due to an accidental importation (possibly from the contemporary Jomon culture of Japan), is controversial.

In any case, pottery seems to have been one of a number of cultural innovations, along with plant cultivation and animal domestication, which induced an acceleration in Indian population growth during the last several millennia before European discovery. Perhaps not by accident the more important of these innovations appeared first in the area that was becoming Nuclear America. Outside Nuclear America cultural progress and the accompanying population increase lagged behind to varying degrees. Little use has been made as yet of these archaeological insights for estimating prehistoric American population size.

The estimates of Indian population that have been made revolve around the year 1492, which is assumed to be the date when the maximum was reached. In large measure these estimates depend upon the earliest European observations and tabulations, adjusted by each estimator according to his own view of their accuracy. It is not surprising, therefore, that the most conservative estimator places the 1492 total at just over eight millions, whereas the most liberal estimator places it near one hundred millions. Although the actual population size was more likely somewhere between these extremes, just where may never be learned.

As would be expected, the number of Indians per unit of land area varied from place to place depending on various factors that encourage or discourage settlement. According to plots of population densities based on the most conservative estimate of maximum population, the areas of most intensive settlement were around the periphery of North America and down the west coast of South America.

Considering the wide variety of environments in the settled parts, the Indians appear to have undergone surprisingly little physical differentiation during the ten to twelve thousand years, at least, that settlement had been under way. Head shape varied from relatively long to relatively broad but without rhyme or reason, except possibly to reflect separate early immigration waves with long heads preceding broad heads. Differences in stature, on the other hand, were both more conspicuous and more orderly. By measuring the living Indians who were least affected by contact with Europeans, anthropologists found the tallest to be in the temperate zones and the shortest to be in the tropical zones. In this respect these recent descendants of the First Americans showed their response to extremes of temperature according to Bergmann's rule, which holds that "within a single wide-ranging species of warm-blooded animal, the subspecies or races in colder climates attain greater body size than those in warmer climates." In no other part of the world has man remained *in situ*, so to speak, long enough to demonstrate so clearly the working of this biological rule.

It is easy to be misled by appearances due to cultural practices, particularly those relating to dress, hair arrangement, mannerisms, and so on, and to conclude from this that racial differences are greater than they really are. Interestingly, in view of this tendency, some of the most discerning early observers of the American scene who made a special effort to discount cultural practices and to ignore the variations in stature, agreed on the similarity in appearance of all Indians. As a matter of fact, their opinions on this score frequently echoed with remarkable fidelity the words of Antonio de Uolla, who in 1772 said, *"Visto un Indio de qualquier region, se puede decir que se han visto en quanto al color y contextura,"* or broadly translated, "He who has seen an Indian from any region, can say that he has seen them all, so much are they alike in color and form."

I have been at pains in the foregoing to outline as graphically as possible what has been discovered of the history of the First Americans up to 1492, primarily because of the remarkable perspective it provides for a conference of this sort. From the standpoint of human biology, on the other hand, the case of the First Americans is remarkable because it is the only one available for study in which a large part of the world was settled in a fairly well-defined period of time by a single strain of people of known origin. And from the same standpoint the European discovery of America in 1492, along with the population shifts that followed, is equally remarkable. The drastic decline in numbers of First Americans that set in rapidly after 1492 was offset almost as rapidly by the increase in numbers of the Second Americans, an increase that was running at full flood by the time the nineteenth century rolled around. Between 1830 and 1920 the United States alone received over thirty-eight million immigrants from Europe. Is it any wonder, therefore, that today the remaining First Americans find themselves a minority group striving for identity in the vast lands which they were the first to discover and settle?

References

Denevan, William M., ed. *The Native Population of the Americans in 1492*. Madison: University of Wisconsin Press, 1976.

Hopkins, David M., ed. *The Bering Land Bridge*. Stanford: Stanford University Press, 1967.

Ingstad, Helge H. *Westward to Vinland: The Discovery of Pre-Columbian Norse House-Sites in North America*. Translated by Erik J. Friis. New York: Harpers, 1972.

Martin, P. S., and Wright, H. E., Jr., eds. *Pleistocene Extinctions: The Search for a Cause*. New Haven: Yale University Press, 1967.

Stewart, T. D. *The People of America*. London: Weidenfeld and Nicolson, 1973.

Stewart, T. D. "Perspectives on Some Problems of Early Man Common to America and Australia." *Grafton Elliot Smith: The Man and His Work*. Edited by A. P. Elkin and N. W. G. Macintosh. Sydney: University of Sydney Press, 1974, pp. 114–35.

Willey, Gordon R., and Sabloff, J. A. *A History of American Archaeology*. San Francisco: Freeman, 1974.

Continuity across Generations: The Adams Family Myth

DAVID F. MUSTO
Senior Research Scientist, Child Study Center,
Yale University; and Lecturer in American Studies and History,
Yale University, New Haven, Conn.

I will define "familial continuity" as a resemblance between parents and children in their personal style, outlook on people and institutions outside the family, and the special meaning they attribute to the family's past and anticipated destiny. That an individual or a family bestows a special meaning on the past or future does not imply, of course, a positive or optimistic interpretation, but rather that this special significance is the possession of a particular family, an important part of one family's or one individual's identity. Although familial continuity might also be defined as physical similarity, like the Hapsburg jaw, I will confine myself to the inner sense of common identity which often, particularly to those outside the family, seems equally singular. For those within a family, their shared sense of the past, their common understanding of the family's place in society now, and their similar way of interpreting and filtering out the myriad events every day brings, is as natural and imperceptible as breathing.

The selective and arbitrary character of any one family's way of looking at themselves and the world is most easily seen by an outsider—who, in turn, may have absorbed without the least doubt an equally arbitrary familial identity. The powerful persistence of familial continuity can be observed among poor or wealthy, distinguished or anonymous, mobile or sedentary families. The tendency toward continuity may be seen at times as unfortunate or advantageous. It has been praised and condemned but, however regarded, the yearning by a family—and other groups as well—to make sense out of life's confusion by clinging to an identity—a psychological map on which is marked everything seen by the mind's eye—is a profound, primeval human trait.

Continuity of identity across generations is one of life's commonplace observations, so obvious that its expression in proverbs has become the tritest among a stale lot: "a chip off the old block;" "like father, like son." This continuity seems such a simple truth that close examination may be justified not only on grounds of its elemental interest to us all, but also because "simple truths" which influence some of society's gravest decisions have occasionally proven neither simple nor true. Certainly the subject of this talk is near the center of social policies in the United States, to look no farther, regarding rehabilitation of criminals, treatment of the mentally ill, childcare, campaigns against poverty and unemployment, mental retardation, and immigration quotas. These social questions underlie the search for a stable, predictable environment; answers to them would ensure a desirable social community, failure would mean descent into chaos.

Common sense and social science have regularly placed both the origin and the remedy for society's ills in that humble demographic unit, the family. Therefore, beliefs about familial continuity, how continuity is achieved or missed, whether it is closely linked to heredity or contact with family members, how tenaciously identity is grasped, and whether a new, improved identity can be created by altering family structure, giving psychotherapy, medication or some other intervention—these beliefs guide far-reaching reform movements.

For about a half-century students of familial and individual identity have stressed the malleability and correctability of that self-perception. Continuity began to appear weaker than the instruments of intervention which could, and ought to, be used to remould or break an undesirable continuity. But before this era of faith in intervention and rehabilitation, society was just as firmly assured that mental illness was as much the result of heredity as was genius and that social improvement would come by letting the weak fall in life's competition. I would like to illustrate this earlier confidence in familial continuity by two statements. The first is taken from an eminent and kindly physician, dean of Harvard Medical School, and a major literary figure of the last century, Dr. Oliver Wendell Holmes. The Autocrat of the Breakfast Table advised that

> I go (always, other things being equal) for the man who inherits family traditions and the cumulative humanities of at least four or five generations.[1]

Here we have a positive outlook on family traditions, an appreciation of what good values they can encourage.

The other quotation is neither cheerful nor advisory. It is rather the law of the land, which approved sterilization for defects claimed to be hereditary for reasons now known to be specious. The source is the Supreme Court's decision in *Buck v. Bell.* There is a double appropriateness to this second excerpt, for not only does it express the darker side of familial continuity, the author is Dr. Holmes' son, Justice Oliver Wendell Holmes, Jr. Carrie Buck was a feebleminded teenager whose mother had been committed as feebleminded and who had a six-month-old baby "supposed to be mentally defective." A eugenics expert testified in 1925 that feeblemindedness was a simple mendelian recessive. Two years later—fifty years ago—Justice Holmes wittily supposed that "the principle that sustains compulsory vaccination is broad enough to cover cutting the Fallopian tubes." He concluded with the stirring affirmation of hereditarian doctrine: "Three generations of imbeciles are enough."[2] I mention the public policy aspect of our topic not because I believe such simple answers as sketched above can be given, but to point out that an assumption, "like father, like son" can become a justification for more than a casual observation or a subject for curious reflection.

Certainly one of the disadvantages of explaining individual differences on the basis of biological constitution is that, in the absence of any biological remedy, the end result can be a paralyzing hopelessness. The physician falls into a therapeutic nihilism. Society at large adopts what George Orwell warned would be "the revival of pessimism" characterized by the conviction that "man is non-perfectible, merely political changes can effect nothing, progress is an illusion." Since the burgeoning interest in family history and search for stabilizing links or "roots" to our American and ancestral origins may be one sign of a return to an earlier confidence in heredity as an explanation for behavior, we should be aware of over-simplification at the end of the path. Although Orwell conceded that "So long as one thinks in short periods it is wise not to be hopeful about the future," he was able to maintain his faith in gradual, hard-won progress toward a "better," not a "perfect," society and not to be thrown into pessimism by the failure of utopian programs.[3]

How can we account for these pendular swings between an almost total hereditarian explanation for family continuity and an equally strong belief that family similarity is due to childhood experiences in that family? Of the possible factors driving the pendulum, I would like to consider just one before passing on to some of the themes which appear when a family is studied over several generations. That factor is the obscurity, invisibility even, of that process responsible for similarity, or continuity, or familial identity. No one has located a genetic element which is a personality-carrier or reproducer. On the other hand, there is no general agreement about which child-rearing practice is responsible for a given specific adult character-type. Child psychiatrists are often hesitant to predict adult character even after study of children and their families; the effects of future events are too complex to permit a confident judgment. I grant that it would be easy to locate environmental and biological adherents who would make predictions or explain the past on one or the other strongly held premise, but the broad trend of family research in the past decade has revealed how difficult it is to separate the two familiar categories, nurture and nature, in any one instance. It is still risky to offer a formula or attempt a detailed explanation of how continuity in a family is achieved.

That so many respected observers of behavior, such as Freud and Jung, have needed to postulate some carrier of continuity across generations in addition to the effect of child-rearing practices suggests at least some good students have been puzzled by the existence of traits they could not attribute only to environmental experiences. In their recognition of some special problem in explaining continuity across generations, Freud and Jung were anticipated somewhat by Aristotle, who rejected the simple material explanation for inheritance in favor of a transmission of immaterial form or essence. This Aristotelian form transmits two categories of characteristics: those appropriate for the species, and those peculiar to the individual parent and, with less force, those of the parent's ancestors. His theory of generation does not reveal how the transmission is effected. Aristotle's closest approach to the conjectures formed more than two millennia later by Freud and Jung is a hierarchical ranking of influences, giving the greatest likelihood of transmission to those traits most primary and widespread among humans.[4]

We could take one further observation from ancient philosophy. Three centuries after Aristotle, the Roman philosopher-poet Lucretius presented a materialist description of the world which included some ingenious speculation on inheritance. Asking his readers to consider what the world would be like if the seeds of any flora or fauna were randomly patterned, he postulated the existence of genetic material which inevitably led to production of similar animals and plants. He reminds us of two facts often overlooked: the dominant characteristic of life is not change, but continuity; second, the continuity extends over time, but not across the full range of conceivable types of living beings—there are gaps in the spectrum of species.[5] This last observation of Lucretius may be applicable to the kinds of human personalities, families, and cultures. When one considers the full range of human expression and interaction that could possibly exist, there seems to be a rather limited number of personality styles, family styles, and cultural styles. An absolute and unexamined assumption that the microcosm of the family—at least in the case of children—and the macrocosm of a culture—in the case of adults —reflects correctly the real world may offer powerful aid to the survival of the human species, for the assumption has been common in history and over the globe.

Praise for stable families and fear of the effect of broken homes and inconsistent childrearing rest on the comfort and social orientation provided by a family or family-surrogate. As we consider the world-view established in families and transmitted by whatever process, though, we might well question how much the good effects of the family's socialization is related to some universal human "truths" inculcated, and how much to an arbitrary, even singular, perception of the world, which could be preserved by a family's psychological defenses against the many subverting challenges a lifetime will offer. The closer the family's world view approximates its society's norm, the more easily is it preserved.

Freud and Jung shared an interest in how the mind could create its own world and successfully defend even the most exposed salients against the attack of reality. Freud has been thought of as explaining the origins of each personal mental world in the traumata of childhood. Anecdotes abound about his ability to discern quickly the probable existence of some specific event in a patient's childhood which the doubting sufferer would then discover, by checking with parents or governess, to be true. Gustav Mahler is said to have had a block in his ability to compose removed when, after an afternoon's consultation, Freud pointed out to him a conflict over the name Mary. Such a simple and popularized understanding of great psychologists does injustice to their work. Here I will concern myself with just one category when I take exception to the oversimplified impression that they considered childhood experiences to be the determinants for adult character. That exception is the reliance of both Freud and Jung on the inheritance of ancient attitudes and modes of thought. I would like to draw your attention to a few statements by them on this less well known element in their psychologies for this reason: the necessity these two observers felt to postulate a sort of psychological inheritance over many generations illustrates the mysterious and fascinating difficulties encountered in studying family continuity. Both Freud and Jung came up against human characteristics which they could not fully explain even after they had taken into account a patient's life experiences.

There is something odd about their hypotheses—we just do not know how specific mental sets or styles of perception could be transmitted by heredity. Their reasoning, however, is analogous to that employed in one of the most astounding discoveries during the nineteenth century. I am reminded of the discovery of Neptune by the great Institution which is our host, for the discovery of Neptune and the establishment of the Smithsonian both occurred in the late summer of 1846. Leverrier of Paris calculated that irregularities in the orbit of Uranus were greater than could be explained by influence of the known planets. He then hypothesized the existence of a more distant planet and predicted its location. On the first night of observation, the astronomer Galle discovered the planet less than a degree from Leverrier's calculation. This is a good point at which to say again that no biological analogue to Neptune has been discovered in humans which could explain the attraction across generations of primeval memories. But a frustration like Leverrier's does exist, that a sufficient explanation for family continuity still eludes the investigator.

Jung's "unknown planet," the archetype, derived from "repeated observation that, for instance, the myths and fairy-tales of world literature contain definite motifs which crop up everywhere." He found "these same motifs in the fantasies, dreams, deliria, and delusions of individuals living today." These repeated images and associations he called "archetypal ideas." Jung was neither as systematic nor as consistent as one would like in his definition of archetype. Early on he termed them "primordial images," not specific ideas with detailed content but rather a "possibility of representation" of "congenital conditions of intuition" in the unconscious. Only if the archetype rises to consciousness, elicited perhaps by cultural stimuli, does it become clothed as it were in language and image. The archetypes are present in everyone and therefore are part of the "collective unconscious."[6]

At times archetypes are large abstract concepts, such as "self"—at other times Jung found evidence for archetypes in very detailed myths. Jung convinced himself that the archetypes were universal after coming to St. Elizabeth's Hospital in Washington, D.C., shortly before World War I. He studied the dreams of black patients in which he detected the same archetypes he had found in the dreams of white European patients and in Babylonian myths. He could only conclude that the archetypes are a common heritage.[7]

Although recently a resurgence of interest in Jung's theories has joined other signs of weakened faith in scientific determinism, Jung's concepts and terminology have never achieved the acceptance of Freud's. Freud never rejected his youthful faith in an ultimate organic or biochemical explanation for human behavior; psychoanalytic theory discussed the conscious and unconscious, gave rules for their interaction and suggested ways to modify them as a necessary simplification awaiting a complete neuro-physiological explanation.

Freud relied until about World War I on a theory of inborn instinctual drives. These unfolded as the child developed; events in the environment were mere occasions for revealing instinctual vicissitudes. This "id-psychology" evolved into the "ego-psychology" of the 1920s and 1930s and extends to our own time in the studies of Anna Freud and Heinz Hartmann. Freud, like his younger colleague Jung, tried to discover what were universal characteristics of the human mind as well as the reasons why each personality was unique. He believed the answers lay in a complex interaction between heredity and environment. Further, he suspected that some apparently universal human characteristics such as the incest taboo had an origin in the early experiences of mankind. He was fascinated with conjectured pre-historic human groups like Darwin's "primal horde" ruled over by a powerful father. From these early social and family experiences, Freud believed, certain attitudes and styles of thought were inherited, somewhat like Jung's archetypes.

In the 1920s Freud postulated a more powerful role for environmental experiences. The child would incorporate the family's expectations, standards, and culture into what Freud called the "superego," thereby providing for each generation a psychological means of transmitting culture. Yet Freud did not find the family's enculturation of children a sufficient explanation for certain deep elements of continuity.

In 1937 Freud argued that "it does not imply a mystical overevaluation of heredity if we think it credible that, even before the ego exists, its subsequent lines of development, tendencies and reactions are already determined. The psychological peculiarities of families, races, and nations . . . admit no other explanation. Indeed, analytic experience convinces us that particular psychial contents, such as symbolism, have no other source than hereditary transmission."[8] In an essay published in 1939, the year of his death, Freud was more specific:

> The behavior of a neurotic child to his parents when under the influence of an Oedipus and castration complex . . . seem unreasonable in the individual and can only be understood phylogenetically, in relation to the experiences of earlier generations. . . . In fact it seems convincing enough to allow me to venture further and assert that the archaic heritage of mankind includes not only dispositions, but also ideational contents, memory traces of the experiences of former generations.[9]

When Freud wrote this he was not relying on the theories of heredity taught him in the nineteenth century, oblivious of new knowledge and attitudes based on mendelian genetics. He frankly states that he knows his position is made difficult "by the present attitude of biological science, which rejects the idea of acquired qualities being transmitted to descendants." His students were embarrassed by this neo-lamarckianism. I quote Freud's acknowledgment that his conjectures on heredity were outmoded to show the awkward position to which one of the most creative and perceptive psychological investigators was driven by a lifetime of observing the remarkable strength of transgenerational identity. He showed his determination to theorize, however tentatively, by "admit[ting] that in spite of this [rejection by biologists] I cannot picture biological development proceeding without taking this factor of [inheriting acquired qualities] into account."[10]

So much remains to be learned about the brain, genetics, physiology, the effects of social relations on the body, and the body's ability to alter perception and mood, that we can easily sympathize with Freud's or anyone's attempt to map out even in large scale a terrain still in shadows. My own effort has been at a lower altitude. I have been studying the private and public documents left by four generations of a family begun by Abigail Smith and John Adams in 1764. Following one trail in the dark forest does permit a pretty close inspection: if we are careful not to over-generalize or to build elaborate theories from experience on one path, possibly study of one reflective, well-documented family will reveal something about continuity. Although an unusual family, the extraordinary accomplishments of some of the Adams family do not remove them from the human condition. Therapeutic work with families in New England and Appalachia has convinced me that the role and endurance of family continuity as well as its dynamics are a common heritage of both noted and anonymous families.

The Adams family in the four generations to which I will refer evolved early a rather unusual perception of itself which dominated the second generation including John Quincy Adams, then the next generation, that of John Quincy Adams' sons, chiefly Charles Francis Adams, Sr., and finally the early years of the fourth generation, until its members gradually and painfully became aware that their household was under the influence of an inappropriate view of the world and their role in it. I would like to borrow a term from family therapists and call this internal stream of identity flowing from one generation to the next a "family myth."[11] If the family myth approximates the norm of the surrounding culture, it will probably continue to bridge generations until dislodged by another way of looking at the world. A family myth seems to follow some psychological equivalent of Newton's First Law of Motion: once established, it tends to continue its course through succeeding generations.

A shared family identity defining and giving significance to what the family does, has done, and will do in its society, and what is the nature of that society is an eagerly sought psychological foundation. People have an imperative need to know where they are on the map. With this knowledge, the family group is united against an often hostile world, filtering the innumerable stimuli flooding in, and thereby maintaining a stable environment. It is not unreasonable to assume that a family or other group could have an increased chance of survival if they reinforced one another's shared perception of themselves and the outside world.

A family's tendency to coalesce around a "myth" is easily triggered; if the shared "myth" coincides with what others might call "the real world" in only a few essential points so as to assure food and shelter it still may be firmly held. I say this because families exhibit an astounding tenacity in holding to their mutual outlook in the face of contradictory information or events. In families where an atypical shared "myth" has been established, clinicians have often been witness to the group's stubborn defense of a self-perception of little apparent social value or even one destructive to family members. Could the Adams family, the four generations just mentioned, illustrate, at least partially, these observations? The answer appears to be "yes," although a full statement of evidence is here impossible. Since the microfilms of the Adams papers stretch over five miles, more space is obviously needed for a thorough analysis. Meanwhile, let me provide some examples of the power of a family myth in those four generations.

The Adams family myth crystallized during the American War of Independence and was transmitted by Abigail Adams to her children Nabby, John Quincy, Charles, and Thomas Boylston. The myth was compounded with John Adams' enormous ambition to guide nations and to receive a justified admiration for his talents. Abigail and John shared a hope that their children would rise to eminent positions in an ordered society.

Abigail created this new myth not with design, but out of a desperate need to justify loneliness and hardships she suffered in wartime Massachusetts while her husband rose to fame in Philadelphia and Europe. At first, in the Spring of 1776, she resented his ridicule of equal rights for women. She chafed at his irritation when he learned she was allowing their eldest child and only daughter, Nabby, to study Latin. Nabby received a letter from her father in April 1776—while he was urging adoption of a Declaration of Independence upon Congress—warning her about the impropriety of a girl studying Latin, the key to the masculine political world. "You must not tell many people of it," he wrote his ten-year-old daughter, "for it is scarcely reputable for young ladies to understand Latin and Greek."[12]

Abigail's eventual response to the hopelessness of her own cause was not unusual: she justified her sacrifice by glorifying her husband and the cause for which he fought until, as the years of his absence accumulated, her children began to picture a stern, perfectionist father who was the key figure in American Independence. Further, she overlooked John's gratification of his personal ambition at her expense as he achieved the very style of life he had thirsted after since at least his nineteenth year. His rise was the reward of merit, she felt, and his work a patriotic responsibility. She began to portray them both as under the same burden of ardent patriotism. She wrote him that "All domestic pleasures and enjoyments are absorbed in the great and important duty you owe your country, 'for our country is as it were a secondary God, and the first and greatest parent. It is to be preferred to parents, wives, children, friends. . . .' "[13]

Her own ambition was transferred to her children, as well as to John. They would achieve greatness under her guidance. For example, she cajoled John Quincy, then twelve and tearfully begging to stay in America, to ask his father for permission to join him on a trip to Europe. John Adams took him through the British blockade so that the boy might benefit in his adolescence from a European education. This was preparation, Abigail told her son, for a "hero and statesman."[14] She conspired with the dashing and romantic Colonel William Stephen Smith in his pursuit of Nabby's hand, for she was sure that he would be another Washington leading his country's defense (but instead he "did more injury to me and my administration," John Adams later wrote, "than any other man")—these were the variegated fruits of her transferred ambitions.[15] She believed that the just, educated, moral, and ideologically pure Adams children would receive merited reward from the great republic, cleansed of European monarchy and social preferment. An important addition to this myth was that merited reward should never be sought by political maneuvers but rather should be awaited patiently and confidently. The bind in which this placed a family member who fully accepted the myth and acted upon it in the American political maelstrom can be readily imagined, and that few family members bore up under the burden, is not surprising.

Into the second generation, Nabby did not marry happily or well—the primary life task she had accepted. Nevertheless, she did not complain. The second son, Charles, died of alcoholism at the age of twenty-nine, deep in debt from land speculation, the myth's very antithesis of proper behavior. The youngest son, Thomas Boylston, did not succeed at the literary life he tried to establish in Philadelphia and returned to rusticate in Quincy, an increasingly bitter man. Only the eldest son, John Quincy, stayed the course and became the only child of a president to attain the same office. He had three children who lived to adulthood, George Washington, John II, and Charles Francis.

Until nearly his tenth year, Charles Francis was raised as an only son, although in fact he was the youngest. Just a baby when his father accepted appointment at the Court of the Czar, he was taken along while his brothers stayed home to go to school. Charles proved to be at least as independent and aloof as John Quincy Adams had been in his adolescence and youth. He did not admire his brothers' talents, nor did he feel as loved as they by his parents. One day in June 1824, after a family row with his Uncle Thomas, Charles went upstairs to read to his illustrious grandfather, then aged eighty-eight. John Adams uncharacteristically chose to discuss with his austere grandson the failures of the young man's uncles, Charles and Thomas, and the blazing success of John Quincy. What the ex-president told Charles Francis is a classic example of defending the family's myth in the face of evidence that its overall effect on the family members was tragic rather than glorious. Charles Francis' *Diary* carries the message:

> He [John Adams] laments the fate which has thrown so much gloom over our house, [but] something was necessary to check our pride and we have suffered bitterly. We should have been crushed, had the Sons all been distinguished, but now while the World respects us, it at the same [time] pities our misfortune and this pity destroys the envy which would other-wise arise.[16]

John Adams saw no problem about the family's goals except the understandable envy of others. The failed sons were fodder for pursuing wolves of public envy, allowing John Quincy to escape.

Charles Francis' generation suffered equal destruction, but he survived. George Washington Adams could not fulfill the eldest son's responsibility to carry on the political tradition. Neither could he release himself from the myth's grip. In April 1829, he fearfully started for Washington to help ex-President John Quincy Adams' return to Quincy and presumed retirement after defeat by Andrew Jackson. George became convinced that a conspiracy against him existed on board the steamer *Benjamin Franklin*. In the early morning hours, leaving his cloak and hat on the deck, George leapt into Long Island Sound and brought an end to his pain. He had just turned twenty-eight.[17]

John Quincy's second son, John, disliked politics and abandoned plans for a legal career. He had "deserted the State," as Charles Francis put it. John preferred to operate—without ability or success—his father's debt-ridden grist mill in Rock Creek Park. John Adams II died after a lingering illness in 1834 at the age of thirty. The youngest son reflected on his two brothers' early deaths:

> I may be called cold in heart, and I have often thought with possible justice, but I cannot regard the loss of either of my brothers as calamity either to their families or to themselves.[18]

Charles Francis lived to the age of seventy-nine, a year short of his father's lifespan. The survival of the fittest, but by whose standards?

Charles Francis, of course, represented the United States to Great Britain during the Civil War. He was thought by contemporaries to come close to the presidential nomination, especially in 1872. Six of his children lived to adulthood, confronting the unusual family role and perception of society they had, as it were, inherited. In his mid-sixties Henry Adams reviewed his life and found his "Education" sadly deficient: the world did not work the way he had been taught. "For some remote reason," Henry Adams mused, "he was born an eighteenth century child."[19] John Adams had set out in the eighteenth century with a youthful ambition to establish the rules of political science and to help—at least help—

establish a great North American Nation. The remarkable Abigail educated their children to believe the family destiny was to guide what John had established. Shortly before becoming president, John wrote Abigail on a note of youthful fantasies achieved: "I have often told you laughing, what may become a real truth, that 'I shall be the great Legislator of Nations and that Nations must learn of me or cut one another's throat.' "[20] In the early twentieth century, Henry Adams recalled a youth in which John's ambition was no longer a laughing matter: he describes in his *Education* a memorable encounter as a child with the family's Irish gardener. He recalled the gardener saying to him, "You'll be thinkin' you'll be President too!" It was not the possibility of such high office that struck him; it was the disturbing element of uncertainty in the man's voice. Henry wrote in the third person: "This made so strong an impression on his mind that he never forgot it. He could not remember ever to have thought on the subject; to him, that there should be a doubt of his being President was a new idea. What had been would continue to be."[21] This was another classic statement of family myth, recalled only decades later when the series of family presidents had without doubt ended.

The fourth generation eventually settled down into a more conventional, less demanding, vision of themselves and their destiny. Less exciting, perhaps, than past power struggles, but also favoring an improved average lifespan. Henry's volatile brother Brooks thought of preparing a book on heredity, demonstrating that personal characteristics persist while the world changes. "It is seldom," he wrote in 1919, "that a single family can stay adjusted through three generations. . . . It is now full four generations since John Adams wrote the Constitution of Massachusetts. It is time we perished. The world is tired of us."[22] Charles Francis, Jr., a one-time president of the Union Pacific, looked back in his autobiography upon his failure to prove the family's ability to guide a great empire of business, the new location of power. The Robber Barons outsmarted him. Reviewing his life, he closed with a humble consolation: he had enjoyed some days of "pure happiness," perhaps not many, "but, more or less, I am very confident they exceed in number those of anyone of my forbears."[23]

In a more primitive world, the myth's intolerance could have survival value. Unquestioning acceptance of the family myth gave tenacity to those who had the extraordinary ability required to approach the myth's standards. In the face of the most bitter personal and political hostility, they held to the myth. John Adams' ambition, Abigail's need to justify her lonely distress, and their faith in a revolutionary promise of a purified society were fused with a certainty and sense of purpose that would have sustained one of Darwin's primal hordes through an ice age.

This family's experiences illustrate some of the intriguing questions which have arisen in our century over the nature of family continuity. They suggest that a family myth can be forged in a stressful period, continue for several generations almost as an inherited set of attitudes, and, eventually, may be restructured under the impact of an incongruous environment.

Notes

1. O. W. Holmes, *Autocrat of the Breakfast-Table* (New York, 1957), p. 23.

2. *Buck v. Bell*: 274 U.S. 200 (1927).

3. George Orwell, *Collected Essays, Journalism and Letters*, ed. Sonia Orwell and Ian Angus (New York, 1968), Vol. 3, pp. 63–64.

4. Cf. *De generatione animalium*, Book 1, l. 159 ff.

5. *De rerum natura*, Book 1, l. 159 ff.

6. C. G. Jung, *Memories, Dreams, Reflections*, ed. Aniela Jaffé (New York, 1965), pp. 380–81. Cf. M.-L. von Franz, *C. G. Jung* (Boston, 1975), pp. 125 ff.

7. C. G. Jung, "Psychological Types," in *Collected Works* (Princeton, New Jersey, 1971), vol. 6, p. 443.

8. Sigmund Freud, "Analysis Terminable and Interminable," in *Collected Papers* (London, 1950), vol. 5, pp. 343–44.

9. Sigmund Freud, *Moses and Monotheism*, (New York, 1955), p. 127.

10. *op. cit.*, p. 128.

11. D. F. Musto, "Youth of John Quincy Adams," *Proceedings American Philosophical Society 1969,* 113:269–82.

12. L. H. Butterfield *et al.*, eds., *Adams Family Correspondence* (Cambridge, Mass., 1963—), vol. 1, pp. 387–88 (April 18, 1776).

13. *op. cit.*, pp. 401–3 (May 7, 1776).

14. *op. cit.*, Vol. 3, pp. 268–69 (January 19, 1780).

15. John Adams to John Quincy Adams, June 26, 1816, *Adams Papers, Microfilm Edition*, Reel 432. Quotations from the Adams Papers Microfilm Edition are by permission of the Massachusetts Historical Society.

16. Charles Francis Adams, *Diary of Charles Francis Adams*, vols. 1–2, ed. Aida DiPace Donald and David Donald; vols. 3–4, ed. Marc Friedlander and L. H. Butterfield (Cambridge, Mass., 1964—), vol. 1, p. 164 (June 2, 1964). Words in brackets supplied.

17. Cf. S. F. Bemis, *John Quincy Adams and the Union* (New York, 1965), pp. 178–84.

18. C. F. Adams, *Diary*, vol. 5, p. 411 (October 28, 1834).

19. Henry Adams, *Education of Henry Adams*, ed. Ernest Samuels (Boston, Mass., 1974), p. 11.

20. John Adams to Abigail Adams, January 2, 1796, *Adams Papers, Microfilm Edition*, Reel 381.

21. H. Adams, *Education*, p. 16.

22. Brooks Adams, "Heritage of Henry Adams," introduction to Henry Adams, *Degradation of the Democratic Dogma* (New York, 1919), p. 93.

23. Charles Francis Adams, Jr., *An Autobiography* (Cambridge, Mass., 1916), p. 211.

The Depression Experience in Men's Lives

GLEN H. ELDER, JR.
and
RICHARD C. ROCKWELL
Visiting Fellows, Center for the Study of Youth Development,
Boys Town, Nebraska

Historical influences are one of the most obvious and neglected facts in the study of human lives, an observation most vividly illustrated by notable research on American youth. August Hollingshead's classic study of Elmtown's youth (1949) pointed out the importance of social class in shaping an individual's life chances, but ignored the influence of historical circumstances. Elmtown's youth had been children of the Great Depression, and when observed as adolescents in 1941–42, they faced the rising military and industrial demands of wartime America. Yet Hollingshead never integrated these historical influences into the description of Elmtown's adolescents. A quarter century later, James Coleman's *The Adolescent Society* (1961) reflected similar historical blind spots. Coleman did not view the adolescents he surveyed in 1957 as members of a cohort with a distinctive life history, marked by changes in family life during World War II—maternal employment, absence of the father during military service, and the strain of family readjustment upon the father's return.

John Seeley (1973:21, 23) may have had such limitations in mind when he recently criticized the "absence of a sense of history" in the adolescent literature. He urged that special consideration be given to "the study of what is to be seen in the simultaneously dual perspective of history and life history." Even before Seeley's critique, the perspective he advocated was emerging in the published works of social historians (Demos, 1970; Greven, 1970; Katz, 1975), life-span developmental psychologists (Baltes and Schaie,

1973), and sociologists (Riley, Johnson and Foner, 1972; Elder, 1974, 1975). A developing sociology of the life course gave fresh insight to historical change in lives by revealing distinctions in the temporal meanings of age: first, developmental time—age as an index of stages in the life course; secondly, social time—age patterns in social roles and events, as in the timing of marriage, parenthood, and worklife events; and thirdly, historical time—birth year as an index of historical location and membership in a specific age group or cohort. Successive cohorts encounter historical events at different developmental and social stages in their respective life spans, and consequently tend to vary in the effects of such events. But even *within* an age cohort, exposure to an event is not uniform; although many children were exposed to economic deprivation in the 1930s, others were spared family misfortune.

Children of the Great Depression (Elder, 1974) explored some implications of this variation in historical experience by studying a longitudinal sample of 167 persons who were born during the early 1920s and grew up in the northeastern sector of Oakland, California. Using data collected annually during the 1930s and at three points in the adult years, the analysis followed members of relatively nondeprived and deprived families from elementary school through adolescence, young adulthood, and the early years of middle age. Families that lost more than 34 percent of their 1929 income by 1933 were defined as relatively deprived; all other families were classified as relatively nondeprived. Family adaptations in the depression, from change in the household economy to role change and emotional stress, emerged as the primary links between income change and the life experience of the Oakland adolescents.

The Oakland cohort experienced adolescence during the 1930s, a time when Hollingshead's Elmtown youth were children; they entered adult roles, including military service, at a point when most of the Elmtown cohort was enrolled in secondary school.

The Oakland cohort was better sheltered from the effects of the Depression than were Elmtown's youth, for its members were beyond the critical years of child development when the economy collapsed, and subsequent war mobilization helped to mitigate the handicap of starting out life from a background of privation. Apart from some disadvantage in the early stages of building a career, economic deprivation did not produce enduring disabilities in the adult accomplishments of the Oakland cohort. Instead, the depression's legacy mainly took the form of shaping values and attitudes. Men and women who had grown up in depression-marked homes were most likely to anchor their lives around family and children, perhaps reflecting the notion of home as a refuge in an unpredictable world. They ranked family activities and parenthood higher in their scheme of values than did the sons and daughters of more affluent parents. Job security and the extrinsic aspects of work, such as income and family convenience, were uniquely important to men from deprived homes only when they were relatively unsuccessful in their own work lives.

The present study broadens this line of research by examining a sample of individuals who were children rather than adolescents during the 1930s. Although little is known about the depression experience of Elmtown's youth, data are available for males born during 1928–29 in the city of Berkeley, who had been selected for a study of normal development by the Institute of Human Development (Macfarlane, 1938). We chose to analyze eighty-seven members of this group who had participated in follow-up studies through the age of forty. As in *Children of the Great Depression*, we divided the group into the deprived and the non-deprived according to the income losses experienced by their families during the 1930s. Forty-four percent of working class families and 55 percent of middle class families in the sample were classified as deprived.

The young age of this cohort when the economy hit bottom implies that, unlike the Oakland group, some were exposed to economic distress during a substantial proportion of their preadult years. We therefore expected children who grew up in the 1930s to have experienced greater disadvantage in life chances and development than did their older counterparts. Preliminary results of our work, reported elsewhere, tend to support this expectation (Elder and Rockwell, 1978); these children of deprived families did encounter greater disadvantage in development and life chances than older boys from deprived households in the Oakland cohort. This essay will compare males within the Berkeley cohort, considering how growing up in deprived rather than non-deprived families influenced the life chances and values of those who were children during the 1930s.

Evidence from our sample suggests that economic deprivation during the Great Depression retarded educational attainment. Boys in the Berkeley cohort left high school at the end of World War II, a time when the State of California offered all youth with a high school diploma a tuition-free place in institutions of higher learning. Nearly four out of five of the young men entered a program of higher education, and about half completed four years, a figure well above the national average. However, those whose families had lost the most during the depression (the "relatively deprived") made less progress in higher education (see table 1), when compared to the sons of more stable families (the "nondeprived"). This difference applies to youth from both the middle class and working class, although the latter were far less likely to continue their education beyond high school. Such effects emerged in prosperous, postwar America, many years after the 1930 decade of hard times, but they were linked to this earlier period through persisting family and developmental disabilities (Elder and Rockwell, 1978), a continuing pattern of socioeconomic instability, misshapen family relationships (mother dominance and an impaired or ineffective father), and personal deficiencies up to late adolescence—self-inadequacy, lack of self-direction and self-assertion, low aspirations, and under achievement in high school.

TABLE 1

Educational Attainment in Relation to Class Origin and Family Deprivation
(in percentages)

Educational Attainment	Education by Class[1] and Deprivation: Middle Class, Nondeprived	Middle Class, Deprived	Working Class, Nondeprived	Working Class, Deprived
Postgraduate	30	25	40 (Postgraduate and College, 4 years combined)	13 (Postgraduate and College, 4 years combined)
College, 4 years	42	38		
Some college	18	31	27	35
High school or less	9	6	34	51
	100	100	101	99
	N=33	N=16	N=15	N=23

[1] Class origin is measured by the Hollingshead index of social position, an index which combines the weighted values of father's occupation and education in 1929. For our purposes, middle class origin is defined by social strata I through III (the lower middle class); working class origin, by strata IV and V.

Despite an unpromising beginning, the sons of deprived families show little evidence of this handicap in their adult years. As a group, they achieved far more in their occupational life than one would have predicted from knowing their early histories (Elder and Rockwell, 1978). By the middle years, about age forty, their occupational position closely resembles that of men from more privileged, nondeprived homes. Between adolescence and mid-life, they also achieved greater developmental growth in self-adequacy, goal orientation, and assertiveness than we observe in the sample as a whole. How did this change occur? Through what process were so many deprived youth from the Berkeley cohort able to surmount the limitations of their early years?

Some clues to this achievement are suggested by strategies in the timing and ordering of early life events, by the pattern of career establishment, and by the developmental value of transitions in the life cycle. For example, Furstenberg (1976) refers to the scheduling of early life events, such as parenthood, as an adaptive strategy in minimizing economic pressures; Sharp and Krasnesor

(1968) identify the "time out" provided by military experience as a potential source of personal growth; and Macfarlane (1963) cites the maturing experience of independence through work, marriage, and parenthood. Economic hardships in the 1930s underscored two adaptive lessions which may have special relevance to the early transitions and work careers of Berkeley men from hardpressed families: income loss reinforced the importance of achieving economic security before the assumption of family responsibilities, as well as the value of establishing a stable line of work. Is relatively late marriage and worklife stability most characteristic of the life course of men who rose above the constraints of a deprived background in the 1930s?

We shall investigate this question in two steps: first by examining the timing and order of early life transitions (work, marriage, education, etc.), and work patterns in the life course of depression-reared men; and then by exploring how their life paths influenced the meaning of both work and marriage. These life paths provide an essential starting point for determining the relevance of depression experiences for "things that matter" in adulthood. As in the Oakland study, one might expect the security concerns of a depression childhood to have adaptive value for men with occupational problems of their own, but not among men with a rewarding, secure occupational position. Both childhood experience and adult situations influence what men come to value about work and marriage.

In late nineteenth-century America, entry into adult roles was distinguished by a considerable time span between achieving economic independence, leaving home, and beginning a family (Modell et al., 1976). By the postwar era of the Berkeley cohort, however, these events had become more compressed. Fully half the Berkeley men were in the labor force as full-time employees by the age of twenty-two (circa 1950), were out of school and married by the age of twenty-three, and were parents by the end of their twenty-fifth year. Nevertheless, the sons of deprived parents generally followed a life course that had more in common with the nineteenth-century pattern of late marriage (table 2). They tended to enter the labor force at an earlier age than the nondeprived, and experienced marriage and parenthood much later in life. As one might expect, those events occurred earlier and more rapidly in the lives of deprived men who did not enter college, but even in this group family deprivation is related to a pattern of early work and late marriage.

TABLE 2

The Timing of Early Life Events by Family Deprivation Among Non-College and College Men (*in mean ages*)

	Timing of Early Life Events by Education and Family Deprivation[1]			
	Less than College		College Entrance +	
Early Life Events	Nondeprived Min. N=7	Deprived Min. N=12	Nondeprived Min. N=31	Deprived Min. N=20
First full-time employment	18.7	17.9	22.9	21.7
Completion of education	21.4	19.5	25.2	25.9
First marriage	20.0	22.4	23.6	25.3
First birth	21.6	25.5	25.7	27.6

1 The effect of family deprivation on event timing is not altered when adjustments are made for variation in class origin.

Among college entrants, deprived men were less likely than the nondeprived to complete four years or more, and yet they more frequently assumed a full-time job before leaving school (48 vs. 37 percent) and entering marriage (61 vs. 41 percent). Also, they let more years pass between the time they started working and the time they married and had children (an average of 3.2 years, for cases in which work came first). One might interpret this sequence of events as a response to economic pressures or needs, stemming from the exhaustion of family resources during the 1930s. However, there is another historical development that could have produced later marriage among men in the postwar years—the military draft and the generalized obligation to serve in the armed forces. Early entry, in particular, is likely to have delayed family events. There is some evidence of this effect across twentieth-century cohorts of American men (Hogan, 1976).

Military service may have been part of the life strategies of men in the Berkeley cohort since the draft allowed some element of choice in scheduling the event, especially before the Korean conflict (1950–53). Most of the men served in the military at some point, generally for two or three years; among those with deprived backgrounds the percentage is slightly higher (77 vs. 67 percent nondeprived). However, the major difference appears to be in the timing of service. By the age of twenty-one (1949–50), fully 60 percent of all deprived men with a background of military service had entered the armed forces, compared to only 17 percent of the nondeprived—a contrast that is even greater among the college-educated. Consistent with this difference, we find a more uniform order of events (military before marriage and education completion) among college entrants from hardpressed families than among the offspring of more affluent families (table 3). This order accounts for the prevalence of late marriage among deprived men and undoubtedly increased their chances for higher education through the financial benefits of the G.I. Bill. Unfortunately, data are lacking on the extent to which men used these benefits.

TABLE 3

Early Status Sequences in the Life Course of Berkeley Men who Entered College by Family Deprivation (*in percentage and mean differences in years*[1])

	Early Status Sequences of Berkeley Men who Entered College by Family Deprivation			
	Nondeprived		Deprived	
Status Sequences[2]	%	Yrs. Between (*means*)	%	Yrs. Between (*means*)
Education exit—work entry				
Education, then work	17	—	13	—
Same year	46	—	39	—
Work, then education	37	6.6	48	10.7
	100 (35)		100 (23)	
		D = .11 (—.51)[3]		

Status Sequences[2]	Nondeprived %	Nondeprived Yrs. Between *(means)*	Deprived %	Deprived Yrs. Between *(means)*
Education exit—marriage				
Education, then marriage	32	3.2	44	3.4
Same year	24	—	9	—
Marriage, then education	44	5.5	48	5.6
	100 (34)		101 (23)	
		D = .15 (.00)		
Work entry—marriage				
Work, then marriage	41	4.3	61	6.7
Same year	18	—	13	—
Marriage, then work	41	2.5	26	—
	100 (34)		100 (23)	
		D = .20 (.64)		
Education exit—military entry				
Education, then military	27	1.1	10	—
Same year	27	—	5	—
education	46	8.4	84	9.2
	100 (26)		99 (19)	
		D = .38 (2.73)		
Marriage—military entry				
Marriage, then military	16	—	10	—
Same year	28	—	0	—
Military, then marriage	56	4.0	90	6.6
	100 (25)		100 (19)	
		D = .33 (2.40)		

1 The average number of years between the timing of one event and another was calculated only for categories with ten or more cases.

2 These sequences are very crudely measured because event timing is measured in whole years of age. We restricted the analysis to ever-married men because first marriage is included in our assessment of event sequences. Only about three-fourths of the men entered the military.

3 The "D" coefficient for each status sequence indicates the amount of case redistribution (across the three categories) which would be required to achieve congruence between the nondeprived and deprived groups; the higher the value, the greater the extent of redistribution. The coefficient is derived from the Duncan-Duncan Index of Dissimilarity, calculated on the basis of cell frequencies. The standardized value of each coefficient is enclosed within parentheses—the higher the value, the more the observed distribution (cell size differences between nondeprived and deprived) departs from randomness (see Cortese, Falk, and Cohen, 1976; Toeber and Toeber, 1976; Cohen, Falk, and Cortese, 1976).

Apart from these effects of military service, the important question is why this event occurred so early in the lives of men who experienced first-hand the family hardships of the Depression. Their adolescent rationale for "joining up" is unknown, and we do not know whether the decision to do so was prompted by an awareness of the educational benefits of the G.I. Bill. However, some clues emerge from their life records and subsequent reflections on military service at mid-life. During adolescence, they were described by clinical ratings as lower than nondeprived youth on self-esteem, assertiveness, and goal orientation, a psychological pattern that reflects the family impact of hard times (strong mother, impaired father, family conflict, lack of emotional support). Though equal to the nondeprived on IQ, they experienced more academic problems and failure as adolescents, a behavioral pattern that may have continued into higher education for some, leading to an early withdrawal and the genuine prospect of military induction. From this vantage point, military service may have offered experiences and options that were largely missing in the lives of men from deprived homes—separation from maternal control through involvement in a masculine culture, a legitimate "time out" from academic and occupational pressures in a structured environment, a chance to sort things out and acquire the confidence and goals for making a fresh start in life.

As we follow these children of the depression into the middle years, one early transition stands out above all others as a critical line of demarcation between the likelihood of achievement and of continuing disadvantage—entrance into higher education. College entrance opened the door to career lines with steady advancement possibilities, and college men from deprived families generally made the best of them. Even when college education amounted to little more than a year or so, it made a significant difference in the career entry and progress of men from deprived families. From early adulthood to middle age, the men who succeeded in entering college also managed to advance well beyond worklife expectations based on their education (Elder and Rockwell, 1978), rising to the occupational level of men from more affluent homes by mid-life (on the seven point Hollingshead index, the group means are identical—2.4, about half, in professional-managerial occupations). Seventy-three percent of the college men from deprived homes, compared to 50 percent of the college men from nondeprived homes, qualified as "high achievers"—that is, as men whose mid-life occupational status was equal to or above predictions based on education, ability, and class origin (Elder and Rockwell, 1978). But when coupled with *less* schooling (most pronounced among working class offspring), Depression hardship forecast an adult life that had some parallels with the 1930s. The economically deprived fared more poorly in worklife (more instability, less advancement) than the nondeprived. They also ended up, at age forty, with a lower occupational position; 50 percent of the less-educated men from deprived families held blue-collar jobs, compared to 29 percent of the less-educated sons of nondeprived families.

College and less-educated men from deprived families followed life paths that tell a very different story of the depression's impact on lives. The most common pathway, through college entrance, is distinguished by adult achievement, by the potential influence of early military experience on educational attainment (via the G.I. Bill and developmental benefits), by delay in marriage and parenthood, and by the early establishment and persistence of a career. These men fulfilled or surpassed the promise of their education. Between adolescence and mid-life, growth in personal adequacy and goal orientation was most striking in their lives, and they ranked well above the adult health of deprived men who were less fortunate in their adult life course (Elder and Rockwell, 1978). These contrasts on work and health are paralleled by evidence on marital stability. Men who rose above the limitations of their deprived background and educational handicap were just as likely to have stable or intact first marriages as successful men from more affluent homes up to the age of forty (70 percent). By contrast, low achievers from deprived homes experienced a rate of marital instability that parallels the instability and frustrations of their worklife. Only a third of their marriages survived to middle age, a figure well below the marital stability of low achieving men (79 percent) who were spared family misfortune in the 1930s.

From the vantage point of mid-life, one might expect markedly different assessments of the past and present among men with different experiences in the Depression and adult years (Elder and Rockwell, 1978). Not surprisingly, the years after thirty do stand out as better times than childhood or adolescence among the high achievers; 78 percent selected these years as the "best time of life," in contrast to 45 percent of the low achievers. Yet even in the latter group, a background of family deprivation enhanced the relative value of the years after thirty (69 vs. 28 percent of nondeprived). Consistent with results from the Oakland study (Elder, 1974:Ch. 8), hard times seem to have meant that any adult experience acquired greater value than dependency in a financially troubled household. However, the most striking contrast appears in the life review of deprived men who overcame the limitations of their background. Nearly four out of five described the years after thirty as the best time of life, and most looked back on adolescence as the very worst period.

Variation in occupational achievement is clearly an important influence on how the Berkeley men described the emotional trajectory of their lives. But what specific meanings are associated with high and low achievement among men who grew up in deprived families? Upward mobility in work generally offers greater opportunity for use of skills, respect from others, and self-direction (Kohn, 1977). However, the significance of these attainments may depend on what men bring to the adult years. For example, we would expect job security and the comfort of home life to be more important than occupational self-direction for those who experienced both depression hardship and low adult achievement.

In an effort to ascertain the specific meanings of adult activity, the men were asked a series of questions concerning work and marital preferences in the forty year follow-up—about 1969–70. High achievers in the cohort were most likely to derive satisfaction from the intrinsic aspects of work (as measured by an index of worklife rewards—use of skills, freedom to develop ideas, opportunity for advancement, etc.) and to regard the expression of interests and ideas as a most important feature of their work (table 4). The low achievers were more inclined to prefer a different career and saw less chance for advancement. Income, security, and family convenience were important aspects of their work, more so than among high achievers. As a life situation, low achievement bears some resemblance to working conditions in the 1930s, and its correlated orientations (income, job security, avoidance of a job change) are those that acquired significance in the lives of men during the 1930s. Accordingly, one might also expect an association between such orientations and economic deprivation. With adjustments for class background and occupational status at mid-life, the results of regression analysis fail to sustain this prediction.[1] Deprived men were more satisfied than the nondeprived with intrinsic aspects of their work (beta = .14), were less likely to expect a career change (beta = —.29) or advancement (beta = —.15). But they were *not* more satisfied with the extrinsic features of work (e.g., "hours of work") and were actually less likely to rank income and security as important considerations in their employment (ave. beta = —.09).

If values are shaped by the imperatives of adult situations, as well as by early experience, their connection to depression hardship is more appropriately assessed within contexts defined by achievement level. The question is not whether deprivation is related to adult values or attitudes, but rather what life patterns increased the adaptive value of lessons from the 1930s. Thus both

TABLE 4

Worklife Orientation (1969–70)* by Men's Achievement
(*in means and percentages*)

Worklife Orientations	Low Achievement N=18	High Achievement N=32	Probability Level (low vs. high)
Work Attitudes			
Worklife rewards (*means*)	3.3	4.4	.00
Extrinsic rewards (*means*)	4.1	3.7	.22
Extrinsic worklife (*means*)	.81	—.69	.00
Would choose different career	45%	6%	.00
Doesn't expect to advance	50%	25%	.04
Important Aspects of Job			
Expression of interests, ideas	50%	81%	.02
Status	25%	25%	1.00
Income	45%	34%	.45
Security, family convenience	40%	16%	.05

* In the 1969–70 follow-up, the men were asked how they felt about aspects of their current job; responses to each of 14 aspects listed in the questionnaire ranged from "dislike it very much" to "like it very much" (five response categories). Two indexes were constructed from inspection of item correlations and a principal component factor analysis, with varimax rotation: *Worklife rewards*—"opportunity for advancement," "respect from others," "use of skills," "supervision of others," and "freedom to develop ideas" (five items, ave. r = .48); *Extrinsic rewards*—"hours of work," "convenience for family," and "leisure time" (three items, ave. r = .62). Item scores per index were averaged, with a high score corresponding to the index label. To obtain a measure of the relative strength of extrinsic versus worklife aspects of work, we subtracted values on the latter index from scores on extrinsic attributes.

The men were asked to check those three aspects of their job which they considered most important. Some men checked more than three, whereas others made no choice—judging none of the items to be appropriate. In lieu of a more appropriate measure of work values, we relied upon these preference data to index what men valued in their work. Four indexes were constructed from item intercorrelations: *expression of ideas, interests*—choice of either or borth "degree to which work involves interests" and "freedom to develop ideas and use imagination" (no choice scored 0); *status*—choice of either or both "opportunity for advancement" and "respect which others give to the job"; *income*—choice of "income job provides"; and *security, family convenience*—choice of either or both "security of job" and "general convenience for the family."

intrinsic and extrinsic aspects of work may be more rewarding to less successful men who encountered the deprivations of jobless parents. As in social learning theory, scarcity of a reward should enhance the value of even small increments of that reward, whether income or job advancement. This is consistent with the popular notion that depression-reared youth were more willing than postwar generations to accept adverse working conditions.

To explore this line of inquiry, we carried out identical multivariate analyses for each worklife orientation in both low and high achievement groups. The main effect of deprivation in each group was assessed with class origin and occupational status (1968–69) included as statistical controls. Deprived men in the low achievement category were distinguished from all other groups by their low expectation of future advancement, security concerns, and satisfaction with extrinsic features of work (hours, leisure time, family convenience). They were less inclined than nondeprived men with low achievement to prefer another career (40 percent average difference), to value ideas, interests, and status (9 percent difference). Income (7 percent difference) and job security (15 percent difference) were more salient aspects of work in their lives, perhaps reflecting the belief that no advancement lies ahead (25 percent difference).

Deprived origins in the Great Depression increased an appreciation of work rewards and extrinsic work benefits primarily among the *least* successful men—the low achievers. High achieving men placed intrinsic considerations well above extrinsic benefits, and their experience in the depression made no reliable difference in this outlook. Job security and family convenience were clearly at the bottom of their priorities. It is noteworthy, however, that "depression thinking" is least evident among deprived men in the achievement category. They were more optimistic about advancement prospects than the nondeprived (17 percent difference), placed greater value on interests (18 percent difference), and showed much less regard for "income" as a worklife value (26 percent difference). As in *Children of the Great Depression* (Elder,

1974:Ch. 7), the value legacy of the depression in men's lives is highly dependent on their adult life course. The more unrewarding this course, the more important were depression values in the adult years.

The basic material concerns of depression life were far removed from the comfortable living standard that most of the Berkeley men enjoyed at mid-life (over two-thirds were employed in occupations above the clerical or sales level). For the sample as a whole, self-expression in work mattered more than job security, and the qualities of marital interaction assumed greater significance than the creature comforts of home life. When asked on a questionnaire (1969–70) to rank five aspects of marriage, more than half of the Berkeley men placed companionship and mutual understanding in first or second place (53 percent; next in popularity came sexual relations and parenthood (40 and 36 percent, followed at a distance by the security and comfort of a home (18 percent). The high achieving men expressed greater satisfaction with their marriage at the time, when compared to the less successful; they valued companionship and mutual understanding more than sex, parenthood, or family comforts. The latter aspects ranked higher in the value schema of men with a troublesome or problematic worklife—the low achievers.

Two marital qualities, in particular (mutual understanding and a secure family life), were relatively scarce in the childhood experience of deprived men, and consequently should have had special significance in their life. A good many of their households expanded as economic conditions worsened (via jobless men, displaced relatives, boarders, etc.), but family relationships also became more strained—conflicted and punitive, unpredictable and emotionally distant or non-supportive (Sacks, 1975). One man from this home situation recalled how his father would talk and talk, but never understood. "I don't think he ever really heard me, really understood me when I talked to him. . . . Usually I related to him as a scared, worried, frightened child."

Another man painfully recalled shouting matches between his parents, extending late into the evening, and the indifference of his father. Even with class origin and adult status controlled, deprived men were more likely to rank "mutual understanding" as the first or second most important aspect of their marriage (60 vs. 47 percent nondeprived), and they were also more inclined to consider the "security and comfort of family life" as a valued source of gratification (25 vs. 12 percent). Mutual understanding assumed priority over "companionship" in the marital concept of men from hardpressed families, and they tended to place greater emphasis on the rewards of parenting than on sexual relations.

However, all of this ignores those life contexts that give options and activities meaning; in particular the crucial difference between the *careers* of deprived men, from low to high achievement. Among high achievers, men from deprived families were more likely to value mutual understanding, the rewards of parenthood, and the security or comforts of home life; they were less inclined to stress companionship and sex than the offspring of nondeprived homes. By contrast, less successful men from deprived families generally made choices reflecting an egocentric view of marriage, a view which differentiates this group from the cohort as a whole. Both work and marriage were least rewarding to these men, and they had little positive to say about the benefits of companionship, conjugal understanding, and "having children." Their concept of marriage is based on the primacy of sexual gratification (four out of five ranked this choice first or second) and on the comforts of home life. Both values were more popular in this group than in any other.

The meaning of work and marriage among the Berkeley men depended on both their depression experience and its consequences for their life course. "Things that matter" in these areas reflect to some degree whether they encountered hard times through family misfortune as a child of the depression or were privileged by the security and nurturance of an economically stable home. Family deprivation is associated with values that assign priority to the security or comforts of family life. However, the fortunes of adult life also made a difference in what men valued, especially in their work. Security was not an important issue among the successful. Intrinsic features of work (self-expression, etc.) are more salient than extrinsic considerations (income, convenience, etc.) in the lives of men (deprived or not) who fulfilled or surpassed the promise of their family background and education; the less successful tended to reverse this pattern. The full implications of these diverse career lines emerge only when life patterns are linked to the depression experience.

Deprived men with divergent career patterns actually display the greatest differences in the persistence of "depression values." Those who managed to surmount the limitations of family hardship and education tended to value work and marriage in terms of personal *and* social fulfillment; both activities were valued in and of themselves. At the other extreme are deprived men who experienced instability and failure through work and marriage; they valued work and marriage less for their intrinsic quality than for what they offered in meeting basic needs—income and job security, leisure time, and sexual gratification.

Since this analysis is based on a relatively small sample, comparisons among subgroups must be viewed with caution. Would similar results be obtained from another, larger sample of men from 1928–29 cohort? It is doubtful whether we shall ever be able to answer this question, owing to the security of long-term longitudinal archives. However, a longitudinal study of an older cohort—the Oakland men who were born in 1920–21 (Elder, 1974) —reports outcomes that do correspond with major themes in this research. Worklife in both cohorts represents an important bridge between family deprivation and adult achievement. A substantial number of the Oakland and Berkeley men from deprived homes were able to counter an educational disadvantage through effective application of their talents in work. Also, the relation between depression hardship and security values appears primarily among the least successful men in both cohorts. Security matters most to men who lacked this basic quality of life during the 1930s and in the course of adulthood.

Overview

The historical time of the Berkeley cohort roughly corresponds with that of younger adolescents in August Hollingshead's classic study, *Elmtown's Youth* (1949). Both cohorts experienced hard times during the vulnerable years of childhood and entered wartime adolescence after a relatively prolonged exposure to family deprivation. Though Hollingshead did not attend to events of the depression or World War II, they most likely influenced the life chances and careers of the adolescents he studied, if we are to judge from the lives of the Berkeley men. Within the middle and working class, deprived youth in the Berkeley cohort were no less able than the nondeprived, but they experienced a substantial disadvantage in life chances through lower formal education and the psychological disabilities of self-inadequacy, low aspirations, and passivity. Consistent with a life stage interpretation, this handicap is more pronounced than that observed in an older cohort which was followed through the depression and into the adult years—males who were born during the early 1920s and grew up in Oakland, California (Elder, 1974). Nevertheless, most of the deprived youth in the Berkeley cohort managed to rise above the limitations of their background, especially if they entered college. By mid-life, their average occupational status closely resembled the position of men who were spared family misfortune during the 1930s.

In this paper, we considered both how Berkeley men were able to overcome disadvantages of early life and how the relationship between family deprivation in the 1930s and later accomplishments influenced values in the realms of work and marriage. From deprivation to adult achievement, the life course of the Berkeley men is distinguished by three events or processes that facilitated achievement: firstly, entry into college at a time of unparalleled opportunity for higher education and career advancement; secondly, early entry into military service, which provided both an economic means for higher education and developmental growth; and thirdly, investments in worklife, reflected by early entry into a stable career and persistence in a line of work. Nearly four out of five of the Berkeley youth entered some program of higher education, and those who followed this course from a deprived background gained access to occupational opportunities which enabled them to utilize their endowment to greatest advantage. Relatively early career entry and persistence were more characteristic of these men than of college entrants from nondeprived homes, a difference which accounts in large part for their noteworthy achievement in worklife up to middle age. Depression hardship entailed a continuing pattern of disadvantage only among the small number of non-college men.

Military service qualifies as a noteworthy bridge between family deprivation and worklife achievement in the Berkeley cohort. Whether middle or working class, deprived youth were more likely than the nondeprived to enter the military, and they did so at a much earlier age, usually before the age of twenty-one. As a result they made the transition to marriage and parenthood at a later age and gained access to the financial benefits of the G.I. Bill at a crucial time in their life. These benefits no doubt weakened the observed educational disadvantage of family deprivation (although documentation is lacking). Time in the military also offered potential developmental benefits, especially to youth who were unsure of themselves and their future. Military service provided male models of competence to boys who grew up without effective fathers, removed them from the control and compensatory interests of their mothers, and established a legitimate "time out" in which to review their life and prospects. Given available evidence, these benefits remain inferential. Nevertheless, it is apparent that military service played a key role in structuring the life course and opportunities of men who managed to rise above the disadvantages of a depression childhood.

The particular intersection of historical times and life history in the Berkeley cohort seems well designed to foster a materialistic life style. Its life span and that of the Oakland cohort in *Children of the Great Depression* is unique in the sense that generalized hardship, which enhanced the value of material goods, was soon followed by economic recovery, that often turned this value into reality. Consistent with this observation, Inglehart (1977:363) refers to the onset of the postwar era in Western Europe as a turning point in value priorities, from "the overwhelming emphasis on material consumption and security" among cohorts which came of age during the scarcity regimes of depression and World War to post-materialist concerns with the quality of life among postwar cohorts, a theme supported by conditions of economic growth and physical security. Some have argued that this value shift may also apply to American cohorts (cf. Bengtson and Lovejoy, 1973). But Inglehart's thesis on historical times is based on two questionable assumptions—that formative historical experiences are relatively uniform across members of a cohort, and that the values "acquired in childhood and youth tend to remain with one throughout life" (pp. 363–64). Both of these assumptions are challenged by intra-cohort analyses of the Berkeley and Oakland men.

Family deprivation was not a uniform event among middle or working class families in the Berkeley and Oakland cohorts, and its implications for adult priorities varied according to the life course of men who grew up in deprived households. For *both* cohorts, security concerns in work and family are related to depression hardship primarily among men who were relatively unsuccessful in their worklife. The interaction of a depression childhood and a troublesome worklife enhanced the importance of income, job security, and the notion of home as refuge. Such concerns were subordinated to life quality matters in the social world of men who rose above the limitations of family deprivation through worklife advancement. In the Berkeley cohort, these men valued work as a medium for self-expression and marriage as a primary relationship based on mutual understanding—experiences often missing from their depression childhood. The value legacy of the Great Depression in the biography of men from Berkeley and Oakland can only be understood within the context of the lives they have lived.

Preparation of this essay was supported by Grant MH-25834 from the National Institute of Mental Health.

Note

1. Regression analysis is a statistical procedure that separates and weighs the independent influence of several distinct variables. In this case it is used to determine the influence of deprivation on work orientation, independent of class background and occupational attainment.

References

Baltes, Paul B. and Schaie, K. Warner, eds. *Life-Span Developmental Psychology: Personality and Socialization.* New York: Academic Press, 1973.

Bengtson, Vern L. and Lovejoy, M. C. "Values, Personality, and Social Structure: An Intergenerational Analysis." *American Behavioral Scientist* 16 (1973):880–912.

Cohen, Jack K.; Falk, R. Frank; and Cortese, Charles F. "Reply to Taeuber and Taeuber." *American Sociological Review* 41 (1976):889–93.

Coleman, James S. *The Adolescent Society.* New York: Free Press, 1961.

Cortese, Charles S.; Falk, R. Frank; and Cohen, Jack. "Further Considerations on the Methodological Analysis of Segregation Indices." *American Sociological Review* 41 (1976):630–37.

Demos, John. *A Little Commonwealth: Family Life in Plymouth Colony.* New York: Oxford University Press, 1970.

Elder, Glen H., Jr. *Children of the Great Depression*. Chicago: University of Chicago Press, 1974.

Elder, Glen H., Jr. "Age Differentiation and the Life Course." *Annual Review of Sociology*. Edited by A. Inkeles. Palo Alto: Annual Reviews, 1975.

Elder, Glen H., Jr. and Rockwell, Richard C. "Economic Depression and Postwar Opportunity in Men's Lives: A Study of Life Patterns and Health." *Research in Community and Mental Health*. Edited by Roberta G. Simmons. Greenwich, Conn.: JAI Press, 1978.

Furstenberg, Frank F., Jr. *Unplanned Parenthood: The Social Consequences of Teenage Childbearing*. New York: The Free Press, 1976.

Greven, Philip J., Jr. *Four Generations: Population, Land and Family in Colonial Andover, Massachusetts*. Ithaca: Cornell University Press, 1970.

Hogan, Dennis P. "The Passage of American Men from Family of Orientation to Family of Procreation: Pattern, Timing and Determinants." Ph.D. dissertation, University of Wisconsin, 1976.

Hollingshead, August. *Elmtown's Youth*. New York: Wiley, 1949.

Inglehart, Ronald. *The Silent Revolution: Changing Values and Political Styles Among Western Publics*. Princeton, N. J.: Princeton University Press, 1977.

Katz, Michael B. *The People of Hamilton, Canada West: Family and Class in a Mid-Nineteenth Century City*. Cambridge, Mass.: Harvard University Press, 1975.

Kohn, Melvin L. *Class and Conformity*. 2nd ed. Chicago: University of Chicago Press, 1977.

Macfarlane, Jean Walker. "Studies in Child Guidance: I. Methodology of Data Collection and Organization." *Monographs of the Society for Research in Child Development* 11 (1938):(6).

Macfarlane, Jean Walker. "From Infancy to Childhood." *Childhood Education* 39 (1963):336–42.

Modell, John; Furstenberg, Frank F., Jr.; and Hershberg, Theodore. "Social Change and the Transition to Adulthood in Historical Perspective." *Journal of Family History* 1 (Autumn 1976):7–32.

Riley, Matilda W.; Johnson, Marilyn E.; and Foner, Anne. *Aging and Society: A Sociology of Age Stratification*. New York: Russell Sage Foundation, 1972.

Sacks, Howard L. "Socialization and Status Change in the Development of Self." Doctoral dissertation, University of North Carolina, 1975.

Seeley, John R. "Adolescence: The Management of Emancipation in History and Life History." *The Sociology of Youth*. Edited by Harry Silverstein. New York: MacMillan, 1973, pp. 21–28.

Sharp, Laure L. and Krasnesor, Rebecca. "College Students and Military Service: The Experience of an Earlier Cohort." *Sociology of Education* 41 (1968):380–400.

Taeuber, Karl E. and Taeuber, Alma F. "Comment on Cortese, Falk and Cohen (ASR August 1976)." *American Sociological Review* 41 (1976): 884–89.

Changing Risks, Changing Adaptations: American Families in the Nineteenth and Twentieth Centuries

JOHN MODELL
Professor, Department of History,
University of Minnesota, Minneapolis, Minn.

Just as the first several generations of historians of the family were content to discover ideal family patterns in legal or literary sources, much current writing consists of the analysis of systematic deviations of behavior from the ideal. Commonly, such divergence from the ideal is understood as adaptive behavior, in the face of constraints which families, with only limited resources, confront in their environment. If the contraints and resources can be examined, and the set of adaptive behaviors charted, we can draw inferences about the experiences of families in historical context. Such inferences we justly call "family history."

The present essay varies this procedure somewhat, but retains its logic at the core. My argument has three main elements. First, drawing upon such fragmentary evidence as carries the account forward, I will assess the extent of uncertainty and crisis faced or reasonably anticipated by American families. One product of the industrial transformation of America in the nineteenth century was widespread externally-imposed uncertainty, experienced by families in the conduct of their daily affairs; but in the twentieth century, such uncertainty has lessened markedly (despite interruptions). This general reduction, I maintain, has resulted in a reorientation in the rhythm and purpose of intrafamilial cooperation.[1]

My second theme involves a conception of cooperation within the family, largely focused on the household as an economic unit.

I propose a distinction between "defensive" and "accumulative" modes of family economic cooperation, suggest some empirical manifestations of these, and argue that industrialization initially imposed the defensive mode upon most families.

My final proposition is that the form of family cooperation affects the internal dynamics of family life. Widespread uncertainty, I argue, broadened the range of family adaptations, and introduced thereby elements of variety into families' interior lives not reflected in ideal statements about modal families under average conditions. The implication of this is that lessened uncertainty over time has reduced the repertory of adaptations carried out by families, and has thereby led to diminished variety in family life.[2]

If this argument is correct, it suggests something of a paradox, for it proposes a direction of change opposite to a widely-accepted sociological interpretation of family history, which argues a change from "family behavior controlled by the mores, public opinion, and law," to a more spontaneous situation of "mutual affection and consensus."[3] The contrasting sequence I here propose is, I believe, especially timely in view of the great interest now being shown in alternative family forms. It seems reasonable to wonder whether our contemporary effort intentionally to vary roles and emotional patterns within the family is not in part owing to the secular decline in unplanned adaptations in the face of uncertainty.

Environmental Risks

An examination of mortality and of one response to it offers us some initial insights. Higher mortality in the past did not simply remove more people from their families than is the case now; it removed them more often at times in their lives and in their families' careers that challenged those families' ways of organizing their resources, material and emotional. Thus, while the age-specific mortality rate for 55–64 year-old white men in major eastern cities in 1880 was only about 1.9 times what it is in similar places in the United States today, the ratio at age 25 was much higher—about 4.3 times higher, in fact.[4] The members dying out of an initial cohort are far more clustered today than a century ago into the years over 65 or so. While in 1880 more than a quarter of the men surviving to adulthood would die during the family-building years (20–44), less than 7 percent of their counterparts today die during that period. Peter Uhlenberg's work has shown in considerable detail that despite increases in voluntary variances from usual family patterns such as divorce, these kinds of demographic changes have created a situation in which "an increasing proportion of the population lives out the life course almost wholly within a family context" and one with full complements at all points.[5]

Propertyless urban families particularly need a buttress in case of the death of the main earner, and in the mid-nineteenth century, life insurance began to supplement traditional succour, eventually to supplant it. Working-men's family budgets indicate that during the 1890s there was a doubling of the prevalence of life insurance among these families, to about two in three in 1901. The upward trend continued at a slightly slower pace until in 1918–19 about seven in eight families had some life insurance expenditures, a level maintained into the 1950s.[6] By this time, Americans had developed a uniquely firm and extensive attachment to the device, which was encouraged both by fraternal insurance and weekly-payment "industrial insurance," and was sanctioned by fear of family disgrace at a pauper's burial and by "many weird stories about 'city' funerals."[7] Initially quite small, by 1900 the average face value of policies had grown to about the average annual wage for American employees; after the 1920s, it was double annual wages.[8]

Once purchased, insurance had of course to be maintained by regular payments, and at nineteenth-century levels of uncertainty even prudential Americans had considerable trouble doing so.

Insurance company records permit us to abstract away from death to whatever other environmental risks led to the failure to renew policies. Data for a large number of American companies for mid-century suggest that perhaps two in ten (not dying) failed to meet the premium on their whole life policies even at the first annual renewal date.[9] By the fifth year, no more than six in ten retained their policies. Persistence in the risk pool improved among those (not dying) who took out their insurance at an older age—up to their forties. *To a point*, age brought security, no doubt in part owing to the maturation of additional wage-earners in the family. Beyond that point, such improvements were offset by lessened physical vigor.[10]

In this context, we should observe that the past century has on the whole seen a marked increase in the ability (or inclination) of families to hold onto insurance once they took it out, probably the product of increased productivity per capita, lower premiums owing to reduced mortality, and generally improved security. Turnover rates seem to have declined by over one-half from the latter half of the nineteenth century to 1940.[11] Although the Great Depression brought a setback to the ability of families to retain their policies, the subsequent return of prosperity permitted the retention rate to climb again; and it has since remained high. If we have correctly understood insurance, American families seem to have gained palpably here in their ability to balance off some of the uncertainties of life.

Since the nineteenth century, the shape of careers has changed, as rewards have been redistributed over the life course. Examination of fragmentary income-by-age data from scattered points suggests that earnings peaks have always been at mid-career, but that the peak has shifted slightly later in life, and that rewards over the life course probably evened out somewhat, largely through increased movement of manual workers into occupations where declining physical vitality is less severely penalized.[12] In the generality of male careers, too, the raw inexperience and energy of the young have become less well-rewarded than once, relative to experience and reputation, which these days fare rather better (contradicting our usual image of this trend). The newer career suggests a system that anticipates and encourages steady application by the worker to his work more than did the older arrangement. The older pattern seemed to capture instead vitality at the early stages of the worklife.[13]

By the early twentieth century, factory reformers had become aware of major costs accruing both to employer and to employee from unpredictable careers encouraged by this system of reward. Rapid labor-force turnover especially attracted reformers' attention, for employee records revealed that (in the New York paper box industry in 1913–14, for example) four in ten employees had been with his or her employer for less than one year. Most of these workers were young, but turnover was widespread in all age groups, and attachment to employer came slowly and uncertainly. Although 35–39 year-old men averaged about fifteen years in the trade, they had been with their current employer on average less than four years. Similar figures were reported in less marginal industries.[14] Generally, layoffs and dismissals accounted for far less of the turnover than did resignations, although these declined with age, skill level, and time at the firm. Only the skilled seemed to recognize a "career ladder," and they only (unlike other employees) cited opportunity elsewhere rather than dissatisfactions as major reasons for resigning[15] (see table 1).

The level and something of the incidence of unemployment in the late nineteenth century can be indicated by 1890 and 1900 figures on unemployment from the United States Census, and from the 1885 Massachusetts state census.[16] None of these censuses fell at the depths of depressions, yet the national figures, taking them at their face value, are remarkably high: about one in five men outside of agriculture lost a month or more, one in ten four months or more. Women, we should note, lost less (but presumably because in many cases they simply avoided or did not report labor-force activity), but this advantage was relatively less true in the tighter year, 1900, and for heavily-industrialized Massachusetts in the depressed year of 1885, it was not true at all. As the Massachusetts materials demonstrate, except before age twenty, maturity brought precious little security against the threat of unemployment, and after age forty, reemployment after layoff came slower. (In the post-World War II period a new age-grading of unemployment has appeared, in which men in the family-building years are considerably more secure than those both younger and older.)[17]

The industrial order of the nineteenth century was filled with uncertainties. Families' plans were at the mercy of numerous

TABLE 1

Proportions Unemployed During Year for One Month or More, by Race and Sex for the United States, 1890 and 1900 (Nonagricultural Occupations Only), and by Age and Sex for Massachusetts, 1885; and Proportions Unemployed Four or More Months, U.S., and Mean Length of Unemployment (*in months*), Massachusetts.

	Proportions Unemployed One Month or More		Proportions Unemployed 4+ Mo.		Mean Length of Unemployment	
	Males	Females	Males	Females	Males	Females
All nonag., U.S.						
1890	18.0%	12.4%	9.1%	6.1%		
1900	23.5%	21.4%	12.2%	11.4%		
Negro nonag., U.S.						
1890	20.8%	11.1%	10.1%	5.6%		
1900	31.5%	23.2%	15.2%	12.6%		
All, Mass., 1885						
10–19	37.9%	38.0%			4.5	4.2
20–29	30.1%	29.0%			3.9	3.7
30–39	27.1%	27.1%			3.9	3.8
40–49	28.4%	23.2%			4.1	4.1
50–59	29.0%	21.8%			4.4	4.4
60+	27.6%	10.3%			5.0	4.9

exigencies outside their control, as a major survey of American workingmen taken in 1901[18]—when unemployment was considerably lower than in 1885 or 1900—indicates vividly. Late attachment to employers and imperfectly developed job markets must explain most of the 17.2 percent of all workers who were "unable to get work" sometime during the year, and their lengthy 2½ month interval between jobs, especially in view of the lesser figures for "establishment closed" and "slack work." We are alerted by reform-centered social history to the considerable extent of industrial accidents, yet fifteen times as many employees lost almost two months apiece because they were sick. The data suggest that, even in periods when the industrial economy was functioning well, those who worked in it were but imperfectly served (see table 2).

If a third of the industrial insecurity in 1901 was owing to sickness, we should look a bit closer at the phenomenon. Systematic investigation began only after public health conditions had some-

TABLE 2

Proportion of Male Heads of Families Idle, by Cause, and Mean Period of Unemployment by Cause, Workingclass Families, 1901

	Proportion of all Family Heads Affected	Mean Period of Unemployment (*in weeks*)
Accident	1.0%	9.6
Bad weather	1.5%	10.2
Drunkenness	0.2%	18.9
Establishment closed	2.5%	8.7
Lack of material, etc.	0.1%	5.2
Sickness	15.4%	8.8
Slack work	6.7%	9.8
Strike	1.1%	9.6
Unable to get work	17.2%	11.1
ALL CAUSES	46.5%	9.4

what improved, but even then, a careful study[19] indicates that in 1919 one in twenty industrial employees missed a month or more for sickness during the year, that one-half missed at least a week, and that overall 1.8 percent of all potential work time was lost through sickness. By analogy with levels of mortality, we may estimate that nineteenth-century sickness figures would be perhaps one-third greater. Heads of workingclass families could well anticipate occasional failures to provide; their families in one way or another would have to compensate. Cross-sectional health surveys of urban populations early in the twentieth century, data for three of which are presented below, document just how pervasive sickness was.[20] They show, too, how much variations in prevalence of sickness by age would amplify change in the conditions of life over the life cycle. One can also estimate synthetic family sickness rates from these data; for instance, a family of five toward the end of the childrearing period had about a one-in-twelve chance of someone's being sick on any given day. But again, sickness was syndromatic, and one could not anticipate when such problems might strike. When they did, the medically under-privileged, the malnourished, the stressed drew undoubtedly more than their share (see table 3).

Extensive investigations of the incidence of sickness in 1921–24 include a study of socioeconomic differentials (although the community studied was a relatively homogeneous one).[21] Age-specific incidence differentials of sickness are striking. If we let the incidence of sickness (per year) among members of "comfortable" families equal 1.00, sickness among people from middling and "poor" families differed from this level (see table 4).

Children from middling and poor families were reportedly more healthy than were those from wealthier families; *but their parents were less healthy.* At the oldest age group there was little socioeconomic differential. Without overinterpreting, it seems fair to say that the lack of economic resources most affected the health of those members of poorer families upon whom family responsibilities fell most heavily. Those whose health was most crucial to

TABLE 3

Percentage Sick at Time of Survey, by Age and Sex, Rochester, Boston, and Pittsburgh, 1915–17

	Rochester, N.Y. Sept. 1915	Boston, Mass. July 1916	Pittsburgh, Pa. March 1917
Males			
—15	0.8	1.1	0.9
15–24	1.4	1.2	1.0
25–34	1.1	1.6	1.6
35–44	2.4	2.1	2.0
45–54	3.2	3.3	3.0
55–64	7.4	5.1	4.4
65+	12.4	10.2	8.2
Females			
—15	1.0	1.2	0.8
15–24	1.6	1.1	1.1
25–34	2.3	1.4	1.6
35–44	2.9	2.2	1.8
45–54	3.6	3.8	2.2
55–64	5.4	5.5	3.5
65+	11.2	11.3	6.9

TABLE 4

Age-specific Incidence Differentials of Sickness (*"comfortable" families = 1.00*)

	0–4	5–9	10–14	15–24	25–44	45–64	65+
Middling	0.92	0.91	0.93	0.92	1.16	1.32	0.97
Poor	0.86	0.85	0.93	1.01	1.32	1.48	1.13

their families took most often to their beds. Their children, of whom less was demanded, had relatively less recourse to the sick role. Since many adult sicknesses were chronic and syndromatic, and had a multivalent affect on family life, we may fairly point to sickness as one systematic link between structured social insecurity and family dynamics. We may presume that this link was even more characteristic of the sickly nineteenth century, and has become less characteristic of life now.[22]

Family Cooperation

We may assume that most families were in touch with the world in which they lived. A "defensive" mode of family economic cooperation was fitted to a world in which the risks to families were many—especially for families with limited resources—and the institutions for softening them few. Kinship, voluntary associations, and formal organizations (such as insurance) served this purpose, but for the most part it was the individual coresident family that, as budgetary unit, adapted in the face of uncertainty. The cooperative family economy of this period—indeed up through the Great Depression—must be understood in part as an attempt to pool risks in what was experienced as a very uncertain world.

Such a perspective often escaped more secure contemporaries, such as the author of a Wisconsin Bureau of Labor Statistics report on child labor, issued in 1900.[23] Reflecting conventional middle-class views of child labor—even when legal—the report insisted upon a major component of parental "greed" in the widespread abuse of child labor. "There are parents who bring children into the world, actuated seemingly by a desire to rear them to the earning age, with as little bother or expense as possible," the report argued. By some unstated principle, "family income is not increased by the toil of small children but invariably reaches a certain standard which would be attained by the head of the household if the children were not allowed to work." Especially galling to this investigator was the fact that many of these families had equity in their own houses.

But house buying was no simple quest for an inappropriate degree of respectability. It was rather a hedge against palpable risks, and one which became increasingly common at and after the end of the nineteenth century. Larger, securely-held houses, at least into the 1920s, were an inducement to older unmarried (or even newly-married) children to remain part of and contributors to the family economy.[24] Control of houses in a tight housing market was a bargaining element within the family, necessary especially in view of the age-earnings curve and the age-incidence of sickness, and it offered a lifetime economic resource through taking in boarders and lodgers.

Home ownership, like multiple family incomes, was part of a defensive strategy oriented, as it were, to hoarding resources—saving for a rainy day, in the quaint phrase. Reformers analyzing nineteenth-century family budgets were generally alarmed at the large proportions of families with a net deficit in a given year, but both their comments and the data they present attest to a recognition which they shared with their clients of the *necessity* of saving. Most families did save; in the 1901 budget study, for instance, 50.3 percent saved at least some money (an average of $121, or 16 percent of the total family income), as compared with 16 percent with a deficit for the year.[25]

The shape of the family economy at any moment was a function of several non-volitional elements, notably labor market opportunities, stage of the family life cycle,[26] and recent or anticipated reverses in family fortunes. But it also followed from at least a pair of elements determined by families' own preferences: sex- and marital-role prescriptions regarding economic activity; and the family's chosen plane of consumption.

External "necessity" did not simply impose itself upon families. Rather, difficulties led families to contemplate modifications in aspiration and the organization of roles to adapt their behaviors without necessarily abandoning their ideals. Herein lay a dynamic that cannot but have affected the content of family life, as experienced.

These various dimensions of the defensive mode of family economic cooperation were surely consequential within the family. At the simplest level, the contributions of each of the contributors were skimmed by that person to a greater or lesser degree, which had to be negotiated. More complex was the potential such arrangements offered for interpersonal conflict. "You never rest until you die," remarked a daughter in New York State who regularly made her contribution to a cooperative family economy, "but I will get out by marrying somebody, but my mother won't marry me off yet. I had a fine chance last week, a nice fellow with a good job who wanted me. But you see I got to work until my brother begins to make some money. I am making $10 and my father $15. It is no cinch I tell you. There are eight of us."[27] Leila Houghteling remarked of Chicago unskilled-labor families in 1927 that "there seems to be no generally accepted principle in relation to the amount a working child should contribute to the family fund," and that such remittances at that time took a wide variety of forms.[28] Such a variety in itself may indicate a challenge to normative consensus within these families.

The expense budget, too, may have often been problematic, and solutions symptomatic of shifting balances within families.[29] A clue to one such process is provided by the exceptionally full data on clothing expenses in the national family budget study of 1918–19.[30] Clothing, after all, in a democratic, industrial society, seems to be connected symbolically with the public identity of family members, as well as with the prestige of the family as a unit. Three striking cross-sectional tendencies accompanied increasing family income. Each is interpretable in part in view of the fact that each income class included greater proportionate contributions of income from members other than the head, generally from children, whose contribution to these workingclass family incomes rose from 8 percent among the poorest to 71 percent among the best-off families.

The budgets reveal that, firstly, wives' clothing expenditures rose relative to husbands'; secondly, children fifteen years and older increasingly exceeded their mothers' and fathers' clothing expenditures; and thirdly, female children fifteen years and older increasingly purchased more apparel than their brothers of the same age, and than their younger siblings. All else remained in roughly constant proportions. As these families prospered, their direct material benefits accrued less to the "patriarch" than to adult and adolescent women. Without presuming to plumb the gender-role significance of all this, we can infer that the family's balance of gratifications changed, to the benefit of working-age boys and girls and to the wives whose reliance upon their husbands was modified.

The 1918–19 budget materials, although they reveal considerable budgetary cooperation within the families, may in important ways resemble current patterns. Indeed, examining together data on family income in 1918–19, 1939, and 1959[31] suggests that the critical element may be acute environmental insecurity. If so, in important respects Great Depression family behavior may have constituted a return to older patterns. We are reminded of the critical distinction between secular but reversible trends (such as the decline in environmental uncertainty) and linear, directional change.

At all three points concerned, proportions of families with supplementary earners was positively correlated with higher family incomes, but not to the same degree. In this respect, the 1918–19 families more resembled those in 1959, than the depression families, for whom the correlation was considerably weaker. In the prosperous years, a close association could be found between a family's economic expansiveness and its ability to send a supplementary worker into the labor force—typically a son or daughter in 1918–19, but a wife in 1959. The 1939 and 1959 data are rich enough to permit some further documentation. Thus, we find that at given family-income levels the 1939 families were far more responsive than were their 1959 counterparts to unemployment of the head, and to family size—a crude approximation to necessary expenses. If the 1939 cooperative family economy had as its logic defense of a standard of living, cooperation in the postwar boom was apparently focused upon accumulating some of the fruits of prosperity. At least since the early post-World War II period (when annual data first became available), there is a near-perfect parallelism in the movements of gross national product per capita, and the proportion of families which have more than one earner.[32] Enjoyment of prosperity by families has depended upon the widespread adoption of an "accumulative" mode of economic cooperation, which, as we have seen, has characteristic ramifications within the family system.

Adaptation and Family Life

Let us for the moment ask what kinds of differences within the family might the widespread "defensive" mode of cooperation have made? We can give no more than a speculative answer, but at least three important areas of family life seem to have been affected: the general flexibility and resilience of the nuclear family unit; the sex-role specialization of the marital partners; and the socialization of children. The impact of uncertainty upon each is illustrated in studies of family adaptation to economic depression, although I suspect that there was nothing special about this particular aspect of risk.

Within months of the economic downturn in 1921, a Children's Bureau study shows,[33] large number of families displayed "defensive" cooperative patterns temporarily put aside in the preceding boom period. Wives and children (especially daughters) entered the labor market for the first time, boarders and lodgers were sought, consumption decisions were made cautiously. That families "coped" is in one sense heartwarming, but we must not assume that adaptability was an inexhaustible resource, a generalized and free good. Robert and Helen Merrell Lynd knew differently:

> Recurrent "hard times" make support of their families periodically impossible for many workers; the wife must make a home for her husband and care for her children, but she is increasingly spending her days in gainful employment outside the home; husband and wife must cleave

to each other in the sex relation, but fear of pregnancy frequently makes this relation a dread one for one or both of them; affection between the two is regarded as the basis of marriage, but sometimes in the day-after-day struggle this seems to be a memory rather than a present help. . . . More than one wife seems to think of her husband less as an individual than as a focus of problems and fears.[34]

Though the Lynds conceive this unhappy state to be of recent origin, such results commonly would seem to flow from externally-induced shifts within the family. Such, at any rate, deserves systematic investigation in historical accounts of families undergoing unemployment, sickness, bereavement, and other forms of crisis.

Virtually all Great Depression accounts discuss the challenge posed to fathers' well-understood role as breadwinner.[35] The challenge was resolved variously, depending upon families' material resources, unanimity about the traditional structure of roles, the father's emotional and physical resilience, his ability to find reemployment; and, affecting all of these, the initial class position of the families. Families which had earlier weathered analogous crises more easily rediscovered temporary but at any rate accustomed responses. Fathers rigidly bound to the basic-provider role coped less well with enforced change than did those whose repertory of family roles was already broad, and who had thereby developed intuitive knowledge of the demands and gratifications of others.[36] Successful family adaptation—given the likelihood of repeated external crises—was in a sense a "career." As uncertainty was widely prevalent in the late nineteenth century, so also, presumably, were successful resolutions of crises. We may therefore posit a wider dispersion of flexible role structures than any ideal image of the rigid (and patriarchal) nineteenth-century family would suggest.

Shifts in responsibilities, gratifications, and even family roles do not, however, necessarily imply long-term innovation in values. Whether or not lasting change results depends on family background, the nature and severity of the crisis, and on the structures in which the adapting family is enmeshed. Thus Earl Koos argues that poorer families will generally resolve crises in a matter-of-fact fashion through a temporary adoption of altered roles and through assistance of "traditional" institutions like mutual aid and kinship cooperation, while middle-class families in effect savor their crises and often place a premium on self-conscious innovation of values.[37]

Melvin Kohn's significant study of family socialization of conformity in the 1950s and 1960s illustrates in another way the chanciness of long-term change stemming unintentionally from family cooperation.[38] Kohn's central argument is that parents socialize their children in ways appropriate to the kinds of situations they themselves have experienced at work. Thus, blue-collar fathers, who have been closely supervised at work, teach obedience and neatness to their children, and discourage curiosity and self-direction. But mothers, too, often worked—for the usual mix of reasons. When they did, they drew from the work experience pretty much what their husbands did. Where wives of blue-collar workers had blue-collar employment, their children were socialized even more intensely in workingclass values. But because of the nature of the job market, most wives worked in white-collar capacities; they learned new values in their work situation and modified accordingly the values they taught their children.

Family misfortune or anticipated misfortune has also often put children to work (especially in the nineteenth century), producing thereby shifts in the distribution of gratifications within the family, and not uncommonly altering family roles. One depression mother reflected upon the shifting configuration of roles within her family:

> Who knows how long my boys will be willing to help pay on the house? Already they are complaining what little they make they can not buy anything for themselves. I don't blame them; it is true. My husband feels badly to see the boys get cross and tried to explain that it is all in the family and what they put in the home it's all theirs.[39]

Often, references to sexual difficulties and to sickness crop up in contexts of sudden economic deprivation, indicating the pervasiveness of crisis throughout the life of the family. The generality of the pattern suggests that these may well be mechanisms by which family roles and emotional balances change. (Sickness, especially, is a social-historical theme badly in need of systematic consideration.) The Lynds rightly heard much when one Middletown wife told them that childbearing would just have to wait "till we get steady work. No, we don't use anything to prevent children. I just keep away from my husband. He don't care—only at times. He's discouraged because he's out of work. I went to work but had to quit because I was so nervous."[40]

The sick role was frequently a part in transitions in internal family structure. The economist E. Wight Bakke describes a classic instance.[41] When Mr. Raparka, eighteen years the patriarch of a Polish-American family in New Haven, lost his job as a moulder's helper, the family responded by economizing, in diet among other ways. The baby, now drinking canned milk, developed convulsions,

> which alarmed the whole family. Mrs. Raparka's pains in the back, present since the birth of the child, suddenly became worse. Her husband, with no money to pay for a doctor, refused to call one. . . . This decision was resented by the whole family. . . . [Soon] he had exhausted his available resources and one day pawned his overcoat. Hunting for work in an early snowstorm, he caught a cold which rapidly developed into a serious illness.

His sickness was the occasion, perhaps the expression, of Mr. Raparka's inability to perform his accustomed family role. With Mr. Raparka debilitated, his wife "took the initiative," receiving from a local social-welfare agency medical assistance not only for her baby but for her husband as well. Mr. Raparka, upon his recovery, was at first sullen, then "desperate" in his search for a regular job. Even after he found public work at his old wages, the children questioned his authority as never before. The transit of authority was completed when Mr. Raparka's eldest son graduated from trade school and obtained a private job that paid so well that his father was cut off the public-employment rolls. Social pathology did not result, and in that sense the family was quite successfully repaired. But much was changed in the family system.

The Raparkas, I am sure, were never quite the same again. Nor, as Glen Elder's study of lives over time shows us, would their children ever be quite the same. Yet, both the depression case studies and Elder's work show us that the Great Depression on the whole did not bring about revolutionary changes within most families. Further, the Great Depression was in no way unique in inducing in families the kinds of adaptive behavior that produced changes in the interior life; in fact, such reactions—including the adoption of the sick role—were quite ordinary and no doubt had long been. I suspect that the systematic application of this perspective will help us understand, for instance, the numerous mid-nineteenth-century accounts of family ruin through spirituous liquor, as well as the less frequently recorded accounts of families preserved.

In the end, we need to project such interpretations onto the population of families, to estimate both the prevalence and incidence of family crises of various sorts. At the same time, widespread environmental uncertainty is an *objective* aspect of family life, one to which families needed regularly to address their planful activity, but also an aspect with an empirically recoverable history. To arrive at a meaningful sense of family careers in the past, I believe we need to assess systematically the changing risks families faced, and with some psychological insight, comprehend the changing adaptations of ideal patterns with which they faced them.

Notes

This essay has benefited from the comments of Professors Clarke A. Chambers, Frank F. Furstenberg, and Eric Monkkonen, in addition to those of my fellow panelists at the Smithsonian Institution seminar.

1. That the rhythm of life has a determinate history is developed informally in Joseph F. Kett, *Rites of Passage: Adolescence in America, 1790 to the Present* (New York, 1977).

2. The historian of the family is considerably in the debt of the sociologist Glen H. Elder, Jr., for indicating both the subtle connections between structure, event, and family experience, and for suggesting paths for empirical investigation. Elder, *Children of the Great Depression* (Chicago, 1974); Elder and Richard C. Rockwell, Jr., "Economic Depression and Postwar Opportunity in Men's lives: A Study of Life Patterns and Health," in *Research in Community and Mental Health: An Annual Compilation of Research*, ed. Roberta G. Simmons (Greenwich, Conn., forthcoming).

3. Ernest W. Burgess and Harvey J. Locke, *The Family, from Institution to Companionship* (New York, 1945), pp. 26–27.

4. United States, Census Office, *Report on the Mortality and Vital Statistics of the United States as Returned at 10th Census*, Part 2 (Washington, 1886), pp. 771–88 (these are registration data); U. S. National Center for Health Statistics, *State Life Tables: 1969–71*, 2 vols. (DHEW Publication 75-1151, 1975).

5. Peter Uhlenberg, "Changing Configurations of the Life Course," unpublished paper prepared for Mathematical Social Sciences Board Conference on the Family Life Course in Historical Perspective, 1975; Uhlenberg, "Cohort Variations in Family Life Cycle Experiences of U. S. Females," *Journal of Marriage and the Family* 36 (1974), pp. 284–92.

6. John Modell, "Patterns of Consumption, Acculturation, and Family Income Strategy in Late Nineteenth-Century America," in *Nineteenth-Century Family and Demographic Behavior*, eds. Tamara K. Hareven and Maris Vinovskis (Princeton, New Jersey, forthcoming), table 19; U. S., Commissioner of Labor, *Seventh Annual Report* (1891), *Eighteenth Annual Report* (1903); U. S., Bureau of Labor Statistics, *Cost of Living in the United States* (Bulletin No. 357, 1924); Survey Research Center, University of Michigan, *Life Insurance Ownership among American Families 1951* (Ann Arbor, 1952), ch. 3; U. S., Bureau of Labor Statistics, *Consumer Expenditure Survey Series: Interview Survey, 1972 and 1973. Average Annual Expenditures Classified by Nine Family Characteristics, 1972 and*

1973 (Report 455-3, 1976). Mark R. Greene interprets this trend (in the post-World War II period) as "support [for] the general hypothesis that Americans are behaving as though they are becoming more risk conscious and risk averting, at least insofar as financial risk is concerned." Other trends Greene cites in support of this argument include social-welfare policies, unionization, and retirement patterns. Greene's overview of the treatment of risk in the social sciences, and his efforts to suggest its societal significance, are valuable, although he explains institutional change *by* public attitudes toward risk, rather than understanding the attitudes as products of their environment. Graduate School of Business, Indiana University, *Risk Aversion, Insurance, and the Future* (Bloomington, 1971).

7. Louis I. Dublin and Alfred J. Lotka, *The Money Value of a Man* (New York, 1930), pp. 138–42; Marion Elderton, ed., *Case Studies of Unemployment Compiled by the Unemployment Committee of the National Federation of Settlements* (Philadelphia, 1931), p. xli; E. Wight Bakke, *The Unemployed Worker* (New Haven, 1940), p. 271.

8. U. S., Bureau of the Census, *Historical Statistics of the United States Colonial Times to 1970* (Washington, 1975), part 2, series X879–962.

9. Actuarial Society of America, *Experience of Thirty-Four Life Companies upon Ninety-Eight Special Classes of Risks* (New York, 1903). The first collated experience data from American insurance companies (1853–74, but with the experience centering on about 1870) reveals the same kinds of effects on persistence in the risk pool by age and duration of policy. Although the effect of duration is about identical to that in the later compilation, the effect of age was even greater. We may ask whether in the earlier set the uncertainties attendant to youth were even more extreme than they would become later in the century. The supposition is strengthened by the repetition of the older pattern in the experience data of a single insurance company covering the period 1846–78. Levi W. Meech, *System and Tables of Life Insurance*, revised ed. (Norwich, Conn., 1886 [by subscription]); [D. H. Wells], *Mortality Experience of the Connecticut Mutual Life Insurance Company . . . from 1846 to 1878* (Hartford, 1884). Although some contemporaries believed that *healthier* insurants often withdrew from the risk pool because they had less to gain by remaining in it, a serious investigation ridiculed this

position, pointing instead to straightened circumstances. Miles Menander Dawson, "Effects of Free Surrender and Loan Privileges in Life Insurance," *Publications of the American Statistical Association*, 4 (1894–95), pp. 84–88.

10. Actuarial Society of America, *Experience*; Association of Life Insurance Medical Directors and the Actuarial Society of America, comp., *Medico-Actuarial Mortality Investigation*, vol. 2 (New York, 1913). Essentially the same age-pattern of persistence appeared in all fourteen nativity and occupational risk classes I analyzed, with the exception of traveling salesmen (who for some reason were extraordinarily prone to renew insurance at all ages) *and blacks*. Reflecting, no doubt, the far wider vicissitudes of life black families faced, the insurance records even of those blacks prosperous enough to insure with major white insurors revealed that for blacks having negotiated the life course even to middle age evidently indicated little about the ability to predict next year's possibilities—and this quite in addition to differential mortality of insurants. Even a special set of tabulations for "colored ministers, teachers, and other professional men" indicated that they, too, did not display the characteristic age pattern of persistence that marked whites' careers.

11. U. S., Bureau of the Census, *Historical Statistics*, comparing series X890 to series X882.

12. Modell, "Patterns of Consumption"; Dublin and Lotka, *The Money Value of a Man*, pp. 164–65; Maurice Leven, *The Income Structure of the United States* (Washington, 1938), pp. 47–53, 156; Herman P. Miller, "Annual and Lifetime Income in Relation to Education, 1939–1959," *American Economic Review* 50 (1960), pp. 962–86; Miller, "Lifetime Income and Economic Growth," *ibid.* 55 (1965), pp. 834–44; U. S., Bureau of the Census, *Sixteenth Census of the United States: 1940. Population. The Labor Force (Sample Statistics). Wage or Salary Income in 1939* (Washington, 1943), table 6; U. S., Bureau of the Census, *Census of Population: 1960. Subject Reports Occupation by Earnings and Education*, Final Report PL (2)-7B (Washington, 1963), tables 2, 5.

13. A closer "econometric" analysis of the fullest wage data I have come across for a relatively early year—for male paper box, confectionery, and shirt workers in New York State in 1913–1914—indicates *no*

reward in weekly wages for length of employment with a given firm. Experience *in the trade*, up to about a dozen years, was recognized in increased wages, in addition to an independent gain in wages per year of age about as much as per year of trade experience. The age reward apparently extended a little beyond age forty, but before age fifty a distinct age penalty in wages could be seen, owing perhaps to perceived diminishing of physical vigor. State of New York, *Fourth Report of the Factory Investigating Commission 1915* (Albany, 1915), vol. 2, pp. 175–338. My procedure depended upon the presence in the report of data of age by wages, by experience in the trade, and with a given employer, and on experience in the trade and experience with a given employer by wages. Regression techniques permitted estimated weekly wage computations for given age groups if experience had explained all the variation in wages by age, and this estimate was then compared with the observed figures to estimate the independent effect of age on wages.

14. Sumner Huber Slichter, *The Turnover of Factory Labor* (New York, 1919), p. 52.

15. Frederick Brissenden and Emil Frankel, *Labor Turnover in Industry* (New York, 1922), p. 55.

16. United States, Census Office, *Eleventh Census of the United States 1890, Population*, vol. 2; U. S., Bureau of the Census, *Census of the United States 1900, Special Report: Occupations*; Massachusetts, Bureau of Labor Statistics, *Eighteenth Annual Report 1887*; Massachusetts, Bureau of the Statistics of Labor, *Census of Massachusetts, 1885,* vol. 2. Unemployment rates, Stanley Lebergott tells us, have not declined notably over the last century and a half. The observation is a striking and important one, but it must not obscure for us the changes in the incidence and nature of the unemployment it subsumes. The growth of the nonagricultural labor force, for one thing, indicates that the same *total* amount of unemployment has been spread over increasing numbers. At the same time, one suspects, the distinctive "secondary labor market" has emerged as more demanding—and predictable—conditions of employment have predominated elsewhere, itself accounting for a good deal of the total unemployment. Stanley Lebergott, *Manpower in Economic Growth. The American Record since 1800* (New York, 1964), pp. 164–90. On the "secondary labor market," see Michael J. Piore, "The Dual Labor Market:

Theory and Implications," in *Problems in Political Economy: An Urban Perspective,* David Gordon, ed., 2nd ed. (Lexington, Mass., 1977), pp. 93–97; Bennet Harrison, "Institutions on the Periphery," in Gordon, *op. cit.,* pp. 102–7; Piore, "Notes for a Theory of Labor Market Stratification," in *Labor Market Segmentation,* Richard C. Edwards, Michael Reich, and David M. Gordon, eds. (Lexington, Mass., 1975), pp. 125–50.

17. U. S., Bureau of the Census, *Census of Population: 1960. Subject Reports, Employment Status and Work Experience.* Final Report PC (2)-6A (Washington, 1963), table 1; for 1930 and 1931 see U.S., Bureau of the Census, *Fifteenth Census of the United States: 1930. Unemployment,* vol. 2, pp. 253–55, 329–30, 383–88.

18. U. S., Commissioner of Labor, *Eighteenth Annual Report,* pp. 290–95.

19. Dean K. Brundage, "Sickness and Absenteeism during 1919 in a Large Industrial Establishment," *Public Health Reports* 35 (September 10, 1920), pp. 2143–54.

20. Lee K. Frankel and Louis J. Dublin, "Community Sickness Survey. Rochester, New York, September, 1915," *Public Health Reports* 31 (1916), pp. 423–38; Frankel and Dublin, *A Sickness Survey of Boston, Mass.* (New York, 1916); Frankel and Dublin, *Sickness Survey of Pittsburgh, Pennsylvania* (New York, 1917).

21. Edgar Sydenstricker, "Economic Status and the Incidence of Illness: Hagerstown Morbidity Studies No. 10," *Public Health Reports* 44 (1929), pp. 1821–33. The entire series is a highly valuable historical benchmark.

22. In this realm, too, blacks seem to continue "nineteenth-century" patterns into today. The overall incidence of illness among nonwhite Americans today is 1.17 times that of whites, but for males 25–44 and 45–64, the ratios are 1.47 and 1.54. Thus, when Robert Coles spoke with southern migrants in Boston in the late 1960s, he noted much talk of death, and remarked that "sickness is for them a heritage of sorts." U. S., National Center for Health Statistics, *Vital and Health Statistics. Series 10: Data from the National Health Survey, No. 90: Disability Days, United States, 1971* (DHEW publication No. (HRA) 74-1517), table 13; Robert Coles, *Children of Crisis,* vol. 3: *The South Goes North* (Boston, 1970), p. 635.

23. "Child Labor," in Wisconsin, Bureau of Labor and Industrial Statistics, *Ninth Biennial Report* (1898–99), pp. 263–406.

24. Howard Chudacoff and Tamara K. Hareven, "Old Age," unpublished paper prepared for Mathematical Social Sciences Board Conference on the Family Life Course in Historical Perspective, 1975; John Modell, Frank F. Furstenberg, Jr., and Douglas Strong, "The Timing of Marriage in the Transition to Adulthood: Continuity and Change, 1860–1975," forthcoming in special number of *American Journal of Sociology*, cosponsored by Russell Sage Foundation, John Demos and Sarane Boocock, eds.

25. U. S., Commissioner of Labor, *Eighteenth Annual Report*, pp. 366–67. On the close tie of bank savings to "the rainy day" in this period, see Meredith B. Givens, "Statistical Measures of Social Aspects of Unemployment," *Journal of the American Statistical Association* 26 (1931), pp. 303–18.

26. Karen O. Mason, Maris Vinovskis, and Tamara K. Hareven, "The Participation of Women in the Labor Force and the Life Course," unpublished paper prepared for Mathematical Social Sciences Board Conference on the Family Life Course in Historical Perspective, 1975.

27. State of New York, *Fourth Report of the Factory Investigating Commission*, vol. 4, pp. 1577–78.

28. Leila Houghteling, *The Income and Standards of Living of Unskilled Laborers in Chicago* (Chicago, 1927), p. 65.

29. "The extreme shortage of money might be thought to rule out quarrels over expenditures because every dollar must be spent on necessities. But this is not the case. The couples quarrel over the order in which bills are to be paid. . . . They quarrel over discretionary expenditures that do remain—beer, cigarettes or clothes. Every minor difference in economic preferences may cause a conflict because the shortage of money necessitates choices." Mirra Komarovsky, *Blue–Collar Marriage* (New York, 1967 [1962]), p. 292. Komarovsky's account (Chapter 13) of the interplay of economic and interpersonal resources among postwar workingclass families is most enlightening.

30. U. S., BLS, *Cost of Living*. The remarkable clothing detail extends from p. 120 to p. 275.

31. *Ibid.*; U. S., Bureau of the Census, *Sixteenth Census of the United States: 1940. Population, Families, Family Wage or Salary Income in 1939*; U. S., Bureau of the Census, *Census of Population 1960: Subject Report PC (2)–4C. Sources and Structure of Family Income*. The 1939 data exclude other sources of income than wages and salary, and thus are not fully comparable. The unemployment comparison involves such heroic assumptions as to be suggestive, at best.

32. U. S., Bureau of the Census, *Historical Statistics*, Series F4; U. S., Bureau of the Census, *Current Population Survey*, Series P-60 annually since 1947 provides a table on "number of earners . . . by total money income" in its number on family income by source.

33. Emma Octavia Lundberg, *Unemployment and Child Welfare . . . During the Industrial Depression of 1921 and 1922* (U. S. Children's Bureau Publication No. 125, 1923).

34. Robert S. Lynd and Helen Merrell Lynd, *Middletown. A Study in American Culture* (New York, 1929), p. 129.

35. E. Wight Bakke, *The Unemployed Worker*; Bakke, *Citizens Without Work* (New Haven, 1940); Elder, *Children of the Great Depression*; Samuel A. Stouffer and Paul F. Lazarsfeld, *Research Memorandum on the Family in the Depression* (Social Science Research Council, Bulletin 29, 1937).

36. On this problem generally, see Aaron Antonovsky, "Conceptual and Methodological Problems in the Study of Resistance Resources and Stressful Life Events," in *Stressful Life Events*, Barbara Snell Dohrenwend and Bruce P. Dohrenwend, eds. (New York, 1974), pp. 245–58.

37. Earl L. Koos, "Class Differences in Family Reactions to Crisis," *Marriage and Family Living* 12 (1950), pp. 77–78ff.; S. N. Miller and Frank Riessman, "The Working Class Subculture: A New View," *Social Problems* 9 (1961), pp. 86–97.

38. Melvin L. Kohn, *Class and Conformity, A Study in Values* (Homewood, Ill., 1969); see also Frank F. Furstenburg, Jr., "Work Experience and Family Life," in *Work and the Quality of Life*, James O'Toole, ed. (Cambridge, Mass., 1974), and Elizabeth H. Pleck, "Two Worlds in One: Work and Family," *Journal of Social History 10* (1976), pp. 178–95.

39. Elderton, *Case Studies*, pp. 229–30.

40. Lynd and Lynd, *Middletown*, p. 125. Earl L. Koos, *Families in Trouble* (New York, 1946), pp. 105–6, reports that sexual activity might well increase in crisis where it had been a reliable source of satisfaction before, but where it was already problematic, frequency declined.

42. Bakke, *Citizens Without Work*, pp. 133–40.

Aging Patterns in Black Families

JACQUELYNE JOHNSON JACKSON
Associate Professor of Medical Sociology, Department of Psychiatry, and Senior Fellow, Center for the Study of Aging and Human Development, Duke University Medical Center, Durham, N.C.
and
BERTRAM EMMANUEL WALLS
Resident, Department of Obstetrics and Gynecology, and Postdoctoral Fellow, 1976–77, Center for the Study of Aging and Human Development, Duke University Medical Center, Durham, N.C.

Unfortunately, the systematic study of social aging (admittedly a recent event) has rarely included Southern aged kinship patterns, a gap especially pronounced for blacks. Most studies about black families and communities (see, for example, Frazier 1939; Lewis 1955; Bernard 1966; Billingsley 1968; Scanzoni 1971; Hill 1972; and Heiss 1975) and about black aging (see Jackson 1971a) have also usually excluded aged kinship patterns. Thus, empirical data about aged statuses and roles in Southern black kinship networks, or, for that matter, anywhere in the United States, are sparse, although impressionistic judgments abound. Further, most generalizations about subjective aspects of kinship among blacks within the familial or gerontological literature are inappropriately based upon fragmented and inconclusive data about kinship structures, as instanced, for example by Hill (1972) and M. Jackson and Wood (1976).

The absence of adequate data about aged kinship development among blacks has retarded considerably theoretical development and testing about them. Inadequate data have also prohibited appropriate comparisons between black and non-black aged kinship networks, and greatly reduced effective social planning for aged blacks.

Purpose and Methodology

In an effort to counteract the trend of spurious generalizations about aging patterns of the later years in black kinship networks, as well as their inappropriate comparisons with white kinship networks, this paper provides an overview of available data about aged patterns in black kinship networks in the South, and, to the extent possible, comparisons of those patterns with non-Southern black kinship networks and with white kinship networks. Finally, we will suggest several types of studies which may be crucial in furthering our sociological and anthropological knowledge and understanding of kinship patterns for aged blacks, the results of which, we believe, could be applied readily to continuing social programs for the aged involving, but not restricted to, blacks.

Overview

Our review of the literature revealed a hodgepodge of operational definitions of kinship networks among blacks, thus reducing meaningful comparisons of the available data. Contemporary definitions of black kinship networks are frequently fraught with strong political overtones, thus increasing definitional problems.

To jump the gun somewhat, we believe that the *aged kinship network* can be operationally defined as including all of the relatives by blood and marriage, as well as all of the fictive kin, whom the aged individual views as kin, *and* who reciprocate in kind. The core of the aged kinship network is the *aged family.* With the aged person as ego, it includes the spouse, if any, and all offspring. Under this definition, of course, an aged person could belong to two aged families—the family of orientation and of procreation, provided in the latter instance, one or both of her or his parents were alive. When both parents are dead, the siblings become members of the kinship network, but not of the aged family.

The aged kinship network contains kin who provide instrumental, affective, or incidental functions. The *instrumental func-*

tion is the provision of goods and services, such as caring for the ill and giving monies, or advice related thereto. The *affective function* is that of emotional support and companionship, including related advice. The *incidental function* is fulfilled by kin who do not themselves provide instrumental or affective support at a given moment, but who influence its distribution, or who happen merely to be physically present when such support is given by other kin.

Following Schneider (1968), the aged kinship network can also be charted by physical distance, socioemotional distance, and genealogical distance. All three influence obligatory and voluntary exchanges between kin.

Anticipated mutual reciprocity—obligatory or otherwise—is also a central component of the aged kinship network. Adult members should be aware of kin expectations, and, to the extent possible, should either fulfill their responsibilities within the tolerance limitations, or some reordering of kin expectations will occur. Within each kinship network, some norms are universal in that they represent those of the larger American kinship system. Others are particular to the specific kinship network.

Prevalent within the literature about black kinship networks and communities is a belief that aging is not a harsh experience among blacks, as well as a related belief that black kinship networks confer high status upon the aged.

Contrary assumptions and findings lead to our basic question. Is the Southern black aged kinship network uniquely different from that of other networks? We think not. Far greater similarity than dissimilarity exists between it and other networks. The few differences which are apparent can best be explicated not by race, but by institutionalized racism, an important distinction.

The patterns of aging uncovered by Jackson in her study of the aged kinship network among Southern urban blacks were not unique. As an instance, although a significant minority of the aged lived alone, and a significant minority also lived only with their spouses (a pattern far more common among the men), the vast majority were not isolated from their kin. But, they were also no more likely than other aged to be in frequent contact with their kin. The slightly higher pattern of multiple generations within the same household were due largely to segregated and inadequate housing then prevailing within the area. In fact, the vast majority of the aged (including those living with either or both their children and grandchildren) preferred independent living arrangements. They, too, believed in "intimacy at a distance."

But, when circumstances warranted other arrangements, the aged and their kin were willing to perform, to the extent possible, their obligatory kinship responsibilities. Most often, when several generations shared living quarters, the aged were the family heads. Socioeconomic variations were apparent. Adult children of parents of higher socioeconomic status living with their parents were more likely to be "problem children," generally the result of marital disruption. Multiple-generational households were more temporary for those parents and children than was typical among those of lower socioeconomic status.

Although very few aged went to live with their children, when they did, the modal reason was poor health or inability to care for themselves physically. The lower the socioeconomic level of the adult children, the greater the likelihood of the parent's living with one or more of the children. The higher the socioeconomic status of the child, the greater the likelihood that the parent was placed in a nursing home. Thus, we see that the extent to which adult children were willing to care for their ailing parents was not a function of socioeconomic status, but rather that the manner in which the obligation was undertaken was a function of such status. That is, their ends were similar, their means were different.

Among these aged, the lines of kinship dependence for instrumental and affective assistance were also not atypical of other kin networks. The married depended first most often upon their spouses. Then, if parents, they depended upon their oldest children, particularly their eldest daughters. If children of both sexes were present, traditional sex-roles in the division of labor occurred. When only daughters or sons were present, sex-role crossing in task performance were apparent. When spouseless, generally through widowhood, mothers tended to increase their instrumental and affective ties with their youngest children. In the absence of spouses and children (the position of a significant minority of contemporary aged blacks), ties seemed to be stronger with siblings, and, in their absence, with kin next closest to them genealogically, kin best known over the years, or, in less frequent instances, with fictive kin. Excepting spouses, these aged tended to rely more heavily upon kin related by blood than by marriage.

When the need arose, parents and children tended to engage in mutual assistance patterns. Variations in these patterns were functions of such factors as their socioeconomic, marital, and health statuses, current locations within their immediate family life cycles, and physical and socioemotional distances. For example, lower-class aged parents and their adult children residing within the same city were far more likely than their middle-class counterparts to exchange direct services, as opposed to gifts, and, in the case of middle-class parents, monies to their adult children and their grandchildren.

While aged blacks and their adult children do attempt to assist each other to the extent they are able, both believe most often that the economic support of the aged is the obligation of the aged themselves or of the government, with those of higher socioeconomic status more likely to believe that adults should be responsible for their own economic support, regardless of age.

Among blacks, as others, women tend to be more responsible for maintaining familial and kinship contacts. This pattern is also typical of aged couples. Aged couples and spouseless aged usually interact most frequently with their kin through exchanging visits in their homes, and joint activities, also usually centered within the homes, on special occasions, such as holidays and birthdays.

"Granny's" significance as an emotional link between kin was present, but her importance in linking kin to other societal institutions was quite minimal in our study. For example, our data showed the diminishing role which these women played over time in obtaining jobs for their daughters. In the past, when most employed black women were domestics, and the demand for them was much higher, many such women operated as employment brokers for their daughters. Various factors have brought about changes in this pattern. The most important ones include the changing occupational patterns of their daughters and greater migration of their employers. But, even this pattern is not unique to blacks. Historically, many white mothers working in factories, for example, "passed on" or obtained similar jobs for their daughters.

In general, then, the patterns of aging within Southern urban black kinship networks do not appear to be significantly different from those of other networks. Kinship obligations calling for the aged to remain independent as long as possible are strong. Economic aid to the aged is regarded primarily as a function of the aged themselves or the government. Whenever necessary, kin, in the expected order, should assist each other, either for obligatory or voluntary reasons. Black communities do not generally bestow high status upon their aged unless they are "famous" people. Black kinship networks bestow high status upon those aged socially vital to them. But generally, as kinship distance increases, kinship obligations decline, and, as earlier noted, consanguineous kin are significantly more important than affinal kin, excepting spouses.

Suggested Studies

Many studies could further our sociological and anthropological knowledge and understanding of patterns of aging in black kinship networks. Among the most important are the following.

First, clearly needed is a study providing for methodological clarification of the concept of ethnicity, setting forth appropriate research use of the term. Included within that study would be a specification of the various ethnic cultures extant among blacks.

Secondly, a cross-sectional survey of patterns of aging in black kinship networks in the United States is needed. Using a representative sample of blacks sufficiently large to permit meaningful multivariate analyses, the focus should be on the identification and affective supports available within the network, and the attitudes and behaviors related to the aged, or to growing old.

Thirdly, a longitudinal study involving several hundred blacks between sixty and sixty-five years of age should be launched to investigate carefully and in depth their kinship interactions. These individuals, representing different sex, marital, parental, socioeconomic, and health statuses, should be followed until they die. In addition to the acquisition of the usual types of sociological data, anthropological data of the type sought by Oscar Lewis in his various studies of Mexican and Puerto Rican families would be extremely important.

Finally, a study investigating the effects of institutionalized racism on patterns of aging among older blacks is clearly needed. Particular attention should be given to systemic discrimination, which involves the application of criteria which are labeled as neutral, but which, in fact, are discriminatory, and which, therefore, produce unequal results. For instance, should Medicare premiums by the aged be the same for all aged, or should they be different, depending upon the income level of the potential recipient? Or, should discounts for the aged in public transportation be made available to all aged, merely because they are aged, or should they be made available only to the aged poor?

Given the phenomenal numerical growth of aged blacks in recent years, it is probably more important now to concentrate upon contemporary patterns of aging in black kinship networks, as opposed to those which may have existed during slavery. It is also important that researchers consider seriously Gutman's (1976) advice to learn much more about the dynamic relationships between kinship, race, and class within the United States over time, noting, as well, at least the increasing convergence of those patterns between various racial and ethnic groups.

References

Adams, B. N. *Kinship in an Urban Setting.* Chicago: Markham Publishing Company, 1968.

Bengtson, V. L.; Kasschau, P. L.; and Ragan, P. K. "The Impact of Social Structure on Aging Individuals." In *Handbook of the Psychology of Aging.* Edited by J. E. Birren and K. W. Schaie. New York: Van Nostrand Reinhold Company, 1977.

Bernard, J. *Marriage and Family Among Negroes.* Englewood Cliffs, New Jersey: Prentice-Hall, 1966.

Billingsley, A. *Black Families in White America.* Englewood Cliffs, New Jersey: Prentice-Hall, 1966.

Cumming, E. and Henry, W. E. *Growing Old: The Process of Disengagement.* New York: Basic Books, 1961.

Dowd, J. J. and Bengtson, V. L. "Social Participation, Age, and Ethnicity: An Examination of the 'Double Jeopardy' Hypothesis. Paper presented at the annual meeting of the Gerontological Society, 1975.

Florea, A. "The New Status of Old People in the Family and Their Relationships." *Age With A Future.* Edited by P. F. Hansen. Philadelphia: Davis, 1964, pp. 455–58.

Frazier, E. F. *The Negro Family in the United States.* Chicago: University of Chicago Press, 1939.

Gutman, H. G. *The Black Family in Slavery and Freedom, 1750–1925.* New York: Pantheon Books, 1976.

Harris, Louis, and Associates. *The Myth and Reality of Aging In America.* Washington, D. C.: National Council on the Aging, 1975.

Hauser, P. M. "Aging and World-Wide Population Change." *Handbook of Aging and the Social Sciences.* Edited by R. H. Binstock and E. Shanas. New York: Van Nostrand Reinhold Company, 1976.

Heiss, J. *The Case of the Black Family, A Sociological Inquiry*. New York: Columbia University Press, 1975.

Hill, R. B. *The Strengths of Black Families*. New York: Emerson Hall, 1972.

Jackson, J. J. "The Blacklands of Gerontology." *Aging and Human Development* 2 (1971a):156–71. Reprinted in *Readings in Gerontology*. Edited by V. M. Brantl and M. R. Brown. St. Louis: The C. V. Mosby Company, pp. 78–97.

Jackson, J. J. "Sex and Social Class Variations in Black Adult Parent-Adult Child Relationships." *Aging and Human Development* 2 (1971c): 96–107.

Jackson, J. J. "Aged Blacks: A Potpourri towards the Reduction of Racial Inequities." *Phylon* 32 (1971b):260–80. Reprinted in *Growing Old in America*. Edited by B. B. Hess. New Brunswick, New Jersey: Transaction Books, 1976, pp. 390–416.

Jackson, J. J. "Comparative Life Styles and Family and Friend Relationships among Older Black Women." *The Family Coordinator* 21 (1972a): 477–85. Reprinted in *Non-traditional Family Forms in the 1970's*. Edited by M. B. Sussman. Minneapolis: National Council on Family Relations, 1973, pp. 109–17.

Jackson, J. J. "Marital Life among Aged Blacks." *The Family Coordinator* 21 (1972b):21–27.

Jackson, J. J. "Ordinary Black Husbands: The Truly Hidden Men." *Journal of Social and Behavioral Sciences* 20 (1974):19–27.

Jackson, J. J., and Walls, B. E. "Myths and Realities About Aged Blacks." *Readings in Gerontology*. 2nd ed. Edited by M. R. Brown. St. Louis: The C. V. Mosby Company, 1978.

Jackson, M., and Wood, J. L. *Aging in America: Implications for the Black Aged*. Washington, D. C.: National Council on the Aging, 1976.

Jericho, B. "Longitudinal Changes in Religious Activity Activity Subscores of Aged Blacks." *Black Aging* 2 (1977).

Lewis, H. *The Blackways of Kent*. Chapel Hill: University of North Carolina Press, 1955.

Neugarten, B. L., and Hagestad, G. O. "Age and the Life Course." *Handbook of Aging and the Social Sciences*. Edited by R. H. Binstock and E. Shanas. New York: Van Nostrand Reinhold Company, 1976, pp. 35–37.

Scanzoni, J. H. *The Black Family in Modern Society*. Boston: Allyn and Bacon, 1971.

Schneider, D. M. *American Kinship: A Cultural Account*. Englewood Cliffs, New Jersey: Prentice-Hall, 1968.

Shimkin, D. B., and Shimkin, E. M. "The Extended Family in U. S. Black Societies: Findings and Problems." Unpublished paper received from the authors, n.d.

Sussman, M. B. "Family Relations and the Aged." In *The Daily Needs and Interests of Older People*. Edited by A. M. Hoffman. Springfield, Illinois: Charles C. Thomas, Publisher, 1970.

Kinship, Community, and Locality in American Culture

DAVID M. SCHNEIDER
William B. Ogden, Distinguished Service Professor of Anthropology, University of Chicago, Chicago, Ill.

The problem of this paper is stated in its title: that is, to spell out the relationship between kinship, community and locality in American culture.[1]

I stress the word "culture," for the problem I have formulated takes its shape from the special sense in which I use that term. By "culture" I mean the system of symbols (or signs)[2] and meanings which inform social action and the norms for social action. I do *not* mean patterns *of* action, nor patterns *for* action when I use the term culture. I specifically mean the system of symbols and meanings which are embedded both in social action and the system of social norms, and I mean this alone. I have discussed this definition of the concept of "culture" at length elsewhere.[3]

For the problem at hand, then, kinship, community, and locality are dealt with here as symbols and meanings and considered in terms of their symbolic and meaningful aspects and not in terms of any other considerations. The problem is to see how they relate to each other as symbols and meanings.

One further comment. What I have to say consists in hypotheses. I do not mean that I am just guessing. What I have to say is based on an analysis of the materials collected in an intensive study of American kinship, undertaken in Chicago starting in 1962, as well as smaller studies done at other times and in other places. Although much of the work was done with middle class white families, a significant portion covered lower class black, Appalachian, and Spanish speaking families as well.[4]

I will begin by reviewing briefly some of the salient features of the cultural definition of American kinship.[5]

At the most immediate level, there are two kinds of relatives in American kinship: there are those related by blood and those related by marriage. Analysis of these symbols—blood and marriage—shows that this pair, in its particular opposition, is but a specific instance of a wider, more general opposition, namely, that of nature and law. This in turn is but a special instance of the broader opposition between substance and code for conduct (which I will often abbreviate as "substance" and "code"). The material or substantive element (blood) is defined as natural while the code for conduct is defined as being part of the order of law. That is, the one, blood, is part of the wider order of nature, the other is part of the wider order of law. The order of law is natural, of course, but it differs in important ways from the order of nature. The order of nature is substantive and consists of objects which are given and fixed, or relatively fixed. The order of law is determined by the will of man; it is changeable at man's will; it consists in rules and regulations, those things which man's intelligence and rationality can create and alter at will.

A further aspect of this opposition between the order of nature and the order of law is that of the opposition between the material and the spiritual. It is true, of course, that under certain circumstances the material can be transformed into the spiritual, or given a spiritual quality. The very fact that this transformation is possible —and desirable—testifies to their opposition in the first case.

Those kinsmen who are related in nature, by blood, by substance, should follow a code for conduct which I have called "diffuse, enduring solidarity." That is, in the terms of native culture, relatives should "love" each other. Love is one of the native symbols which can be translated as diffuse and enduring solidarity. That only means that relatives should be kind to each other, do what is good for each other, should "stick together." There is no place for self-interested motives: these are ignored or explicitly set aside in the cultural construct. In fact, in the fullness of daily life, which includes more than just the culture, of course, it is just the failures to be kind, to love, to behave according to the highest canons of diffuse and enduring solidarity, of which the very stuff of novels and tragedies is made. But I speak here, as I have indicated before, purely at the cultural level, so we can say that at the cultural level there is no place for self-interested action, for the manipulation of others exclusively for the gratification of one's own ends. One maintains solidarity with kin because they are kin, and there should be no question of right and wrong. It is precisely here, in the fullness of daily life (which includes people's motives, the organization of society, and the actual context within which action takes place), that the richness of the mixture of culture, society, motive, and the expediency of the concrete situation makes for tragedies and for the conflict which we can often observe between relatives. But at the level of culture alone there should be no question of right and wrong, only of helping a relative, only of being kind and of loving one's kinsmen and thereby only doing what is good for them.

Note, however, that I am not describing "ideal" patterns for behavior. The contrast between "ideal" patterns for action and the so-called "real" observable patterns of action is a quite different matter which only appears, superficially, to look like what I am talking about when I speak of culture. There is no space to enter into a full discussion of the difference here, but I do want to point out that what I am talking about when I speak of culture is not "ideal" patterns of behavior.

The blood relationship, then, has two qualities: it has a material and substantive aspect; it has also a distinctive code for conduct, the native name for which is "love," and the analytic term for which is diffuse, enduring solidarity.

Now, code and substance are hierarchically ordered. That is, in different contexts these two aspects of the blood relationship may take different degrees of valorization or positions of priority or primacy, as well as different forms. In certain contexts it is the substantive, material aspect which is held crucial and of the highest value, while the code for conduct is treated as subordinate or even hardly noticed, although in fact it is always implicit. In other contexts the material, substantive aspect of the relationship may be overridden, while the code for conduct is given primacy and such relevance that it might seem that the material, substantive element is absent although it is present at an implicit level.

Let me be clear about what I am saying here. I am *not* saying that in certain circumstances it behooves a person, for reasons of expediency, to stress the substantive aspect of a relationship and to ignore the code for conduct, while at other times a person may gain some advantage by stressing the code for conduct and ignoring or slighting the substantive aspect. People do in fact do just that. But I am not dealing here with the strategies people undertake in *using* their culture. I am instead trying to define in what their culture consists in the first place, before they come to use it. How they use it, and to what personal or other ends, depends first on what is there to be used, and so is a different problem. To know the grammar, syntax, and vocabulary of a language is one thing; how a particular person uses it and the different ends to which he can put it is quite another. What is most important is that people can use what is there and what in fact exists before they arrived on the scene, except of course where they invent or create some part of it. As I am using the term culture, it is the customary signs and significations out of which social action is built. And by the same token it is the same code of signs and meanings out of which new culture and creative acts can be built as well. But these are always there before the actor is even born; these are the tools of social action which the actor finds at hand and learns to use as he grows up.

Two aspects of the blood relationship, then, the substantive and the code for conduct, are in balance only under certain limited conditions. More usually one is primary and the other subordinated, one is salient, the other subordinate under certain conditions, while the relation may be reversed under other circumstances.

A final point about kinship can be made which illustrates the way in which the symbols and meanings I have outlined operate.

Consider the situation of adoption. How are we to understand this? We can begin at the beginning. One can be a relative by blood or by marriage. Those related by marriage are, of course, "in-laws," or, to put it more generally, they are related by law. This is a special instance, as I have said, of the wider order of law in American culture. One of the major ways of becoming related by law, then, is through that particular legal act, marriage. (I do not mean getting a marriage license from the town clerk; law is far wider than that alone, although it includes it.) But there is another way in which a person can become related by the bonds of kinship and that is by adoption. Adoption is not a form of marriage and the relatives of the adopted person do not become "in-laws" to the adopter. But it is most certainly a relationship established and validated by law. In fact, when I first learned that in colonial times, among the Puritans of New England, an adopted son was sometimes referred to as a "son in law," it came as no surprise and made perfectly good sense. We can understand adoption, then, with reference to the fact that American kinship is defined by two, not just one, criteria: blood as substance and law as a special code for conduct. In many situations blood as substance has a higher value than code for conduct, and so it is said "blood is thicker than water." No matter how badly persons may adhere to the proper code for conduct, the substantive tie will take precedence and the relationship will be maintained. Where adoption takes place it is clearly the code for conduct, as a special case of the relationship in law, that takes precedence, and so long as the parent and child play those roles then the absence of the substantive aspect of the relationship is not counted as an insuperable impediment. That is, the code for conduct is valorized above the bio-genetic relationship. Taken as a whole, therefore, it can be said that under certain conditions the hierarchical relationship between substance and code favors substance, while under other conditions as defined in the particular culture, it is code which is favored and takes precedence.

The different symbols of American kinship seem to say one

thing: they are all concerned with unity of some kind. The unity of those related by blood, of those joined in love, of the parent and child, in the face of the child's growing up and going off to found a family of his own, of man and woman as husband and wife (a point I have not stressed sufficiently here), and so on. All of these different kinds of unity are expressed as or symbolized by the unity of substance or the unity engendered and required by the code for conduct as diffuse, enduring solidarity.

If we turn now to the meaning of "community" in American culture it is immediately apparent that unity is one of the most prominent of its meanings. A community is a group of people who have something they deem important in common: they may live together in the same place, they may hold something jointly, or they may have a common undertaking. They may be a community of scholars, or a village, or a neighborhood, or a body of persons interested in a particular kind of endeavor—perhaps they are a community of those who seek to preserve the environment or to exploit it in some way. Threading through these various notions, however, there remains the commonality, the unity of something, the identity of each person with the other in some important respect. Indeed, the family can be considered as a special kind of community, whether we think of the small nuclear family of just husband, wife, and children, or the whole family including all the relatives. And it is in this sense that community as well as family in American culture are defined by the same symbols and meanings.

Of course, a particular community may be made up of different families, which may be of differing kinds, backgrounds, sizes, and political or religious persuasions. But it will remain a community so long as it can be designated as a unit either by those outside or by those within it: two different but complementary perspectives.

This last point is important. Regardless of how it is internally differentiated, it is the commonality, the unity, of the community which marks it as a community and not just a collectivity or an aggregate to those both inside and outside it. The same can be said of the family and of kinship: at one level it is a single undifferentiated entity, at another it can be seen as highly differentiated into different nuclear families, different kinds of kin—mothers, fathers, brothers, sisters, cousins, grandparents, and so forth. I will return to this point below.

Thus far, then, kinship and community are culturally linked by the fact that common to their definition is the idea of a unity, of commonality (common blood or common outlook, common aims or values, for example). With this, there obtains that individual sense of belonging, of being a part of, at its extreme perhaps a sense of mystical participation, but at least the sense of belonging and being immersed as an inseparable part of a unit. What Victor Turner has described as "communitas" is a fair description from the point of view of community but is also apt for the sense of diffuse, enduring solidarity of both community and kinship.

There is a condition of the cultural conception of a community which also ties it to the family and to kinship and this basis for its commonality entails the particular code for conduct of diffuse, enduring solidarity. The mere existence of a body of people who live in a neighborhood does not make it a community. It may be said that it is not a *real* community. It becomes a community when, on the one hand, belonging means something positive and something valuable to its members, and there is, on the other hand, that sense of their commonality, as an aim, common goals, common commitment to the community, or the sense of their unity expressed in some form. And all of this is based on a code for conduct which entails diffuse, enduring solidarity. For instance, the community may have a baseball team which has the united support of the hometown. It may be no more or less than this that makes for some degree of community. But crucial to unity, as it is culturally defined, is the fact that members of the community maintain diffuse enduring solidarity precisely similar to that which is defined as appropriate to kinship.

Yet another symbol runs through the conception of the community, in some circumstances prominently displayed, in some subordinated to other conditions. This is the idea of place, of locality, of physical locus, of the specific piece of the face of the earth with which there is a link conceived of as physical, or as once having been a physical link. ("We came from there," for example.) It can even be a place which does not exist and never existed, but has the form of a place in some context: the "heavenly city," for example, or the white man's conception of the Indians' "happy hunting grounds." A community is a group of people, but not in limbo and not on cloud nine. It is a group of people who are identified with a place, where the place stands for the group as the group stands for the place. Assuming Washington, D.C., to be a community, it is the combination of the people, the place, and the people's commitment to the unity of their relations of diffuse, enduring solidarity that make it a community. The place without the people is merely a city, a place. The people without the place are just people. And the two without that sense of unity, that sense of commonality, that sense of belonging that is entailed in the code for conduct of diffuse, enduring solidarity, make it merely a commercial or work oriented entity.

The American cultural concept of "home," in one of its important meanings, brings the ideas of place, kinship, and community together into a single unit. For "home" can mean either or both the place and the people who are unified as kin or community into a single entity. An American may ask "Where's your home," and be told "Down south," or "In Ohio," just as he may answer "1234 Main Street." The folk song "Lookin' for a home . . ." makes this same point. And so the immigrant, coming from abroad, is looking for a new home—a new place, a new group of people with whom he can be identified and feel "at home" (that is, share a sense of diffuse, enduring solidarity). These may be both or either relatives or persons not related by kinship but only by bonds of common origin, such as common birth in the same foreign country or the same town.

The significance of place is clearly to be seen in the way in which immigrants to America behaved. They came, on the whole, from lands where different languages were spoken, where different customs obtained. Generally, advance parties or persons came and set up some sort of establishment. They then constituted "catchers" as well as links to the old country, in that they either brought over at their own expense members of their family or they constituted the first stop, the first contacts which oriented the newcomers to their new surroundings. But the newcomers were either kinsmen or "landsmen" or "Landes Leute," that is, they were either kin or they came from the same town or the same community. They came to these "catchers" precisely because the same sense of trust, of diffuse, enduring solidarity, marked kinship and community. In many cases, of course, the trust was mistaken, but such are the ways of the world. But the cultural presumption for the immigrants was, as it remains for their descendants, that you should be able to trust your relatives and you should be able to trust people from your home town, which was, in most cases, a community in the sense in which I have been speaking.

Kinship and community thus replicated and so supplemented each other for the immigrants to America, the one providing a narrow but firm basis for trust, the other providing a wider basis for the confidence that was necessary to learn how to take the first steps in the new land.

But place and its representation of community did more. Many immigrants did not come to New York and just sit tight. Vast numbers of them came to New York speaking Swedish or German, Polish or Gaelic, and were met by people from their home towns (from their locality, to be precise), and were then handed along in a kind of aboveground railroad, in which the railroad was, in fact, an important instrument. Many Swedes and Poles, for instance, landed in New York, were picked up either by kinsmen or by people from their home places in the old country, taken in for a period of time, and "taught the ropes." Then railroad tickets were obtained for them and they were put on the right train and put off by the conductors at their destination where again relatives or people from their home locality in the old country were waiting for them. They were once more taken in, fed, taught the rudiments of how to get on, and then either settled there or moved on to some place where they could settle permanently. Some took years to learn to speak English because they were merely transplanted from the home country to this country and continued to live among their kinsmen or their countrymen—which means, simply, people from their community as composed of both a locality and a place of birth.

Locality has become very popular this year in one of these senses and closely linked with the other in the term "roots." Roots are both place and a set of special links to the particular people of that place. Community and kinsmen come together in a place or from a place, and one's identification with all of these constitutes one's roots. They make one's identity, they signify who one is, and they identify one as against all other kinds: people of different places, different kin groups, different nations. And so the sense of belonging that I spoke of earlier consists in the symbols of the place, the nation, the kinship group, the family, the home, and above all the love and confidence in these which I have characterized in my anthropological jargon as diffuse, enduring solidarity.

Locality—in all the senses in which I have been using the term—has an interesting link with blood and birth which is worth noting.

In an earlier publication I noted how kinship, nationality, ethnicity and religion were defined in terms of both birth and love. Thus, one is a member of a country by birth or naturalization (adoption is used too, as in "the country of one's adoption"), and one loves one's country. I need not expand on this point, partly because it is obvious, and because I have spelled it out in some detail elsewhere.[6]

But the point that should be raised is that being born in a country does not seem quite the same thing as being born of a particular mother. In one of its meanings this is true. But it has other meanings as well, and it is these other meanings which serve as the crucial links among these cultural constructs. In fact, it is just the element of *substance* in the concept of place or locality which mediates this seemingly different set of conditions. The close symbolic identification of country (nation) with kinship is seen in many ways, not the least of which is the use of the so-called "kinship terms" for both, as mother and motherland, father and fatherland. But it is the special definition of place or locality in terms identical to those of common substance—blood, for example—that shows the two to be parts of the same cultural construct. Place, land, locality, home in the sense of place, substance; place stands for one as one stands for one's place; place is the source and represents the difference between people. The substance of which people are made is thus closely identified with the substance of which the place is made.

The definition is that just as one is a member of a family by being born into it, one is a member of a nation or ethnic group by being born into it. And "born" in this sense is not to be understood merely as the emergence from a womb, although that is no small part of it. It is not pertinent to bring in Navajo cosmology, and I do so only because I think the analogy helps to clarify the point: the Navajo believe that they first came into the world through a hole in the ground. Americans do not state their relations to their country in quite that way, but their way is very close to it, for being born in its widest sense means either or both having a substantive origin and having the bio-genetic substance of one's parents and the substance of one's country.

Day to day living has created a situation in which there is a high degree of spatial mobility and a large number of people who see themselves as rootless. This may seem to have devalued these fundamental cultural definitions, but they are by no means debased, and they are certainly not lacking. The most rootless yearn for roots; the most mobile bemoan their placeless fate; the most isolated yearn for kin and community, for these represent the basic things that for many Americans make life worth living. The continual stories in the newspapers of people who search and search for their own real fathers or mothers, and make pilgrimages to the towns and villages of their ancestors (to kiss the Blarney Stone, for example), is testimony to the existence and salience of these symbols.

It is the replication, or better, the availability for substitution of kinship, nationality, religion, ethnicity, and community which mark it off as a special galaxy of American culture. And its hold on Americans should not be underestimated.

Thus far I have tried only to suggest that the cultural categories of kinship and community are defined, at one level of contrast, by the same set of symbols and meanings, and thus belong to the same cultural galaxy.

I will now approach essentially the same material with a different question in mind. Do these symbols and meanings form a coherent, systematic structure, and if so, how?

Code for conduct, specified as diffuse, enduring solidarity, applies without qualification to both kinship and community, and substance, the other element in the opposition, does too. In this sense kinship and community are the same, for they are defined by the same symbols and with the same meanings. However, there is a sense in which kinship is quite distinct from community, and that is the sense in which blood characterizes kinship, while locality is the symbol which distinguishes community. But the other element in the opposition, code for conduct as diffuse enduring solidarity, remains the same. Thus the distinction between kinship and community starts with the distinction between two kinds of substance: blood for kinship, locality for community. Each of these two is further differentiated internally, and the contrast between kinship and community no longer applies, since it is now embedded in every aspect of these subunits as an implicit condition. The contrast is rather between relative and non-relative, and below that in further specification, family versus non-family, blood relatives versus those related in law, and below that father versus mother, brother versus sister, and so on. Correspondingly, when we follow out community and examine its internal differentiation, kinship is no longer relevant at that level of comparison, and instead the internally differentiated units of community become the units of comparison. These units are of variable kinds, for community is not necessarily made up of any particular kind of unit. The significance of the fact that kinship is highly internally differentiated as compared with community, and that its internally differentiated units are culturally precisely specified (relative, family, mother, and so on), while community is not necessarily made up of any particular kind of unit, so long as members of a community all share the common code of diffuse enduring solidarity and some reference to locality, is an interesting and important question which I cannot pursue here but which should not be overlooked.

Kinship and community belong to the same cultural galaxy as nationality, ethnicity and religion (at least), and all of the units in this galaxy are defined by a common code for conduct (diffuse, enduring solidarity) and common substance.[7] The meaning of common substance is that of identity, unity, and equality. The code for conduct specifies a special kind of cohesion between the constituent persons.

But the galaxy as a whole is internally differentiated (into kinship, community, nationality, ethnicity, religion, etc.) by various forms of substance while the code for conduct (diffuse, enduring solidarity) remains the same for each unit within the galaxy; it is the substance of each sub-unit which differs and so distinguishes it from the others. Kinship is distinguished by blood; community by locality or place (without specific boundary); nationality by a special kind of locality or place called "a country" or "a nation" (which is to say, a political boundary); ethnicity is a special form of nationality within one country (a bounded place) which is linked to a place outside of the country—a variation on the place of place or the locality of the locality; religion is marked by a special transformation of substance, or a special kind of substance of spiritual quality.[8] It has always been obvious that community, nationality, and ethnicity are three very closely related units in American culture. If I am correct in this analysis, their closeness can be specified as variants on the symbol of place or locality in the code/substance opposition. They represent respectively a place without boundary, a place within a boundary (country, nation), and a place within one boundary which derives from a different place elsewhere.

One further point should be made about the American cultural symbol of substance in this particular galaxy. The different kinds of substance which distinguish the different sub-units of the galaxy are culturally constructed so that differences between them are defined as minimal and no distinct, sharp, unbridgeable lines are drawn between them. Blood and locality might seem, to some eyes, entirely different things, and in some culturally defined contexts they are indeed so defined. But in other settings they can be interchangeable and can be substituted for each other, or very nearly so. Thus blood, land, earth, place, "stuff," "born," and "come from" are all slightly different ways of designating substance and the fact that they are encompassed by the more general term makes them suitable, under specifically defined conditions, for substitution one for another with relative ease. For example, the symbol of birth can be treated in its sense of emergence from the womb, or in its sense as the continuity of bio-genetic substance, or in its sense of being of a certain place, as in "I was born in the United States," or "He is foreign born," or "We were born in this community," and so on. Being "born" in the United States brings together in one meaningful whole emergence from a particular womb, the continuity of bio-genetic substance, and the place or locality, by the fact that in American culture all are conceived of (that is, they "mean") as aspects of substance, and in that sense equivalent. Thus the bridge between kinship and nationality can be understood in just these terms.[9]

A second device which helps tie the whole galaxy together into a single unit is that of hierarchy. Hierarchy applied to symbols and meanings, as I am using the term, refers to the relations of the elements of an opposition with regard to their differential cultural valorizations or the primacy or dominance of the value of one over the other element in an opposition.

Hierarchy and any particular opposition are really two different orders of things. A particular opposition puts elements in a particular relationship—of opposition. But hierarchy modifies that relationship so as to give higher value to one element than the other, to make one element in the opposition more salient or less so. Hence even to discuss hierarchy it is necessary to deal with a double set of oppositions: A versus B, and High versus Low. Perhaps the best example is the relationship between physical place (and however it is represented, as "land," "ground," "soil," "home," "country," "where one lives," "where one is free") and the unity of those so associated.

It is not simply that those associated as a unity must necessarily be in the same place, for, as I have said, they may be dispersed over a wide area and be in many different places while still having that unity which marks community. Conversely it is not simply that those who are in one place must necessarily form a community; propinquity, by itself, does not make a community.

Now consider hierarchy. In certain contexts it is place which stands for the unity of community. In other contexts the unity of community may take precedence and place is subordinated so that it may hardly be noticeable. Indeed, it is not uncommon to speak of a dispersed community in such terms as "we all stand together despite the fact that we are scattered all over the country." A classic example of this is, of course, the Jews in the *diaspora*. They formed a community on the basis of their religious unity, but what they held to be their place, which was also their place of origin, was never missing, even though it was of necessity subordinated in value.

Another example of this double opposition of place versus unity on the one hand and the hierarchy of the elements of the opposition is found in the sacredness of Jerusalem in Christian belief. In some contexts for Christians the real Jerusalem is the heavenly one. The earthly one is at best no more than a pale reflection, if that. In other times and contexts it is the place where sacred events took place, and it takes its sacred origin from that. Thus Jerusalem "above" is "the mother of us all," and a quite different place from the Jerusalem below. But the relationship between place, whether conceptual or material, remains clear: it is explicitly or implicitly associated with the community, whether merely as "where it happened" or as "the mother of us all."

I am not concerned here with the details of Jerusalem. I only use it as an example of where locality or place can, under certain defined conditions, be seen to have the higher valuation on its physical locus, while in other contexts the higher value is on its significance in a cosmological scheme and its physical locus recedes into the background (although it never entirely disappears; just as Jerusalem's cosmological significance for Christians can never entirely disappear no matter how omnipresent its physical existence is). There are also, of course, special situations in which it is hard, if it is even possible, to determine the rule which governs and which has evaluative priority, as is the case for a present day pilgrim who actually walks along the Via Dolorosa.

The more usual example, and one I have used in previous publications, is that between code and substance in kinship.[10] There are those contexts in which blood is of the utmost significance and the code for conduct recedes although never to the point where it ceases to exist. For example, the adult child whose parent has mistreated it, even after that child has left home and has broken off all contact with that parent, still remains the child of that parent. In collecting a genealogy from that child, the parent will usually be named. Although the code for conduct is not followed, its presence is still very much in evidence in the very nature of the accusation, explicit or implicit, in the child's breaking off all interpersonal relations. On the other hand, there are situations in which people say that although they know there is no blood relationship between themselves and an adoptive parent, they insist that that is of no concern, for the adopting parent "acted just like a real mother (or father)." They may go on to show that whereas the real (by blood) mother or father abandoned them for adoption, they were never abandoned by the adopting parent. Again, although there is no blood in the relationship, the reference to the blood, the substance, makes it clear that this element in the opposition is always present, though, in this latter example, diminished, while the code is given the highest value.

There is one final point to be made. If kinship, community, nationality, ethnicity, and religion are all part of the same galaxy in American culture, is that galaxy distinguished from other galaxies of American culture?

The special feature of this galaxy is the code for conduct which enjoins diffuse, enduring solidarity. The feature which distinguishes units within the galaxy are particular forms of substance —blood, locality, and so on.

It is the code for conduct which entails diffuse, enduring solidarity which distinguishes this whole galaxy from that of work, of commerce, of industry, of the rest of American culture. For that other part of American culture is characterized by the primacy of a code for conduct which entails enlightened self interest, calculation of personal advantage, the dominance of rationality, and the rational orientation of means to ends. I have spelled out elsewhere the contrast between love and work which characterizes this opposition and so need not go into it in detail here.[11] But the opposition between the sphere dominated by love or diffuse, enduring solidarity and that dominated by work, or the rational orientation of means towards self-interested ends, is quite clear. These are two major divisions in American culture, and it is within each of them that further differentiation at a cultural level takes place, as I have suggested for the segment of diffuse, enduring solidarity.

But if one thing is sure, American culture is materialistic. It is concerned with the material in ways which are as profound and pervasive as they are laden with the gravest emotional commitments. It is materialistic in that it explains life in material terms and only brings in the spiritual as a special form of materialism. The whole area of work is concerned with material—with transforming material into goods which in turn take a key role in commerce. And "material" in American culture is just another way of saying what I have called "substance."

To explore the meaning of materialism, the signs and symbols of substance, the place of the concrete in American culture should be the next task, for it is the crucial bridge between the spheres of solidarity on the one hand and of rationally oriented means toward self-interested goals on the other. For, as I have tried to show, the galaxy of diffuse, enduring solidarity is structured by its opposition to substance, and material or substance thus appears in both galaxies, albeit in various special forms.

Notes

1. This paper is part of an ongoing attempt to analyze and depict American culture. A number of publications have preceded it, and it is expected that others will follow. The works which have preceded this paper are listed in the bibliography under my name. Readers familiar with my earlier papers may find that the first few pages restate (sometimes in slightly altered form) certain of the main points which are made in detail in the previous publications. Such readers may find it expedient to skim over these pages. For those who are not familiar with the earlier publications, these few pages are a necessary prerequisite to the analysis which follows.

2. I have used the term "symbol" in my definition of culture for many years now. I began using it when the term "symbol" was understood as the most general form of signification, and special kinds could be comprehended under that general term. Since then the term "sign" has come to mean the most general form of signification and "symbol," like "icon," has (following Pierce) become a special kind of sign. I will stay with my previous usage in this paper; "symbol" is the most inclusive and general form of signification and is the equivalent of the term "sign"

for those who follow Pierce and the newer usage. This should create no difficulty since I am not interested in studying the different kinds of signs but only in signs (or, as I call them, "symbols") in general.

3. Schneider 1968, 1972, 1976.

4. See Schneider 1968 and Schneider and Smith 1978 (1973) for a minimal account of this material. Schneider 1972 has a more complete bibliography.

5. The material which follows immediately, confined entirely to American kinship, is based on, and highly condensed from, Schneider 1968.

6. Schneider 1969 spells this out in detail.

7. Schneider 1976 defines the concept of "galaxy."

8. Steven Zuckerman has pointed out in an unpublished paper that Geertz (1963) following Shils (1957) contrasts those collectivities based on "primordial attachment," that is, on shared language, race, religion, blood ties, and the like, with "civil" groupings based on nationhood. Nationhood is, of course, a relatively modern phenomenon in the form of the nation-state as we know it today. The two bases of solidarity were seen by Geertz as antithetical, the "primordial" attachments involving a kind of basic social identity while the "civil" or "national" involved a kind of political commitment of a very different order. Zuckerman quotes Fallers (1974) and develops the point that the "civil" bonds of solidarity not only themselves create "primordial" bonds but are very closely related to, and are possibly even built upon, the "primordial" forms of attachment. My analysis is of course confined entirely to American culture, but insofar as the point can be generalized it would seem to support Zuckerman and Fallers' point that the so-called "primordial" symbols are by no means antithetical nor do they contradict the so-called "civil" symbols but are rather transformations of each other.

9. This is not a matter of interlocking and overlapping connotations with distinct denotations. It is certainly a matter of interlocking and overlapping meanings so that one can go from meaning A to meaning D in such a way that A and B overlap and interlock, and B and C overlap and interlock, and C and D overlap and interlock, but A *seems* to be of an entirely different order from D. But to put it in terms of connotation

versus denotation is to accept a theory of meaning to which I am not at this time prepared to subscribe.

10. Schneider 1968, 1972.

11. Schneider 1968:45 ff.

References

Fallers, L. A. *The Social Anthropology of the Nation-State.* Chicago: Aldine, 1974.

Geertz, C. "The Integrative Revolution: Primordial Sentiments and Civil Politics in the New States." In *Old Societies and New States.* Edited by C. Geertz. New York: Free Press, 1963.

Schneider, D. M. *American Kinship: A Cultural Account.* New York: Prentice-Hall, 1968.

Schneider, D. M. "Kinship, Nationality and Religion in American Culture: Toward the Definition of Kinship." *Forms of Symbolic Action: Proceedings of the 1969 Annual Spring Meeting of the American Ethnological Society.* Edited by V. Turner. 1969.

Schneider, D. M. "What is Kinship All About?" *Kinship Studies in the Morgan Centennial Year.* Edited by P. Reining. Washington, D. C.: Anthropological Society of Washington, 1972.

Schneider, D. M. and Smith, R. T. *Class Differences and Sex Roles in American Kinship and Family Structure.* New York: Prentice-Hall, 1973. Reprinted, with new introduction, as *Class Differences in American Kinship.* Ann Arbor: University of Michigan Press, 1978.

Schneider, D. M. "Notes Toward a Theory of Culture." *Meaning in Anthropology.* Edited by K. Basso and H. Selby. Albuquerque, New Mexico: University of New Mexico Press, 1976.

Schneider, D. M. and Cottrell, C. B. *The American Kin Universe: A Genealogical Study.* Chicago: Department of Anthropology, University of Chicago, 1975.

The Making of a Community: The Role of Women in an Agricultural Setting

SEENA B. KOHL, Ph.D.
Professor of Anthropology,
Webster College, St. Louis, Mo.

Women's participation in the settlement of the West has been traditionally overlooked and ignored by historians. This is a consequence not only of male bias but also of the preoccupation of historians with the "movers and shapers." Historians are trained to be uninterested in the daily lives of ordinary people, the stage on which women's part in history is, in large measure, played out. This myopic, impoverished view provides the vista for others besides historians, such as sociologists and anthropologists.

My data on women's participation in the settlement of the West was collected as part of a larger study of family life and agricultural enterprise development which has spanned more than a decade, beginning in 1962. (See Bennett, 1969, and Kohl, 1976.) Although the locale of the study was the southwestern region of Saskatchewan, Canada, to which we have given the pseudonym Jasper, the processes of homestead settlement and enterprise establishment have been repeated over and over again in other North American prairie communities.

This region has had three generations of development, in which each generation faced a unique set of problems. (Bennett and Kohl, 1975). The first generation of pioneers had as its primary task the establishment of an enterprise and the process of settlement itself. For the second generation, the primary task was the maintenance of the enterprise in a period of severe economic depression and ecological hardship. For the third, contemporary generation, the primary task was and remains the development of the enterprise and the maintenance of a community which can provide the expected amenities of social life. In each generation the participation of women has been consistently important in two directions: first, in the agricultural enterprise, and secondly, in the making of the social community.

Furthermore, each generation—or period of time—set particular economic, ecological, and national structure constraints which called forth particular responses, and which formed the background of changing expectations for women, their families, and community life.

Some of the original homesteaders were still alive in 1962, when fieldwork began, as the study region was a recently homesteaded one. We were able to collect oral accounts of the settlement process from them. In addition, we made great use of written accounts of the frontier and homestead experiences culled from the numerous district history books, which had been compiled and published by local women's clubs. Most of these accounts emphasize family history: births, deaths, marriages, the establishment of the family enterprise, and the development of social amenities important for community life, such as post offices, stores, schools, and roads. They celebrate the family's survival in the face of hardship, and force the reader to take note of the characteristics necessary for survival: courage, strength, and mutual aid and support.

These qualities are set forth in the recollections of the difficulties experienced during the 1930s:

> In one way such hard times were good for a community, as folks made their own fun . . . visited . . . and shared. Card parties, social evenings and dances were the usual thing. There were no shows, no driving fifty miles to go to some show or dance. Those were the days when away we would go with lots of robes, blankets and hot rocks in cutters or bob-sleighs; where there was no such thing as baby sitters; where young and old danced to Darling Nellie Gray and Red Wing and Clementine.

The importance of these qualities is reiterated by Jasperites in the interviews taken in the 1970s, in which they stated why the region was a good place to live. Their views are also shared by the fourth generation. In response to our request for essays contrasting life in Jasper with that in other places, one student wrote:

> In the building of the curling rink, the people of the community donated money, nails, lumber, food, and their own help to make this possible. Even the teenagers helped. In a city . . . the occupants would hire someone to do it for them . . . living in a community like ours means togetherness, and that is what a community is for. The sharing of one's feelings and ideas.

The homestead-settlement period can be divided into two phases: first, the early frontier period of the open range; second, the period of the closing of the range and heavy homesteading on the prairie. In both periods, the first generation was faced with the task of the establishment of an enterprise.

In both situations women's tasks varied. Women were important in ensuring the continued survival of the family household and its associated members through the familiar domestic tasks of cooking, washing, cleaning, and giving birth to and taking care of children. These necessary tasks are the hidden aspects of production (Rowbotham, 1974).

The work women do in the household has rarely been included in economic analyses. Rather, women's domestic tasks are considered to be personal services to other family members. John Kenneth Galbraith has described women in this situation as "crypto-servants." Moreover, women's participation even in economic enterprises has been ignored or considered as private services to a male owner. Such a view of women is not only a serious error in the analyses of economic development, but also misrepresents women's contribution to society in general.

Women were full participants, albeit taken-for-granted ones, in the development of an economic enterprise which laid the base for contemporary agriculture. It was not uncommon for men to leave the homestead for extended periods of time for cash employment. Women and children remained at home. One woman recalled:

> The winter I stayed on our homestead alone I shall never forget. Good thing I was young, with lots of courage and ambition, and afraid of nothing. I must admit it would have been most lonely many times if it had not been for Mrs. P. L. P-, our neighbor a half mile north. . . .
>
> I recall one time in the fall when I had tethered Bessy the cow, and she broke loose. I took Helen in my arms and off I went to hunt for her on the wild prairie. . . . Finally I found her two miles from home near a herd of wild ranch cattle. What a chance I was taking. I am sure those cattle had never seen a woman on foot before, but I had little fear and soon chased the cow home.

Women's labor was crucial, and even when they had no past experience or skills, they responded to the tasks at hand. In particular, they played a significant part in survival on the frontier through their activities as nurses and midwives; even those without skills functioned as such.

There are two common and opposing views of the frontier woman. One regards her as overburdened, overworked, and an object of pity. The second regards her as a heroic figure. R. Bartlett, in his book *The New Country* (1974), makes the point that, for many women, life on the frontier was a continuation of the life they knew in other farming settlements. In both settings it was a life of continuous work. Few of the settlers regarded themselves as heroic. "They did what had to be done." Numbers of them regarded themselves as overworked but saw no alternative, and in later years they recalled their struggles with pride.

While the women's primary task was a continuation of similar home and farm tasks she had done before, the requirements of survival on the frontier necessitated the learning of new skills and the putting aside, or holding in abeyance, the traditional concepts of feminine behavior. One has only to look at the early mail order catalogues to become aware of the incongruity of urban constraints upon women in their daily lives on the frontier. No pioneer woman could milk six cows, drive a horse team, or plaster her house in the corsets and skirts of that period—and they did not.

The loosening of sex role definitions did not release women from their primary tasks: the maintenance of the household and the care of the children. However, the frontier did permit greater variation from accepted behavior and ideology—a tendency which has continued into the contemporary period.

While the frontier experience called forth extraordinary responses from both men and women, it would be a mistake to consider only the hardships and costs that were involved in settlement. The frontier offered both men and women new opportunities, which they grasped. For both, the opportunity to own land represented the opportunity of a lifetime. There are numerous accounts of women, widows and heads of families (homesteads were not available to single women, other than women who were heads of families), who came with their kinsmen to homestead land which they had bought "for practically nothing."

Isolation was an important component of the life of the settling families. It was most severe for those who settled during the open range pre-homestead period prior to 1905. The early ranchers settled in isolated areas of the region along creeks in protected coulees. In that pre-homestead period, families were isolated for months at a time, and the older regional residents speak today with nostalgia of the annual or bi-annual trip to town. Travel was by buckboard or horse, and social calls could last from three days to a week or more.

The cost of isolation from others could be lessened by adopting the ideology that it was "good" to live apart, setting an example of self-reliance. Socially, the cost could be lessened by the rewards of visiting, the demonstrations of hospitality, and the fact that while one could count on one's neighbors, one need not be restricted by them.

At the same time, even where there were desires for a less

isolated life, there were few expectations of urban amenities, such as stores, schools, and medical care. Due to extensive land use, ranch families isolated for months at a time were forced to find individual solutions to problems usually solved socially: schooling for children was one, medical care another. The solutions to these problems varied. When necessary the family members either did without such social amenities or moved into town (Jasper). One pioneer recalled what he had heard of the arrangements made for his birth:

> In the fall of 1891 I was born. Having no nearby neighbor or hospital, arrangements were made for a room at the International Hotel in town [Jasper] with Mrs. H—a local midwife—and the doctor from the barracks [The Royal Canadian Mounted Police].

The closing of the range and the advent of homestead settlement created "instant" communities on the prairie. Isolation was not valued. Houses were built with access to neighbors and to the road. Neighbors were welcomed. The homestead farm population came to build a society. They were on a frontier, but the frontier experience was considered only a phase in the development process.

One woman wrote:

> The people were all young couples, and those that were older were so ambitious and anxious that they forgot they were old. Everyone had visions of a growing and prosperous community. Neighbors helped one another build houses and barns and went to [town] together for their loads. The community spirit was wonderful. Everyone had a smile and a cheerful word at all times. . . . This was truly a county that could not fail.

In this period the greater numbers of women and children created demands for social amenities based upon past experiences of nucleated settlement. They wanted schools, churches, stores, and the establishment of a community social life. The demand for schools and their establishment created a focal point of social life. Schools were established where there were a minimum of ten children in an area of six square miles. These schools became centers of social life and were used for church services, concerts, dances and parties, box socials, showers, weddings, wedding receptions, funerals, and anniversaries.

As part of the development of a social community, women organized themselves into a variety of women's groups almost immediately, some connected to a church denomination, others non-denominational. The ostensible function of these groups varied and changed over the years from the purchasing of school equipment to the sending of parcels overseas to the maintenance of a women's rest room in town. They provided the opportunity for women to meet together, to share their problems, and to consider, even if minimally, the wider world and their relationship to it.

Women's participation in women's groups was always important; however, the degree of importance and activity changed in direct relation to the need for their physical labor at home. In the early homestead period these women's groups provided one respite from daily drudgery. The meetings were all-day affairs, and it required great ingenuity, in some instances, to get there. In later years, with the mechanization of farms, greater ease in transportation, and greater economic prosperity, women's clubs proliferated, and women's community activities then became a much more important and regular part of their routine.

Throughout the open range and homesteading periods, women were at a premium. Reminiscences exist that at some of the dances the men would outnumber the ladies four to one. The balance was restored by tying a white handkerchief around a man's arm, thus making him a "lady" for a period of time. In both periods, women were important components of a developing social order, and they were highly valued as such. Women were expected to "make a home," a concept which implied warmth and comfort and the niceties of life, including literacy skills and cultural attributes such as music, books, and church attendance. In the absence of local schools, women supervised their children's lessons, served as teachers in private homes, and when necessary moved into town for the winter so the children could attend school.

In the past as well as today, women had a higher level of educational achievement than the region's male population. This differential stems in part from the fact that an important source of wives on the frontier was the single schoolteacher. Approximately one-half of the first generation of women were schoolteachers who entered the region unmarried, married almost immediately, and remained as part of the growing community. In later periods the differential in education has been due to the fact that women are not considered potential successors to the economic enterprise. There are higher educational expectations for them than there are for young men. Young men are encouraged to, and commonly do, succeed to their father's enterprise, staying within the bonds of the family, and remaining without additional schooling. By contrast, if the young women do not marry either prior to or upon graduation from high school, they are expected to leave the region for further training in one of the traditional female occupations, teaching, nursing, or secretarial work. For the most part these young women and their families recognize that completion of the twelfth grade and further education is necessary for successful emigration. Each decade, approximately two-thirds of the young women leave the region; fewer than one-third of the men do so. The visits home of both men and women, and their continued ties with their family, are important links by which this rural region is connected to the wider society. Thus the contemporary women, like their frontier grandmothers, continue to be a major source of broader expectations of social and cultural life.

Perhaps most relevant to the development of a community was the importance of family ties in the early settlement period. Like that of most frontiers, the frontier population was composed for the most part of single young men, many of whom did not remain to establish an enterprise but moved on to other frontiers. Those who remained either arrived with a family and friends and a ready-made network of social support or, through their marriage to the daughter (sister, widow) of a homesteader neighbor, were quickly included in a network of mutual aid.

The homestead and depression periods were both times of extended deprivation, of learning to defer household and personal wants in favor of the enterprise. Women as the household managers and quartermasters were and remain the "gatekeepers" for consumption wants. The family agricultural enterprise was dependent upon family household members' willingness to share and participate in work activities. This required a modicum of satisfaction for all members. Women were the moderators of demands and set the style and level of consumption. One of the important differences between the homestead and the depression periods was the differing view of deferment. Homesteading was a time of optimism and hope; the depression period provided little hope. Of course, during both periods women were an important factor in the decision to leave or to "stick it out."

The increase in mechanization and the general increase in economic prosperity of the 1950s and the contemporary period has meant that the need for women's physical labor has declined. Women's tasks in the enterprise remain, but they have changed. Women are now the business-manager-bookkeepers, a function of their higher educational skills as well as of the need of agricultural enterprises to keep business records. Whereas formerly women were important members of the enterprise labor force, today they are more likely to work in town, contributing their cash income to the family enterprise and in particular using that income to fulfill family household wants. Women are still consumption gatekeepers, but they are also part of a national system and are responsive to pressures to consume. Rural women can now maintain living standards similar to those of their urban counterparts. This recent feature of rural life makes for community continuity.

The history of the Jasper region (similar to other plains agricultural settlements) since the depression has been one of continued population decline and population dispersal. The decline in population and concomitant consolidation of farm enterprises, while ecologically and economically sound, meant inevitable consolidation of service facilities and the disappearance of the local school, the local post office, and the local village. Most rural communities have experienced this decline.

However, despite the dispersal in population, the sense of "community" has remained intact through the evolution of an effective communication system which operates through a series of overlapping social networks based upon kinship, friendship, work associations, and formal organizations. There are multiple connections between people, which means there are few impersonal relationships. The behavior of everyone is considered relevant and important. There is constant comment and discussion about others, and there is little anonymity or privacy. This concern with the behavior of others can be viewed as oppressive and has been the hallmark of the pettiness of the small town (and mind). The constant talk and speculation about others serves as an important means of social control and social constraints on individual behavior. For some, the only solution is to leave. The tradeoff, however, is seen as a loss of community in exchange for the anonymity of city life. At the same time, concern about others is an indication that people "care" about one another.

In the present, as in the past, Jasper agriculturalists are faced with important economic and social needs which cannot be met within the associated household or households, nor, given the private character of family agriculture, are they met by national entities. The survival and maintenance of an agricultural enterprise depends upon a system of local instrumental exchanges. Both men and women participate in numerous social and work activities with kinsmen and friends in order to gain access to needed resources for the continuity of the enterprise. These exchanges are embedded in a social matrix based upon shared agreements about work, reciprocity, friendship, and kinship, and they can never be considered merely in terms of their economic utility. These exchanges also, and importantly, reinforce and maintain the sense of community.

The work of the agriculturalist for the most part excludes women, whose primary tasks are within the home. Similarly, the social opportunities for women, based upon the women's world of home, club, and kin, largely exclude men. Men and women have separate social and work activities through which they establish independent ties with others. However, due to the limited number of alternatives, these ties are complementary, and they incorporate different members of the same household.

Whereas men have important work exchanges with other men, it is the women who, for the most part, organize the social relationships between the household, the kin group, and the community. They establish the social context of the household by determining the relationships of household members with other members of the kin group and the larger community.

Through the continuous effort of meeting the social demands of others—kinsmen, neighbors, friends—shared goals develop and social ties are maintained and reinforced (or attenuated and destroyed). These are processes which have wider consequences than the fulfillment of personal and private needs. They can be conceptualized as behavioral correlates of the existing contemporary "community."

Within this frame of reference, a community is seen to be not so much a place as a process of relationships which are constantly forming and dissolving: relationships which serve a myriad of functions for both individuals and the larger regional social system. These are relationships based upon shared ideas of reciprocity and mutual aid, ideas which are rooted in the early period of settlement and the homestead experience. They are relationships based upon shared experiences of the economic hardship of drought and depression in the thirties and the fact that the agriculturalists and their families survived. They are relationships based upon goals of the maintenance of continuity of the family and the enterprise, goals which are shared by the whole community within this particular geographical setting. These relationships embody the conceptualization of community. Clearly, women have played, and continue to play, a key role in the formation and maintenance of this community.

References

Bartlett, Richard A. *The New Country*. New York: Oxford University Press, 1974. pp. 350–54.

Bennett, John W. *Northern Plainsmen: Adaptive Society and Agrarian Life*. Chicago: Aldine Publishing Co., 1969.

Bennett, John W. and Kohl, Seena B. "Characterological, Strategic and Institutional Interpretations of Prairie Settlement." In *Western Canada: Past and Present*, pp. 14–27. Edited by A. W. Rasporolch. Calgary, Canada: McClelland and Stewart West Ltd., 1975.

Kohl, Seena B. *Working Together: Women and Family in Southwestern Saskatchewan*. Toronto: Holt Rinehart and Winston of Canada Ltd., 1976.

Rowbotham, Sheila. *Hidden from History*. New York: Random House, 1974.

Caring for the Insane in Ante-Bellum Massachusetts: Family, Community, and State Participation

BARBARA G. ROSENKRANTZ
Professor of the History of Science, Department of the History of Science and School of Public Health, Harvard University, Cambridge, Mass.
and
MARIS A. VINOVSKIS
Associate Professor, Department of History, and Associate Research Scientist, Center for Political Studies of the Institute for Social Research, University of Michigan.
Associate Staff Director to the United States House Select Committee on Population

The role of the family in America's past is now one of the most exciting and rapidly growing areas of research. Though much of the impetus for family history came from the work of colonial historians, most of the recent studies of family history are set in the nineteenth century. There is an outpouring of studies on various aspects of the family life course such as childrearing, adolescence, marriage, labor force participation, old age, and death. Although these analyses have tried to place their investigation of the family within the context of the larger society, many of them have focused almost exclusively on either the family or the family member and have paid scant attention to the interaction of the family with the rest of society. Furthermore, many of these analyses of the family are based on either prescriptive literature, such as domestic and childrearing manuals, or on demographic data, such as vital statistics and census returns. Families are probably best understood when we are able to examine contemporary statements about desirable conduct in the context of actual behavior. Very few studies of family history have integrated quantitative data with literary evidence in order to investigate the interplay between ideas and behavior in ante-bellum America.

We propose to examine a small, but significant, area that illuminates interaction among families, their local communities and the state in nineteenth-century Massachusetts—the care and treatment of the insane. This is a particularly interesting issue because dramatic shifts in the attitudes toward insanity in the late eighteenth and early nineteenth centuries led to the development of specialized institutions for the insane and provided new alternatives for handling the mentally ill in Massachusetts. By comparing attitudes toward institutionalization of the insane with the extent of their commitment to those institutions available, we will be able to show how provision of custody and care for the insane reflected changing beliefs about the nature of family, local community, and state responsibility.

Care of the Insane in Colonial America

The family was the center of colonial society. Everyone in Massachusetts, and in most New England and central seaboard settlements, was expected to live with a family; the community relied upon the family to carry out such functions as the socialization of the young and care of the elderly. It was expected, therefore, that family members would take care of their insane although they might seek advice and guidance from their minister or physician.[1] When there were provisions to replace the family with community responsibility for indigent or deviant individuals, this obviously reflected a variety of concerns in colonial America. The pursuit of order in the community, the threat of unaccustomed financial burdens, and differences in the behavior expected from the poor, the criminal, and the sick, all in some way determined the characteristics of institutional arrangements.

Following the traditions of English Poor Law, Massachusetts towns were held accountable for the welfare of their residents.[2] Although the fundamental principle of public relief was that responsibility lay with the local community in which the dependent person lived, the Commonwealth gradually did become the resource for those persons who had no legal residence. Since most communities were reluctant to spend large sums of money to care for their less fortunate residents, every possible effort was made to maintain arrangements that were as cheap as possible. As a result, although colonial Americans attempted to rely on families for the care of their own insane, they did not hesitate to break up poor families if it appeared that this would reduce the burden on the public treasury. We find the town of Braintree, Massachusetts, voting in 1698 "that Samuel Speere should build a little house 7 foote long and 5 foote wide & set it by his house to secure his Sister good wife Witty being distracted & provide for her."[3] In return, the town obligated itself to repay Speere for taking care of his insane sister. A few years earlier, in 1653, Plymouth colony intervened quite differently in the face of a family's impending poverty. The court ordered the town of Taunton "to order the especiall affaires" of Thomas Braydon, who was, "by reason of a distracted condicion," unemployed. At the same time his wife was "putt forth to service, beine younge and fitte for the same, and haueing noe other way soe likely to procure her mayntanance."[4]

In a few of the larger communities, almshouses had been built to take care of the dependent population. In these urban areas, the insane were often placed in those almshouses since it was considered to be a much less expensive way of maintaining the poor than boarding them out in the community. This policy had the obvious disadvantage of mixing the sane and the insane poor together under conditions which were not conducive to the recovery of either group. Although Boston looked into the possibility of building a separate facility for the insane as early as 1729, nothing was done during the colonial period.[5]

Massachusetts was not eager to accept financial responsibility for any group of indigents—sane or insane. The harmless insane who were supported by their kin were expected to live without assistance from the community. Reluctance to deviate from this custom is seen in the statutes directed to the violent insane whose behavior threatened standards of safety. The first Massachusetts law specifically concerned with the insane stated in 1676 that

> Whereas, There are distracted persons in some tounes, that are unruly, whereby not only the familyes wherein they are, but others suffer much damage by them, it is ordered by this Court and the authoritye thereof, that the selectmen in all tounes where such persons are hereby impowred & injoyed to take care of such persons, that they doe not damnify others.[6]

By the end of the next century the state was not willing to accept financial responsibility even for insane persons committed to a house of correction. The law declared that even when a person was jailed by reason of insanity because he or she was declared "dangerous to the peace and safety of the good people. . . . every person so committed shall be kept at his or her own expense, if he or she have estate, otherwise at the charge of the person or town upon whom his maintenance was regularly to be charged if he or she had not been committed: and he or she shall if able to be put to work during his or her confinement."[7] If dangerous behavior was less likely than dependence to remove the victim of insanity from family responsibility, the hope of rehabilitation treatment was even less persuasive.

Seventeenth and eighteenth century Americans often attributed insanity to supernatural factors. The insane were seen as either possessed by demonic powers or cursed by God's judgment. Although by mid-eighteenth century, colonial physicians were more apt to interpret insanity within a medical framework, contemporary theories of disease did not lend themselves to the cure of insanity through distinctive therapy.[8] Institutional care of the sick was largely limited to infirmaries associated with almshouses. In

Philadelphia, where the first colonial hospital was established in 1751, the ward for pauper insane was more the object of vulgar curiosity than medical attention. Although physicians often resorted to the customary therapies used for fevers, including bleeding and dosing with depletive drugs, they were quite pessimistic about curing their patients. As a result, colonial Americans spent little time and effort on medical treatment of the insane.

The family, therefore, remained central to the welfare of the insane throughout the colonial period. If insanity threatened to create dependence the community might intervene, but only minimally. The catalyst for community involvement was the threatened disruption of the family unit; when insanity imperiled social stability, traditional criteria and means of relief were used. The needs of the insane and the needs of society were not in conflict and both were best served through supporting traditional roles for the family.

Changing Attitudes and Behavior Toward the Insane in Nineteenth-Century America

There were several dramatic changes in ideas about insanity and care of the insane in the late eighteenth and early nineteenth centuries. Probably most important for the insane themselves, their families, and society as a whole, was the new conception of insanity as a curable disease. While this idea had complex origins and was intimately associated with interest in identifying the physical and psychological causes of insanity, an important consequence of this concern was the conviction that recovery would follow medical intervention in a new environment for therapy. As the pessimistic view of the curability of insanity gradually was replaced by the expectation of rehabilitation through the moral treatment advocated by Philippe Pinel in France and Samuel Tuke in England, the central role of family responsibility for care was challenged.[9] American physicians and enlightened laymen came to share this perspective and shifted their reliance from the home and family to the asylum as institutional environment for the insane.

At the same time, as the proponents of moral therapy for the insane dismissed the family from its effective role in restoring the deviant to health, enthusiasts for "the cult of domesticity" stressed the beneficial aspects of family life and saw the family as the refuge from the competitiveness and bustle of the rest of society.[10] Where colonial Americans had ordinarily left the insane with their own families, reformers both abroad and in the United States insisted that treatment of the insane required a special therapeutic environment. The champions of asylums viewed family life as hectic when compared with the quiet and ordered atmosphere needed for recovery from insanity. While we found little direct evidence of confrontation between these two judgments about family life in the early nineteenth century, discussion of how the insane might respond to their home environment suggests an underlying tension. At a time when most Americans did not believe that a sick person would be best cared for away from home and among strangers, removal of the insane from family care was justified specifically by noting the adverse effect of family expectations upon the afflicted. The home, rather than being a place of comfort and support, could retard or prevent recovery.[11]

A medical handbook published in 1822 went further to reassure the public of the safety and desirability of asylum care. Since general hospitals remained for most of the nineteenth century repositories primarily for the indigent, asylums for the insane were distinguished as necessary for the treatment of those whose financial means would have made home care permissible in other illness. This *Treatise on Domestic Medicine* spoke directly to answer the fears of harsh treatment, found "both among the highest and lowest classes of society," and pronounced them "groundless." The asylum provided the environment conducive to calming the furious maniac, no matter what his or her social background; by contrast "the patient confined at home naturally feels a high degree of resentment when those whom he has been accustomed to command refuse to obey his order. . . ."[12] Family order and the health of the insane would both be needlessly at risk if the patient were not given access to the humane and scientific treatment available through commitment to an institution.

This insistence that the insane should be treated in asylums minimized the role of families and encouraged the development of private and public hospitals. The proper medical and moral regimen could only be organized in these circumstances. Kind consideration and appropriate response to disordered behavior was best assured once the patient was committed. The view that insanity was amenable to rational treatment attracted Americans under different circumstances than those in England and in France where large hospitals had traditionally incarcerated the indigent sick without differentiating the origins or nature of their illnesses. In the United States the argument for moral management gained adherents in part because of fear that insanity was increasing as the population grew and the manner of life changed. Enthusiasm for constructing asylums, in which treatment could be made available to all insane, reflected hope and expectation that Americans would thereby affirm the opportunity for better health and life in the New World. Americans would adopt the moral and medical principles advocated abroad in new circumstances.[13]

In general, advocates of insane asylums devoted very little attention to the problems and needs of the families of the insane. While superintendents of newly established hospitals were anxious that families send their insane member to the asylum as quickly as possible, since insanity in its early stages could be cured more easily than later, they were not particularly concerned about the home environment. No effort was made to alter the family arrangements that may have contributed to the insanity of the patient by counselling the other members of that family. In fact, although the superintendents of these asylums used their annual reports to inform the public on a wide variety of issues, almost no effort was made to advise the family and friends on how to deal with the insane person other than to have him or her committed as quickly as possible.[14]

The insane were not only to be removed from their families, but they were not to be visited by them in the asylum. Although superintendents and trustees of these institutions acknowledged that relatives and friends might want to visit, and although clothing and other comforts from home were often solicited, visiting was discouraged since this was most likely adversely to affect the convalescent. Only in the later stages of recovery, when reason was well established, were occasional visits from family and friends anticipated with favor.[15]

The insistence on distinguishing the environment of the hospital as different from the home was important because it minimized the role of the family in care for the insane and encouraged support of public and private asylums. One gets the impression that superintendents and trustees, who ultimately authorized admission and family visits, had little confidence in the ability of family and friends to understand the nature of insanity. Complaints were frequently made that patients were removed prematurely from the hospital; any sign of improvement was misinterpreted as an indication of cure. Superintendents, therefore, tried to eliminate interference in the hospital routine by physicians, family, or the local authorities who had initiated the original commitment. The public was expected to accept the advice and guidance of the medical superintendents who were expert in treatment and prognosis. Yet the superintendents of asylums had to pay homage to the family in principle, since anything less than the proper reverence for that hallowed estate would have created serious difficulties with legislatures and charitable contributors to hospital endowments.

Advocating the merits of insane asylums was one thing, but raising the money necessary to build them was another problem. Since the asylums were expected to be large enough to permit the classification of patients and spacious enough to provide individual rooms for the patients, they were quite expensive. Nevertheless, sufficient enthusiam for these institutions was generated so that several private hospitals for the insane were built in the first three decades of the nineteenth century.

In Massachusetts a group of wealthy philanthropists undertook to construct a general hospital in Boston as well as McLean Asylum, a separate hospital for the insane nearby. Although the Commonwealth of Massachusetts chartered the hospitals and assisted them to some degree financially, almost all of the money was raised by contributions from wealthy Massachusetts citizens.[16] From the time the Asylum was opened in 1818 most of the patients were sent and supported by their own families and friends. McLean was willing to accept some poor patients sent by their local communities if they supported them. Since the cost of patient care at McLean was considerably higher than that of confining the insane paupers in jails or almshouses, the number of town paupers at McLean was never very large.

As the value of placing the insane within asylums became increasingly evident, efforts were made to construct a public hospital as well. McLean was simply too small to accommodate the growing demands for institutionalizing the insane and too expensive for most Massachusetts families and communities. It was uneconomical for local communities to construct their own asylums because most of them did not have enough insane persons to justify the construction of such a large facility. Therefore, under the legislative leadership of Horace Mann, Massachusetts built its first state institution for the insane in 1833—the Worcester State Hospital.[17] With the completion of the Worcester State Hospital, the interrelationships among the family, the local community, and the state in the care of the insane became even more complex. The primary responsibility for an insane person still rested with the family. But it was now considered desirable, if possible, to send that insane individual to either McLean Asylum or the Worcester State Hospital. In either case, it was the responsibility of that family to pay for the cost of that care.

If an individual had no immediate family or if the family did not have the financial resources even to maintain them at home, then it was the responsibility of the local community to take care of that person. The local authorities now had the option of sending the insane person to the Worcester State Hospital and supporting him, placing him in a local jail or almshouse, or auctioning him to a private family. With the great increase in the local almshouses in the first quarter of the nineteenth century, towns were now more apt to use these facilities for their insane than in the colonial period. Although towns were strongly urged by medical experts to send their insane to the Worcester State Hospital, very few of them did so because of the much higher cost of maintaining them in the hospital rather than in an almshouse, jail, or private home. The reluctance of the local communities to provide good medical attention for the pauper insane created a serious problem in the Commonwealth. Increasingly during the 1840s and 1850s, reformers such as Dorothea Dix urged that the state accept the responsibility for all insane paupers since most local communities failed to provide them with adequate medical attention.[18]

The role of the state in the care of the mentally ill had greatly expanded since the colonial period. Although Massachusetts had assumed the responsibility for paupers who had no legal residence in the eighteenth century, the number of paupers supported by the state had not been very large. With the growing number of immigrants to the Commonwealth in the nineteenth century, the number of state paupers, sane and insane, greatly increased. The state could either send these lunatic paupers to the Worcester State Hospital or reimburse the local communities for taking care of them in their almshouses or jails. In addition, the state subsidized at least part of the cost of maintaining all patients at Worcester State Hospital by charging private patients only the estimated cost of accommodating them rather than a larger sum which would have included an amount to cover the capital costs of that hospital. Thus, the state was now very deeply involved in the treatment of the mentally ill and exercised a large amount of influence in determining the nature and quality of care for the insane that would be available in the Commonwealth.

The interests of the family, local community, state, and superintendents of the new asylums did not always coincide in providing care for the insane. Whereas the superintendents stressed the importance of their asylums as therapeutic rather than custodial institutions, the state and local authorities were often more interested in using them simply as convenient places for accommodating patients who were too dangerous to be kept at home or in a local almshouse. As a result, the superintendents of the public hospitals complained that the therapeutic action of their institutions was being undermined by the type of patients they were obligated to receive. Furthermore, while the superintendents and reformers were not particularly concerned about the high cost of maintaining the asylums, local and state officials often hesitated to send patients to the hospitals rather than to the much less expensive alternatives such as local almshouses or county jails. Even when the families or local authorities did make a decision to send someone to these hospitals, they were often tempted to remove the patients before they were fully recovered in order to save money.[19]

While selectmen and overseers of the poor worried over the expenses incurred through the support of indigent insane in these new hospitals, some individuals of means and influence were reluctant to give up their traditional family responsibilities. Thus, in a long article in the *Independent Chronicle* in 1817, a correspondent argued against building an asylum because it would crowd together lunatics of all sorts and separate families.[20] Furthermore, although the necessity of institutions for the furiously mad and violent was most generally agreed upon, and the advantage of moral management for the recently incapacitated seemed to offer the best hope for cure, family medical advice books continued to recommend that tractable patients should be kept within the family circle:

If . . . a patient is quiet and manageable without coercion, and his disease partakes more of the nature of melancholy than fury, then the attendance of an affectionate wife or husband, brother, sister, or friend, at his own home, or any private house, may, with proper instructions, be able to do much more than can be expected where a number are to be attended to.[21]

Despite the widespread publicity in behalf of asylums, many writers of these books did not encourage their readers to send their insane friends among strangers for treatment. Whether this was because they were not fully aware of the care provided, or did not think that institutions could replace the loving care of friends, is not clear. In any case, many of the best-selling antebellum literature of advice did not prepare the public to seek comfort from asylums.[22]

Although the superintendents of asylums were usually careful not to make negative remarks about the relatives and friends of specific inmates, there were frequent complaints in the annual reports of the McLean Asylum and the State Hospital at Worcester that families and local physicians reduced the chances of curing some insane by finding reasons for delaying commitment. In some cases, for instance, patients were sent to the hospital only as a last resort, when it was necessary to relieve the family and friends of responsibility. Typically, Dr. Merick Bemis, superintendent at Worcester, complained in 1857:

Epileptics I regard as the most troublesome patients admitted to an asylum. When admitted they are generally very much worn out. They are usually kept in the family until there is no hope for them, when they are moved to an asylum to relieve the friends of a burden. . . .[24]

Although our research to date has only pinpointed some of the areas of potential and actual friction between these different images of the nineteenth-century family, we suspect that it is an area of investigation that can and should be pursued much further. By studying these incongruent perspectives on the home and its intimate associations as set forth in family advice literature by proponents of the new asylums and spokesmen for the somewhat apprehensive public, we will develop a richer and deeper understanding of family and institutional life during the first half of the nineteenth century.

Care of the Insane in Mid-Nineteenth Century Massachusetts

In the first sections of this paper we discussed changes in attitudes towards the insane that were recorded in the writings of physicians, reformers, trustees and superintendents of asylums, and authors of domestic literature. In this section we investigate the reported prevalence of insanity in ante-bellum Massachusetts, and the provision of care by families, local communities, and the Commonwealth. It is very different even today to evaluate the extent of insanity and its treatment because it depends upon the definition of insanity as well as the reliability of the procedures for ascertaining who is insane. The problem becomes more complicated since we cannot resurvey the population. As historians we are dependent upon surveys of the insane that were conducted under less than ideal conditions and based on different conceptions of insanity.

The most widely known and available series of data on nineteenth-century insanity are the federal censuses which began to record the number of insane persons in 1840. Unfortunately, the quality of those data is extremely poor. The federal census marshalls who gathered the information were usually political appointees who had little or no knowledge of insanity and who sometimes did not even bother to record such information. Furthermore, most families were reluctant to admit to a census marshall that one of their members was insane. As a result, the federal census information on the number of insane persons in ante-bellum America is useless for estimating the prevalence of insanity in that society.[25]

Fortunately, there is an unusually comprehensive survey of insanity among the general population of Massachusetts that was done in 1854. In an effort to determine the need for constructing a third state hospital for the insane, the Massachusetts legislature in 1854 commissioned a survey of the extent of insanity and of the capacity and efficacy of existing facilities. The survey was conducted by Edward Jarvis, a prominent physician and statistician who already had considerable experience in analyzing the extent of insanity from the federal census returns.[26]

Jarvis argued that previous efforts to survey the number of insane were hopelessly flawed. Rather than relying on the federal census marshalls or trusting to the self-reporting of insanity by households, Jarvis enlisted the help of local physicians, superintendents of public and private hospitals, keepers of jails and houses of correction, and some clergymen and selectmen to identify every insane individual in Massachusetts in 1854 by name, nativity, age, means of support, place of residence or confinement, degree of insanity, and prognosis for the future. Altogether, over fourteen-hundred individuals co-operated with Jarvis in providing information on the insane by responding to his questionnaire. The results are an unusually comprehensive effort by relatively knowledgeable and concerned individuals to describe the insane population. The Jarvis survey indicates the extent of insanity as perceived by selected contemporaries in mid-nineteenth-century Massachusetts. By re-analyzing the results of the Jarvis survey in conjunction with the characteristics of the Massachusetts population from the state census of 1855 and those of the local paupers from the returns of the poor in Massachusetts towns in 1855, we developed a different measure of mental illness as well as the likelihood of a person's being committed to a public or private institution designed specifically for the insane.[27]

Jarvis found that there were 2,632 insane persons in Massachusetts in the autumn of 1854. Or, using the population figures for 1855, about 232 insane persons per 100,000 population. This is considerably lower than the prevalence rates of mental illness in eleven community studies that have been done for the twentieth century. This does not necessarily indicate, however, that there was less mental illness in mid-nineteenth-century Massachusetts than today. Rather, that difference is more likely the result of applying different definitions of mental illness in the two time periods as well as using different methods for surveying the population.[28]

The insane in Massachusetts in 1854 can be subdivided according to the source of their support (see chart 1). Their family and friends were supporting 41.8 percent of the insane. Thus, even as late as the 1850s, the care of nearly one half of the insane in the Commonwealth was being financed by their friends or family.

CHART 1

Number of Insane in Massachusetts in 1854 by Source of Support

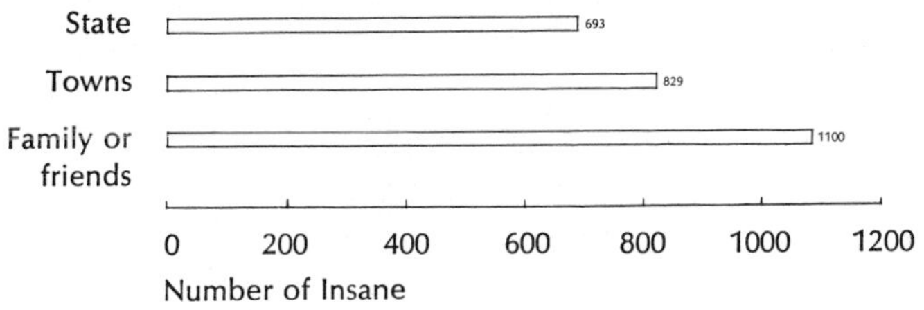

Source	Number
State	693
Towns	829
Family or friends	1100

0 200 400 600 800 1000 1200

Number of Insane

The local communities continued to play a large role in caring for the mentally ill who had no family or whose family was too poor to support them. Almost a third of the insane (31.6 percent) were supported by their local communities.

Finally, the state assumed financial responsibility for the remaining 26.4 percent of the insane. Whereas the state had not been heavily involved in the care of the mentally ill in the colonial period, by 1854 it provided support for about one quarter of all the insane. The state's direct responsibility for providing assistance for the insane was largely the result of its willingness to support foreign-born paupers who had been unable to establish a legal residence in any community. Of the state insane paupers, 90.2 percent were foreign-born.

In general, the foreign-born insane were unable to be supported by their family or friends. Of the foreign-born insane, 93.0 percent were paupers, almost all of whom were wards of the state rather than local communities. On the other hand, of the native-born insane, 53.1 percent were supported by their family or friends and most of the rest were cared for by their local communities.

The Commission on Lunacy not only surveyed the extent of insanity in Massachusetts, but also where the insane were being kept. Therefore, we can see to what extent the family, local community, and state had accepted the idea of institutionalizing the insane by sending those under their jurisdiction to these new facilities.

In 1854, Massachusetts had three large asylums for the insane—a private hospital at McLean and two public hospitals at Worcester and Taunton. In addition, there were two small private institutions for the insane at Dorchester and Pepperell which accommodated about forty patients altogether.

By the eve of the Civil War, Massachusetts provided what was considered relatively good institutional care for nearly one half of its insane. These private and public hospitals were considered the ideal locations for treating the insane in mid-nineteenth century Massachusetts. Although renovations were needed to maintain these institutions, especially at the Worcester State Hospital, these asylums were considered among the best facilities in America for treating the insane. Altogether, these hospitals contained 1,141 patients or 43.4 percent of the insane (see chart 2).

However, some of the insane, particularly those who were deemed incurable, were kept in one of the three county receptacles for the insane, or in one of the eight houses of correction or jails, or in the state prison, or in the recently constructed state almshouses at Monson, Tewksbury, and Bridgewater. It was less expensive to maintain the pauper insane in these institutions than in one of the hospitals, but there was no pretense of treatment. The receptacles, jails, houses of correction, state prison, and state almshouses were simply custodial institutions for the insane where

CHART 2

Number of Insane in Massachusetts in 1854 by Location

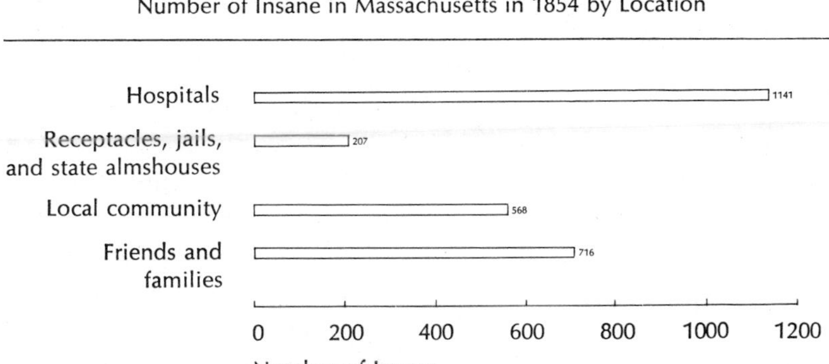

they could be accommodated at less expense than in the hospitals. Some of these institutions were the ones which Dorothea Dix had strongly condemned in 1843 as being unfit to accommodate the insane because they did not provide for the basic comforts or needs of those patients.[29] Altogether, only 207 insane persons (7.9 percent of all Massachusetts insane) were confined to these institutions.

The remaining 48.8 percent of the insane were maintained in either one of the local almshouses or in a private home. The Commission on Lunacy did not give detailed information on the exact location of these insane persons, but we can be almost certain that all of the 716 insane who were supported by their family or friends and were not in one of the hospitals, county receptacles, jails, and so forth, were either at home or with one of their friends. Thus, at least 27.2 percent of the insane in Massachusetts in 1854 were still living with their families or friends.

Of the 568 insane who were supported by their communities but were not in one of the hospitals, county receptacles, jails, and so forth, we cannot ascertain whether they were being kept in a local almshouse or auctioned off to live with a private family. We can obtain another perspective on the relief provided by local communities by examining the Massachusetts Poor Returns for

1855.[30] Considering the great increase in the number of towns with almshouses in the Commonwealth in the nineteenth century, it is likely that many of these insane were kept in one of the local almshouses. Most towns supported their paupers by maintaining an almshouse as well as by providing outdoor relief; almost every community had some form of outdoor relief, and 67.1 percent of them kept an almshouse. Although the number of persons who received outdoor relief in the Commonwealth was twice as large as those who were assisted within an almshouse, we suspect that the proportion of insane supported within almshouses was even higher since many of the insane paupers may have been confined for their own safety as well as for protection of the public.

The cost of maintaining insane paupers in local almshouses was considerably less than sending them to one of the private or public hospitals. Most communities were able to accommodate their insane paupers in a local almshouse at less than 50 percent of what Worcester State Hospital would have charged them. For example, in 1854 the state charged local authorities $3.00 per week for patients during their first six months and $2.75 per week after the first six months.[31] Most local communities operated their almshouses at substantially less cost per week for each pauper (see chart 3). Only 5.2 percent of the towns maintained their local almshouses at a cost of $2.50 or more per week. As a result, it is not surprising that many local authorities refused to send their insane paupers for treatment at one of the new asylums.

Having considered the perceived extent of insanity in Massachusetts, the sources of support for the insane, and the distribution of the insane in various institutions, we now consider some of the factors that determined whether one received treatment in a public or private asylum. Again, we can use the Jarvis data since they provide information on where each insane person was confined as well as some of their socio-economic characteristics. We will focus on three possible predictors of whether a person was in one of the asylums—their source of support, their marital status, and their age. These three factors have been selected because of

CHART 3

Distribution of Average Weekly Costs in Dollars Per Pauper in Local Almshouses in Massachusetts in 1855

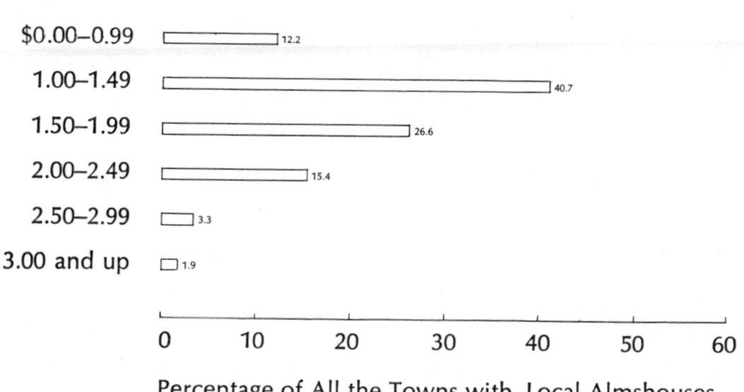

their particular relevance to our discussion of the role of the family. There are many other factors which may have influenced whether someone was treated in one of these hospitals. Therefore, we included four other variables in our analysis that seemed important and that were readily available—the sex of the patients, their place of birth, their present and usual condition, and the length of time since their last attack of insanity. These four variables will be introduced in our analysis as controls; however, in order to keep this paper within a reasonable length, we will not analyze them in any depth at this time, but will merely incorporate them as appropriate controls.[32]

There are many different factors which influenced the likelihood of an insane person's being sent to an asylum; any statistical procedure which can examine only one or two variables at a time, such as the cross-tabulation of data, cannot adequately take into consideration the variety of factors we want to investigate. We use demographic data to examine empirically the likelihood of a family, community, or the Commonwealth sending someone to an asylum. Using multiple classification analysis, a statistical procedure which permits the use of several independent variables, we can analyze the effect of the source of the support for the insane individual on commitment to an asylum, after controlling for the effects of their marital status, age, place of birth, sex, present and usual condition, and duration of present insanity.[33]

Of the state insane paupers, 72.0 percent were being treated in one of the asylums (see chart 4). However, this may tend to exaggerate the effect of state support since state insane paupers were also considered more dangerous (a condition which encouraged institutionalization) and were more apt to be foreigners who had no legal residence in a community which might have sent them to an almshouse instead. In fact, the results of the MCA analysis supports such an interpretation—after adjusting for the effects of the other independent variables, only 59.7 percent of the state insane would have been in an asylum.

The towns were the least likely to send anyone to an asylum. Only 36.7 percent of the town insane were in one of the hospitals. Even after controlling for the effects of the other variables, the percentage of town insane that would have been in an asylum is only 41.7—nearly ten percentage points less than the insane supported by their family or friends and eighteen percentage points less than the state insane. Our analysis clearly confirms that the local communities were the most reluctant to send someone to an asylum—mainly because of the higher cost of supporting them. Reformers such as Dorothea Dix were, therefore, correct in their assessment that one of the best ways of increasing the likelihood of sending the insane to an asylum was to shift the burden of financial responsibility from the local community to the state.

About half of the insane supported by friends or family were in one of the public or private asylums, and this figure does not change much after we control for the effects of the other variables. Thus, a large segment of the insane under the care and protection of their families and friends were being treated in a hospital even though the cost of the treatment was a major financial strain on most households. Although some families may still have harbored doubts about the advisability of institutionalizing an insane member, by 1854 most families were probably willing to try one of these asylums if they could afford the additional expense.

CHART 4

Percentage of Massachusetts Insane in Asylums by Source of Support

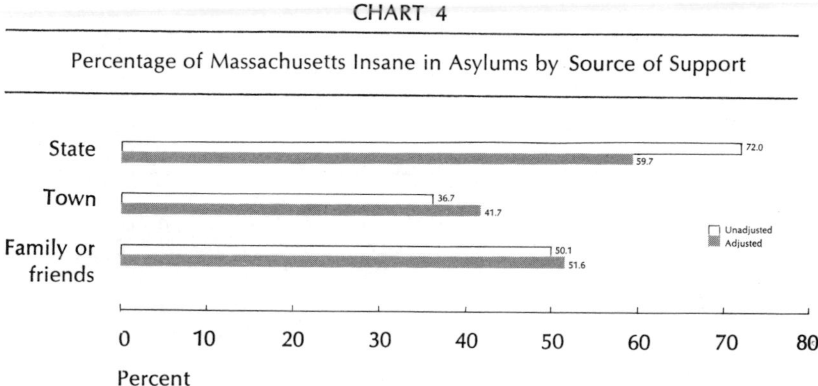

We can gain another perspective on the role of the family by analyzing the likelihood of being in an asylum after taking into consideration one's marital status. One might suspect that the marital status of an insane person might be an important factor in the decision to commit him to an asylum, because single people often had very different obligations and resources from married individuals. However, the popular and medical literature of the period does not discuss this issue at all, leading us to doubt whether this was an important explicit consideration in most families or communities.

The percentage of Massachusetts insane in asylums in 1854 by marital status does indicate some differences. Single and married individuals were more apt to be in an asylum than their widowed or divorced counterparts. On the other hand, the unadjusted percentages in this situation are quite misleading since there is very little difference in the likelihood of being in an asylum by marital status after we control for the effects of the other variables. The apparent reason that widowed or divorced individuals are less likely to be in one of these asylums is that they are generally older than the single or married insane—a serious handicap in a society where the elderly insane were much less likely to be treated in a hospital than their younger counterparts.[34]

CHART 5

Percentage of Massachusetts Insane in Asylums in 1854 by Marital Status

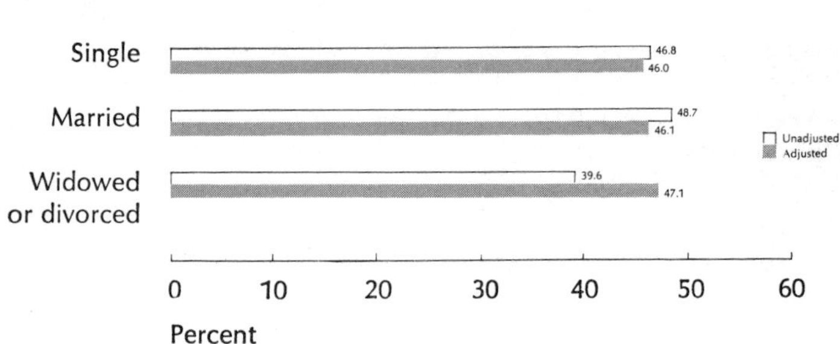

Finally, we will briefly analyze one more factor which may have affected both their family life and the probability of being institutionalized—the age of the insane person. Two separate, though related, issues in an individual's life course will be considered: the likelihood of being insane and the probability of being treated in an asylum.

Most superintendents of the asylums as well as other medical writers assumed that the prevalence of insanity was the greatest for persons in their twenties, thirties, or forties. They arrived at this conclusion by noting the large number of insane in asylums who were in those age-groups.[35] These impressions of the prevalence of insanity by age were incorrect. The physicians greatly underestimated the number and the proportion of elderly insane who were not in the asylums. In fact, if we recalculate the reported prevalence of insanity in Massachusetts in 1854 by age-group, the highest rate of insanity is not among individuals in their twenties, thirties, or forties, but those in their sixties and seventies (see chart 6). As we have argued elsewhere, the elderly insane were the "invisible lunatics" of the nineteenth century because most contemporaries underestimated their numbers as well as their plight.[36]

CHART 6

Number of Insane Persons in Massachusetts in 1854 by Age

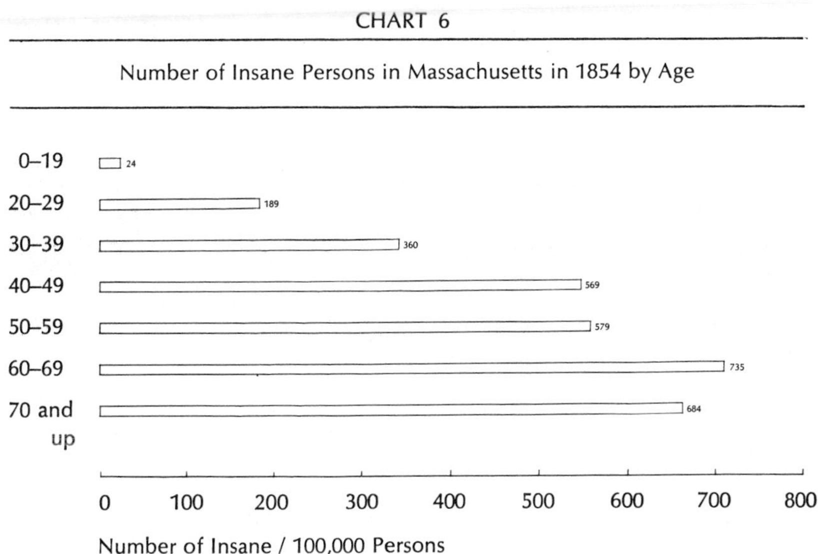

We can also calculate the percentage of each age-group that was in an asylum in 1854 (see chart 7). The results suggest that the probability of an insane person's being treated in an asylum was a life course phenomenon. Those who were young or elderly were much less likely to be in an asylum than those who were middle-aged. This pattern remains basically the same even after we control for the effects of the other variables.

The relative absence of young people from the asylums is not surprising. Many of the insane persons under twenty were young children living with their parents. Since the proportion of persons under twenty who were insane was never very high and given the prevailing notion that young children should be cared for by their own parents, the advocates of the asylums did not try to encourage parents or local officials to send very young children to the hospitals. As a result, the likelihood of an insane person under age twenty being in an asylum was relatively low.

The more interesting finding is that the elderly insane were much less likely to be in an asylum than their younger counterparts. Even after controlling for such factors as the length of time since the previous attack of insanity, the elderly were still less apt to receive treatment in an asylum.

CHART 7

Percentage of Massachusetts Insane in Asylums in 1854 by Age

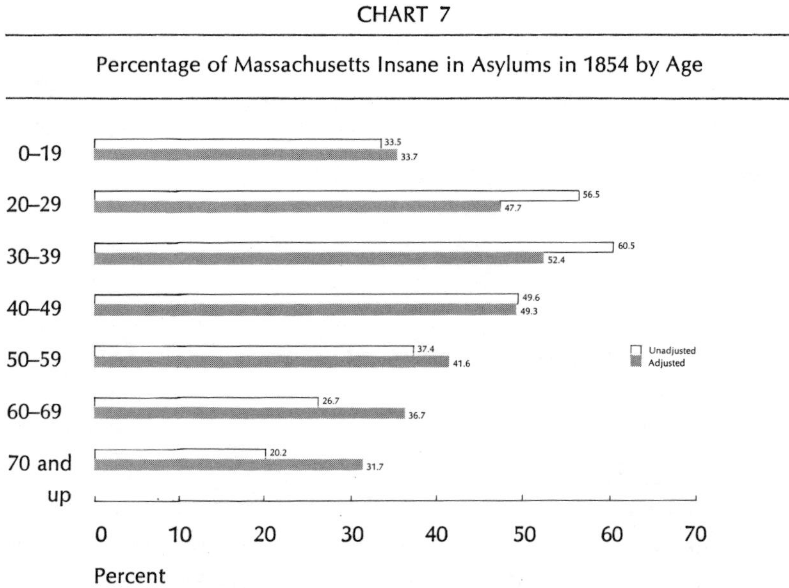

The under-representation of the elderly insane in the hospitals can be explained by the increasing prejudices against them in the general population as well as among the superintendents of the asylums. By the 1850s, the superintendents of these hospitals assumed that elderly patients were less likely to be cured than other patients due to their old age. Although our detailed analysis of the case records of the Worcester State Hospital and the

McLean Asylum suggests that the chances for curing old patients was actually quite good, the superintendents of these hospitals thought otherwise. By the 1840s and the 1850s the superintendents at both of these hospitals began to discourage the admission of elderly patients.[37]

The superintendents were mainly interested in preserving a therapeutic rather than custodial institution. They discouraged the admission of the aged patients because they began to consider them incurable. However, they rationalized their decision to exclude the aged patients by suddenly extolling the benefits of family life:

> We received during the year several aged people, suffering simply from mental decay, and whose friends are ready to admit that the patients are brought here to die. All treatment in such cases must be quite unavailing. Proper attention to hygenic rules is all that can be suggested. . . . There is an obvious impropriety in committing this class to our care. They cannot recover, and but seldom improve. Their waning existence should be made cheerful and attractive, by all the delicate attentions of home. Although, from inability to associate the ideas connected with things going on around them, they may not suffer keenly the loss of home with its accustomed pleasures. Still, a hospital in its best estate is but a poor exchange for the kind offices of love and affection.[38]

It is ironic that one of the very few positive statements by a superintendent of an asylum of the value and benefit of love and support for the insane from members of their own family should be used to justify the exclusion of a group of the insane that the superintendents regarded as incurable—the elderly.

Families in ante-bellum America had never enthusiastically accepted the idea of sending one of their members to an asylum since it separated the family and was a large expense for most households. Nevertheless, under admonishment from the superintendents of the hospitals that the insane could only be cured within the new asylums, ante-bellum families in Massachusetts often made the necessary financial and emotional sacrifices to send their insane members to these hospitals.

By the eve of the Civil War, Massachusetts had a complex system of providing care for its insane population. Although the family and local community still supported the majority of the insane, the state assumed a much larger role than ever before. About a quarter of the insane in Massachusetts were now supported by the state. Furthermore, by 1854 the state had constructed hospitals for the insane at Worcester and Taunton, state almshouses at Monson, Tewksbury, and Bridgewater which housed some insane, and the legislature was considering the erection of a third hospital. Although all of the Massachusetts insane were not accommodated under ideal conditions, a large proportion of them were receiving treatment that was considered to be exceptionally good by the standards of the day. In fact, the decade of the 1850s may have been the high point of good treatment for the insane in nineteenth-century Massachusetts.

The future did not bode well. The state did assume a larger role in providing support for the insane, but the nature of that support deteriorated. Reacting to ever-increasing costs as well as the increasing proportion of foreigners in the state hospitals, the state moved away from its policy of trying to provide therapeutic facilities for a large proportion of its insane. Instead, the state developed a series of custodial institutions where the insane could be accommodated very cheaply even though they received little treatment in those institutions.

This shift in state policy toward more custodial institutions for the insane was paralleled by the growing pessimism in the medical profession about the curability of insanity. Reacting against the claims of the early superintendents that 80 or 90 percent of recent admissions to their asylums could be cured, physicians in the second half of the nineteenth century argued that a much smaller percentage of cases could ever be cured as their views of insanity shifted more towards a strictly somatic interpretation.

Since these cases were likely to be diagnosed as incurable,

their friends and family had little hope of their recovery. As a result, insane persons in late nineteenth-century America faced a much bleaker prospect than those in the ante-bellum period. Families were more likely to send their insane to one of the custodial institutions provided by the state in order to relieve themselves of the burden of supporting an incurable member indefinitely. Since the insane person was deemed incurable, their relatives saw little reason why they should sacrifice to send their afflicted member to one of the more expensive private hospitals such as McLean. Although the state was now prepared to accommodate a larger number of insane persons than ever before, it did so under conditions which were not likely to improve the patient. Gradually, the state policy of large custodial institutions for the insane and the willingness of the public to tolerate them as well as to send their own friends and relatives to these institutions helped to create an atmosphere in our society which designated the mentally ill as non-persons who did not deserve the kindness and treatment that earlier reformers had sought to provide.

Funds for this research were provided by NIH Grant LM-02355 and we are indebted to Mary Vinovskis for programming the data.

Notes

1. On the role of the family in early America, see John Demos, *A Little Commonwealth: Family Life in Plymouth Colony* (New York, 1970); Edmund S. Morgan, *The Puritan Family* (New York, 1966). On the care of the insane in colonial America, see Albert Deutsch, *The Mentally Ill in America*, 2nd ed. (New York, 1949), pp. 24–54; Gerald N. Grob, *Mental Institutions in America: Social Policy to 1975* (New York, 1973), 1–34.

2. For an analysis of early poor laws in America, see Robert W. Kelso, *The History of Public Poor Relief in Massachusetts, 1620–1920* (Boston, 1922), 91–142; Marcus Wilson Jernegan, *Laboring and Dependent Classes*

in Colonial America, 1607–1783 (New York, 1931), pp. 175–209; David J. Rothman, *The Discovery of the Asylum: Social Order and Disorder in the New Republic* (Boston, 1971), pp. 30–56.

3. Quoted in Deutsch, *The Mentally Ill*, p. 42.

4. Quoted in Kelso, *History of Public Poor Relief*, p. 96. It is interesting to observe that most of the new histories of the early American family do not mention or discuss the willingness of colonial authorities sometimes to break up families if they became an economic burden to the town. Just how prevalent this practice was or what it says about early American attitudes toward family life remains to be explored.

5. Carl Bridenbaugh, *Cities in Revolt: Urban Life in America, 1743–1776* (New York, 1955), pp. 125–26.

6. Quoted in Deutsch, *The Mentally Ill*, p. 43.

7. *Acts Prov. Mass. Bay*, 1797, ch. 62.

8. For the most important early nineteenth-century American text on insanity, see Benjamin Rush, *Medical Inquiries and Observations on Diseases of the Mind* (1812). Rush, a typical eighteenth-century physician in his "heroic" treatment of fevers, advocated rational and humane treatment of the insane as a departure from traditional custody.

9. On the impact of European reform ideas on insanity in the United States, see Grob, *Mental Institutions in America*, pp. 35–50; Norman Dain, *Concepts of Insanity in the United States, 1789–1865* (New Brunswick, N. J., 1964), pp. 3–52.

10. There is a growing literature on the "cult of domesticity" in the nineteenth century. For example, see Barbara Welter, "Cult of True Womanhood," *American Quarterly* 18 (1965), pp. 151–74; Nancy F. Cott, *The Bonds of Womanhood: "Women's Sphere" in New England, 1780–1835* (New Haven, 1977).

11. George Parkman, *Proposals for Establishing a Retreat for the Insane* (Boston, 1814; reprinted in *The Beginnings of American Psychiatric Thought and Practice*, ed. Gerald N. Grob (New York, 1973)), p. 11. McLean was opened in 1818, and from the start primarily admitted paying patients, as contrasted with the predominantly charity or sponsored patients cared for at MGH which opened in 1821.

12. Robert Thomas, *A Treatise on Domestic Medicine* (New York, 1822; revised ed. by David Hosack), pp. 230–31.

13. Theodric Romeyn Beck, *An Inaugural Dissertation on Insanity* (New York, 1811; reprinted in *The Beginnings of American Psychiatric Thought and Practice*, ed. Grob), pp. 27–28.

14. The superintendents of the hospitals acknowledged that the public was often very dissatisfied by the way in which they were not allowed to visit their friends in the asylum. However, the superintendents were not particularly upset by these reactions. Instead, they were more concerned about the welfare of the patients as well as their own interests. Thus Daniel H. Trezevant, superintendent of the South Carolina Asylum, noted that "much dissatisfaction exists in the community at my refusal to permit them to visit their friends, while under medical treatment. I have tried the experiment, and have so uniformly found it injurious, that while there is a chance of their restoration, I never allow access. It often irritates, seldom soothes, but mostly leads their thoughts to home, where the source of the trouble is usually centered, and makes, of quiet, well-disposed and orderly patients, restless, unhappy, and violent maniacs. Another objection to their receiving the visits of their friends, is the incorrect opinion they sometimes go away with as to the treatment of the patients. . . ." *American Journal of Insanity* 2 (October 1845), p. 163.

15. Philippe Pinel encouraged occasional visits to the insane when they were recovering. "When they are in a convalescent state, the occasional visits to their friends are attended with manifest advantage. Such an intercourse imparts consolation, and presents views of future happiness and comfort." Philippe Pinel, *A Treatise on Insanity*, trans. D. D. Davis (Sheffield, England, 1806), p. 216.

16. On the early development of New England hospitals, see Leonard K. Eaton, *New England Hospitals, 1790–1833* (Ann Arbor, Michigan, 1957); Grob, *Mental Institutions in America*, pp. 35–83; Rothman, *The Discovery of the Asylum*, pp. 109–54.

17. For an analysis of Worcester State Hospital, see Gerald N. Grob, *The State and the Mentally Ill: A History of Worcester State Hospital in Massachusetts, 1830–1920* (Chapel Hill, N. C., 1966).

18. Dorothea Dix was instrumental in arousing public support for the

construction of asylums in the 1840s and 1850s. For analyses of her career, see Helen E. Marshall, *Dorothea Dix: Forgotten Samaritan* (New York, 1937) and Dorothy Clarke Wilson, *Stranger and Traveler: The Story of Dorothea Dix, American Reformer* (Boston, 1975).

19. There are numerous complaints by the superintendents that families removed patients from the hospitals prematurely. For example, see *American Journal of Insanity* 7, No. 2 (October, 1850), p. 173; *American Journal of Insanity* 12 (January 1856), pp. 282–83.

20. *Independent Chronicle*, February 6, 1917.

21. Thomas, *A Treatise on Domestic Medicine*, p. 231.

22. Our preliminary investigation of advice manuals suggests that some of the medical manuals did recommend that insane persons be sent to asylums while the more general advice literature, such as Catherine Beecher's works on domestic economy, did not make explicit references to the new asylums. On the methodological problems of using such manuals, see Jay Mechling, "Advice to Historians on Advice to Mothers," *Journal of Social History* 9, No. 1 (Fall 1975), pp. 44–63.

23. Most physicians assumed that the longer an insane person went without proper treatment, the less the chances of recovery. Hence, it was essential that the patient be sent to an asylum as soon after an attack of insanity as possible.

24. *American Journal of Insanity* 15, No. 1 (July 1858), p. 114.

25. For a discussion of the under-registration of the insane in the early federal censuses, see Gerold N. Grob, "Edward Jarvis and the Federal Census," *Bulletin of the History of Medicine* 50 (Spring 1976), pp. 4–27.

26. Massachusetts Legislative Documents, *Report on Insanity and Idiocy in Massachusetts, by the Commission on Lunacy, under Resolve of the Legislature of 1854*, House Document No. 144 (1855). For an extensive introduction to this report, see the discussion by Gerald Grob in Edward Jarvis, *Insanity and Idiocy in Massachusetts: Report of the Commission on Lunacy*, ed. Gerald N. Grob (Cambridge, Mass., 1971), pp. 1–71.

27. The original data from the Jarvis survey have been preserved in manuscript form in the "Report of the Physicians of Massachusetts,

Superintendents of Hospital . . . and Others Describing the Insane and Idiotic Persons in the State of Massachusetts in 1855. Made to the Commissioners on Lunacy," Mss. volume in the Countway Library, Harvard Medical School, Boston, Mass. As part of a larger study of insanity in ante-bellum America, we have computerized and analyzed the individual returns on insanity that were sent to the commissioners.

28. On the prevalence of insanity in the twentieth century, see Peter K. Manning and Martine Zucker, *The Sociology of Mental Health and Illness* (Indianapolis, 1976), pp. 34–42.

29. Dorothea Dix, "Memorial to the Legislature of Massachusetts, 1843," in Dorothea L. Dix, *On Behalf of the Insane Poor: Selected Reports*, ed. David J. Rothman (New York, 1971).

30. Since a few of the towns did not send in their poor returns for 1855, we also used those for 1854 and 1857 to fill in the missing data.

31. Worcester State Lunatic Hospital, *Annual Report* 24 (1856) pp. 10–12.

32. The complete results of our multiple classification analysis will be presented in our forthcoming re-analysis of the Jarvis data.

33. Since many of the readers of this essay may not be familiar with multiple classification analysis, we will try to provide a brief introduction to this technique in order to facilitate a better comprehension of our results. Multiple classification analysis (MCA) is a form of multiple regression analysis with dummy variables which express results in terms of adjusted deviation from the grand mean (overall average) of the dependent variable of each of the various classes of the predictor variables. For example, MCA answers the question: how much of the likelihood of going to an asylum was associated with being supported by the state, while controlling for such other variables as the age of the person, his marital status, and his place of birth? Similarly, it also provides an approximate answer to the question: *ceteris paribus*, what is the effect on going to an asylum of the age of the person? In other words, MCA allows one to study the relative importance of a subcategory of an independent variable in predicting some dependent variable. MCA "controls" for other variables by assuming while it looks at one class of

a predictor variable that the distribution of all other predictor variables will be the same in that class as in the total population, thus "holding constant" their effects. Although traditional multiple regression programs also do this, MCA has three advantages: it does not require variables to be interval variables, it does not require or assume linearity and thus can capture discontinuities in the direction of association, and, finally, it is useful descriptively because it presents the reader with the unadjusted effects of a predictor class, that is, the actual mean of each class, as well as the mean after adjusting for the influence of the other variables.

For an introduction to the use of MCA analysis, see Frank M. Andrews *et al.*, *Multiple Classification Analysis*, 2nd ed. (Ann Arbor, Michigan, 1973). For an example and discussion of the use of multiple classification analysis in historical studies, see Carl F. Kaestle and Maris A. Vinovskis, "From Fireside to Factory: School Entry and School Leaving in Nineteenth-Century Massachusetts," in *Family Processes in an Historial Perspective*, ed. Tamara K. Hareven (Academic Press, forthcoming).

34. On the likelihood of the elderly insane being treated in an asylum, see Barbara G. Rosenkrantz and Maris A. Vinovskis, "The 'Invisible Lunatics': Old Age and Insanity in Mid-Nineteenth-Century Massachusetts," in *Aging and the Aged: Humanistic Perspectives in Gerontology*, eds. Stuart F. Spicker *et al.* (Humanities Press, 1978).

35. *Ibid.*

36. *Ibid.*

37. *Ibid.*

38. Worcester State Lunatic Hospital, *Annual Report* 25 (1857), pp. 55–56.

Roots of the American Family: From Noah to Now

FRANCIS L. K. HSU
Department of Anthropology, Northwestern University

Much has been said about the many problems which beset us today, such as crime and violence, and their causes. The quality of television, drugs, economic fluctuations, and even weather changes have been blamed. More recently, a finger has been pointed at the family. That is, at least in part, why the august Smithsonian Institution is elaborating the theme of "Kin and Communities" in its bicentennial celebration.

But what is the link between the American family and our basic problems? I suggest that the key is to be found in the highly discontinuous way in which we relate to each other. Here an analogy may help.

In physical matters glue is used when we want to join objects together. There is the usual household paste which is a mixture of flour and water, and there is Elmer's glue, which is supposed to hold diving boards together. Objects stuck together by household paste can be separated by soaking in water. But Elmer's glue is stronger than the power of tractors: the objects it holds together cannot be pulled apart without destruction.

If we transfer the glue analogy to the human scene, we might say that the glue which glued Romeo and Juliet together was some kind of Elmer's glue, while that which bound the Midnight Cowboy to any of his clients was no more than the thinnest of household paste.

In all societies human beings relate to each other by two kinds of glue: role (or usefulness) and affect (or feeling). We understand role in terms of skilled or unskilled labor, white collar or blue collar, dentists and diamond cutters, housekeepers and politicians, customers and salesmen. As our society has grown in complexity, the number and variety of roles have grown with it. In fact, role differentiation is the major concomitant of the growth in societal complexity. For example, in today's conditions, giant corporations often have more diverse personnel and more workers and specialists on their payrolls than do many small member states of the United Nations.

On the other hand, while our roles have evolved in number and proficiency with the complexity of our industrial society, our affect has not. We still have the same kind of feelings as our ancestors had many thousands of years ago: love, hate, rage, despair, endurance, hope, anxiety, forbearance, loyalty, caring, betrayal, and so forth. The list is not long, and many of the terms describing them are partially or wholly subsumable under each other.

That is why, in contrast to old books on science and technology, which are useless to us except as curiosities or as material for histories of science and technology, great literature (fiction, poetry) and great art (painting, sculpture) and even great philosophy and ethics survive the ages, for we moderns experience the same agony and joy and the same loyalty and duplicity as the ancients. We can relive their lives through what they have written and they, too, were they alive today, would have been able to discuss with us our problems with our children, parents, friends and enemies, employers and employees, sweethearts and spouses.

To return to the glue analogy. Role works like household paste. Humans linked by it are easily pulled asunder and can be replaced. Affect is like some more tenacious Elmer's glue. Humans linked by it cohere to a far greater degree, and replacement cannot be made without psychic cost or disturbance.

Culture and Affect

However, the *patterns* of affect which operate among Americans are different from those which motivate people of other cultures, such as the Chinese and Japanese. Americans and Asians may experience the same love, hate, and despair, but the ways in which they express love, hate, and despair, and especially what makes them love, hate, or despair, differ greatly.

Literature is one of the best evidences for this. I will not detail the spectacular differences between Western novels, drama and art, and their Chinese and Japanese counterparts. I have done this elsewhere (Hsu 1970:17–41; 1975). Briefly, the two outstanding psychological characteristics of Western and American novels and drama are: freedom of the individual to the extent of egotism and preoccupation with sex. The former expresses itself in characters in search of identity such as Holden Caulfield in *The Catcher in the Rye;* in those who go it alone to prove themselves by conquest, such as Captain Ahab in *Moby Dick* and the old man in *The Old Man and the Sea;* or in those striving to be something they can never be, such as Herzog in *Herzog*. More extreme manifestations of egotism are found in *Papillon* or *On the Road* or *Easy Rider*.

Freedom of the individual has given Western men their singleness of purpose and their absolute zeal in pursuing many objectives of which they may justifiably be proud; conquest of space, exploration of the high seas, spreading social benefits through their missionary spirit, elimination of poverty and disease via science and technology, and many more. But it has also led to the shrinkage of affect and the tendency to substitute role for affect altogether.

The Shrinkage of Affect

Shrinkage of affect takes many forms: loyalty becomes scarce, friendship turns shallow, people refuse to consider each others' needs or to be involved in their affairs. It is also linked to the fact that American males have a strong aversion to contact with each other, except in emergencies (such as mouth-to-mouth resuscitation) or in certain sports (such as wrestling). This aversion is the external symptom of an inner inability to form deep friendships. American men will combine to conquer the external world but they must shun lasting and undying attachment to each other.

Why? Could not the answer lie in a fear of homosexuality? If sex is everywhere, then the only safe area for intimacy is between members of the opposite sex. This is why Holden Caulfield, the young hero of J. D. Salinger's *The Catcher in the Rye,* bolted out of his favorite teacher's apartment with haste when he found the older man sitting on the edge of the couch and stroking his hair. This is also what the other itinerant farm laborers suspected when, in John Steinbeck's *Of Mice and Men,* they questioned Lenny and George as to how long they had been traveling together. The more our culture is preoccupied with sex, the less persons of the same sex have been able to develop and maintain *affective* relationships with each other. At first this inability was confined to males, but our females have been catching up. They too are seldom to be seen walking hand in hand with each other.

We have then an atomistic situation in which humans become emotional islands to themselves. The individualist may need others for his rise to power or fame or fortune, but he cannot afford to be slowed down by affective baggage in his quest for success. In order to make breaks with the past more clearly and easily, he must have few affective involvements. In such a context, one man's gain is necessarily viewed as another man's loss. Our news media and popular publications make much of the exploits of many successful individuals. But for every girl who is crowned Miss America there will be thousands or even hundreds of thousands of disappointed and heart-broken damsels. A psychological climate favoring driving individualists bent on cut-throat competition will hardly enable them to develop genuine and lasting friendships with each other. This is the root of what Philip Slater speaks of as *The Pursuit of Loneliness* (1970).

Externalization of Human Relationships

An effectively atomistic situation leads to more than individual loneliness. It necessitates the escalation of role, and of externalized inducements or restraints, at the expense of affect.

Externalization of human relationships finds expression in diverse ways. Our principal approach to crime and violence is one example. We rely on surveillance, detection and control: more secure locks and fences, more hidden cameras, more guards, more electronic alarms. We develop mugger-proof public vehicles, vandal-proof schools, shoplifter-proof supermarkets, and rapist-proof co-eds, all the way to child-proof medicine bottles and crash-proof automobiles. Yet crime and violence continue to increase year after year so that it is an elaboration of the obvious to quote statistics on the subject. The ingenuity of the externalized means for stopping crime and violence will surely be outmatched by the creativity of those bent on more ingenious means for breaking the law.

Externalization of all relationships has inevitably changed the nature of discipline in our society. It is often cried that America lacks discipline. This is not true. There is ample evidence of discipline in American life. Take a look at our super-highways and the thousands of cars which ply them at high speed twenty-four hours a day. This would be impossible without discipline. Our huge hotels, officies, water works, mines, air lines, and atomic plants cannot be run without discipline.

What is wrong is that this discipline is increasingly externally imposed and is less and less due to a desire to respect or care for others: their rights, their safety, and their happiness. Driving within a speed limit because cops are there to catch me is one thing, while doing so because I do not want to injure someone is quite another. Operating a machine strictly according to instructions for fear it will blow up in my face is one thing, while doing so because I do not want to harm my fellow employees is quite another. We emphasize rules of survival, not rules of morality.

Kinship and Behavior

Roles are first learned in the family, but the individual's capacity for role mastery continues in schools, in work shops, in factories and offices, and through diverse other networks and situations of life. An old Chinese proverb says: "He who works throughout old age, learns throughout old age."

That is not, however, the way we acquire our patterns of affect. The real hothouse for such patterns in every society is the kinship system, at the core of which in America is the nuclear family. The kinship system is the first web of human relationships for the individual. It sets the basic feeling tone and establishes the affective foundation for all subsequent interpersonal patterns because it comes first, because it catches the individual *tabula rasa,* and because it conditions the individual when his or her cerebral development is faster than at any later time. The family is the arena through which the individual develops feelings about himself, about his fellow human beings, and about the rest of the world. Such feelings, in turn, determine what roles he or she chooses and how well he or she is motivated to perform them throughout life. In the broadest sense the kinship system is the psychic cell of every society. It holds the key to social and cultural development in the same sense that the germ cell holds the key to the adult biological organism yet to appear (Hsu 1971:3–29).

Many observers speak of the decline of the family in America. High divorce and separation rates, generation gaps, prevalence of single parent households, increasing numbers of couples living together without marriage, unwed mothers, abused children, runaway fathers, juvenile delinquents, children returning to empty homes because their mothers are working: these are among the symptoms of it. These symptoms led scholars such as Urie Bronfenbrenner to say that "the family is falling apart" (Bronfenbrenner 1977:41), and Dr. Margaret Mead to urge the need "to redesign the whole social structure with the family at the core" (Mead 1976).

However, when we come to the question of why "the family is falling apart" and how to reconstruct our family for a better America of the future, I am at variance with a majority of other social scientists. For example, Bronfenbrenner says:

What's destroying the family isn't the family itself but the indifference of the rest of society. The family takes a low priority (Bronfenbrenner 1977:42).

My question is, is not the society which is so indifferent to the family run by Americans who are products of that very family? What transformed them into such monsters who want to destroy the social grouping of their origin?

Others are more specific and claim industrialization or modernization to be the prime mover of social and cultural change, including changes in the family. I think this view is a misapprehension. It is based on the Western fallacy of another era, that Christianization of the world was the means to free mankind from greed, violence, and war. Christianity has not merely failed to free the Western peoples, who took to it in droves, from greed, violence, and war; it has failed, despite Western pressure, to gain many converts among the rest of the world, especially in Asia.

In the first place, I do not agree that the American family was once very different from what it is today. American fathers certainly seem to have exercised more authority over their wives and children in the frontier days, but how did they themselves become so independent of their own parents to begin with?

Besides, the "extended family of several generations, with all its relatives" (Bronfenbrenner 1977:41), never really existed on any grand scale in America. Mary J. Bane, in a piece of recently published research, shows that only 6 percent of households in America contained grandparents, parents, and children, and that the percentage of such households remained the same in 1970 (Bane 1977). Bane also opines that it is doubtful that Americans move more often today than they did in the last century. If mobility is decimating America's family and social fabric, she concludes, it has been doing so for a long time, unrelated to the extent of industrialization. Whether industrialization or mobility is compatible with some sort of extended family has been the subject of sociological debate (see, for example, Parsons 1949:191–92 and Litwak 1960:385–94).

What I wish to point out, in the second place, is that American society is not, as many would claim, a "young, rambunctious society, only 200 years old" (Bronfenbrenner 1977:42). Every society consists of three basic elements: cultural heritage, social organization, and individual behavior. The first consists of everything handed down from the past, from ethics, myths and ideas about gods to games, artifacts, and skills. The second refers to the way the individual members of society are organized into groups, such as families, clubs, classes, and castes, both to act and to transmit the cultural heritage from generation to generation. The third element, individual behavior, is generally so strongly influenced by the cultural heritage transmitted through the social organization that it is predictable on a probability basis.

Once this is understood, it will be easy to see that American society it not merely two hundred years old. In fact it is much older than Chinese society. Its cultural heritage came from the Chaldaeans, the Sumerians and the Babylonians, not to mention the ancient Israelites, the Greeks and the Romans. The American social organization descends directly from Anglo-Saxon and Teutonic Europe. Most of American society's individual members speak English, and those who were native born were socialized by immigrant parents who rambunctiously claimed their society in America to be new because they had rejected the societies of their origin and because their old cultural heritage and social organization encouraged them to be adventurous and to seek the new.

The germs of this Western development, allegedly brought about by industrialization, were inherent in the Western psychocultural orientation long before the appearance of the Industrial Revolution. In fact we can go straight to the myth of Noah and the flood.

To punish the wickedness of men, God decided to flood the earth and kill all except the chosen man Noah and his family. Noah made an ark into which he packed his wife, his three sons and their wives, together with seven pairs of all "clean" animals and one pair of all other animals. After they had floated around for some forty days, the flood subsided and the ark landed on Ararat, where Noah at once thanked the Lord by appropriate rituals. Next, Noah drank the wine he had made and, while under the influence of liquor, he masturbated in his tent. Ham laughed at his father's condition and called in his two brothers. They all expressed disgust toward Noah but covered him up. Some kind of quarrel ensued. Noah then cursed Ham and condemned his son Canaan and future descendants to be eternal slaves but blessed Shem and Japheth and told them to disperse in their separate ways to people the earth.[1]

We have in this most celebrated of Western myths, still being taught in churches and schools, dramatized on the stage and screen, thematized in literature and serialized in comics, all the ingredients which some of our social scientists claim to be the results of industrialization and therefore of recent origin. Ham's lack of reverence for his father did not originate with him, for when the flood came Noah left his own parents to perish. And his son's lack of reverence for him was more than matched by Noah's vindictiveness toward his own flesh and blood. The evidence for mobility is equally strong. Not only did Noah and his family escape the disaster by boat but they never returned to their old home after the flood waters subsided. Despite the fact that they were the only eight people left in the world, Noah and his kin could not stay together.

There is even in this myth clear indication of Western absolutism, in which role approach has erased all affect considerations: a God who decided on his own final solution, a solution that another notorious dictator was later to attempt on the Jews. Myth is not, of course, reality. But myths, like art, inform an audience of traditional values, reflect the fantasies of the people, and may consciously or unconsciously give direction for future courses of action. That is why President Carter, in response to public objection, recently had to amend his remarks concerning who killed Jesus (reported in *Chicago Sun-Times,* May 14, 1977). That is why Black Muslim leader Wallace D. Muhammed is trying to convince black Christian churchmen that depicting Christ as a Caucasian is harmful to non-Caucasians (reported in *Chicago Sun-Times,* May 27, 1977). The contents of such myths are, at the very least, as reliable indices of how people feel about themselves, each other, and the rest of the world, as are the results of the public opinion polls or even some of our scholarly questionnaires.

The significance of this myth becomes even clearer when we realize how the contents of its Chinese counterpart point to another totally different pattern of affect, also under no industrial or modernizing influence. In the reign of the Emperor Yao (said to be about 2357–2258 B.C.), a terrible flood devastated China. Yao appointed a certain Kun to control the flood but the latter, after nine years of work, was unsuccessful. Yao took full responsibility, resigned from office, and offered the throne to Shun (said to have reigned between 2258 and 2206 B.C.). Emperor Shun executed or exiled Kun for his failure but appointed the executed man's son Yu in his place. Yu worked all over the country for thirteen years, during which time he passed by his wife's door three times. Being absorbed in his official duties Yu did not once go in to see his wife. After Yu's success, Emperor Shun gave Yu his throne. Yu became the next emperor, thus exonerating the name of his father, and the Chinese lived happily ever after.

The Chinese myth reveals how differently they felt about themselves, about each other, and about the rest of the world. For one thing, the Chinese legend named no chosen man. Instead all Chinese suffered from the disaster together. It did not provide for an escape by boat to a new world. Instead all the Chinese stayed where they were born and raised and did the best they could. There was no question of sons going in different directions from their parents. Instead the son worked hard to succeed where his father failed. In his toils Yu did not visit his wife even when convenient, for larger duty took precedence over matters of his own heart. Finally it is most significant that the supernatural had no place in this Chinese story: no Chinese god would impose the final solution on all Chinese as punishment for their faults.

In both cases, the myths contain the basic psycho-cultural germs which were to grow, unfold, spread, and proliferate in their respective kinship systems independent of economic developments. In both cases the central themes of the myths and the perceived solutions of the problems are consonant with the two societies' broad, historical development.

I am aware of the fact that there is variation in kinship patterns among Western peoples. There is zadruka in Yugoslavia. The French pattern of dowry is absent in the United States. The German father is more stern than his English counterpart. The Spanish and Italian style of chaperoning their daughters before marriage is inconceivable to most American parents. But if we take a broader and longer historical view, it should become clear that Western society as a whole is centrifugal or outward looking, and that centrifugality is rooted in a kinship situation that was centrifugal long before the Industrial Revolution. The society did not destroy the family. Instead, the family nurtured individuals with an affective pattern which threatened to dismantle itself and the society with it.

The Chinese society, on the other hand, has always been centripetal or inward looking. That too was rooted in a centripetal kinship pattern since ancient times. That is why there are today more people of European origin outside than inside of Europe, while less than 3 percent of Chinese are outside of China. To many, the Chinese appear to be the largest racial group in the world, but this is only because most ethnic Chinese are still in one contiguous area, whereas Europeans are scattered over all parts of the globe.

Noah's power over his children looks excessive to us today, but if parental power were really that absolute, Noah would not have been able to condemn Canaan and his future descendants to eternal slavery *without permission from his own elders*. The facts that Noah left his own parents to perish in the flood and had such a free hand in dealing with his own progeny are clear indications of discontinuity between the generations and of freedom of the individual. In such a context, figurative children of Noah would naturally be moved to escalate the same discontinuity and individual freedom even further. What has happened in the American family is the inevitable growth of the Western kinship roots. Those roots explain why the American family, though different in spectacular ways from its European ancestry, remains part of the same psycho-socio-cultural development.

Can We Save Our Family?

I do not think we need to worry about the disappearance of the American family as a physical fact. Unisex marriages, cohabitation without marriage, generation gaps, and singlehood notwithstanding, Americans living in matrimony still constitute the majority. Even increasingly high divorce rates do not threaten the family with extinction. For example, divorced and widowed persons are most likely to get married again. The desire to possess the loved one is so pervasive that most young people will still seek the marital contract as a way of securing a predictable affective relationship, especially in a society where other relationships are subject to change without notice.

What we must ask ourselves instead is, what can we do to reshape our kinship system so as to make our families less centrifugal and to give future Americans more, rather than less, trust in each other?

I am aware that some scholars regard the present woes of our society as the necessary price to be paid for "the limitless opportunities of the future" (Slater 1966:94). To them, the instability of our primary group is a necessary condition of more creativity and imagination and of maximum commitment to larger groups and issues.

To some extent I agree with this position. For example, the Chinese, who were oriented to seek their security and their life's satisfaction in human involvement, failed to develop industrialization, in spite of their considerable and varied achievements in science which are reported in the monumental works of Joseph Needham.

But perhaps the temporariness of our family and the de-personalization of our human relationships have gone beyond the point of no return.

Given the foregoing analysis it seems clear that one fundamental task is to reevaluate the boundary, content, and worth of our value of privacy. Privacy is an essential attribute of individualism. It can mean many things, physical, social, or psychological, and have many degrees, from keeping one's health problems secret to making career decisions by oneself.

In the parent-child context the American way in privacy expresses itself as follows. Before the children come of age their parents have exclusive powers over them and tend to shield them from intensive interaction with all others. Even when grandparents live in the same house, they are only guests, with no jurisdiction over their grandchildren. Parental authority among the poor may be more diffuse. Recently I met a student who was born and raised in the small Alabama town of Mount Vernon. He told me that when he was a child his grandfather or a non-family member could punish him for such wrongdoings as stealing watermelon from another's field. When his own parents learned of his misdeeds they would give him another thrashing. However, this pattern no longer obtains in his home town today. My informant says it is because strangers have moved in who do not share the same standard of judgment. He finds no explanation for why grandparents today are also excluded from the authority to discipline their grandchildren.

Certainly among most middle class Americans everywhere today the custom is for the mother to write out a list of do's and don't for any baby sitter to follow, whether or not the sitter is a relative. In short, whoever else is allowed a hand in the child's upbringing is merely acting at the command of the parents. Recently a fourth grader who asked her mother about her grandparents because they were doing genealogies in school received the reply: "Tell your teacher it's none of her business." Teachers, too, are supposed to deal only with areas that parents have given permission for and nothing else.

At the same time children begin to guard their own privacy early. They learn more from what their parents do than from what their own elders say. Their parents also give them encouragement in that direction since training children for independence is the American thing.

In pre-school years the situation is manageable. Parents have the last word and children can express their demand for privacy and independence in limited areas. But, as children move into pre-teen and teen years and demand larger and larger spheres for privacy and independence, a conflict between the generations is inevitable. The more exclusive parents' control over their children, the less likely the parents are to contemplate with pleasure their children's freedom. This often leads to strong adverse feelings between parents and children which preclude rational management.

This conflict has far-reaching consequence. It has been repeatedly observed that peer pressure is great, so great that much of the juvenile delinquency and drug problems are attributed to it. What we must see is that submission to peer pressure is not universal, as some social scientists would have us believe, but a function of the separation of parents and children. The greater one's need to separate from one's parents, the greater one's need to belong to peer groups.

Thus the exclusive parental control is at the root of generation gaps and peer tyranny; it prevents the cultivation in the young of the affective need for a mixing of ages which so many authorities see as desirable. In the circumstances efforts to turn us into our own family historians will lead to no more than a new form of pastime. Unless the interest in our own genealogies is matched by affective links with our own forebears, it will have no bearing on the actual shape of our families to come.

We ought at least to try some truly revolutionary ideas. In an earlier connection I have already explained the importance of a society's literature as evidence of its pattern of affect. I now wish to say that literature is also the main carrier of that pattern and transmits the pattern from generation to generation. We need, of course, to inform our young of the traditional pattern of feeling about ourselves, about each other, and about the rest of the world, the pattern which is central to the cultural heritage of Western man. We need also to offer them the knowledge that the traditional Western affective pattern is not the only one possible. We need to see, for example, that there are alternatives to unconditional surrender or absolute victory, to total *individual* failure to total *individual* success, and to leaving home as a way of solving life's problems.

How many Americans know that there is no counterpart of *Moby Dick* or *The Old Man and the Sea* in Chinese literature, or that the Chinese did not have first person novels like *The Sun Also Rises, The Great Gatsby* and *The Deer Park?* Or again, how many know that relatively few Chinese novels dealt with sex or romance, and that those that did always let the social requirements overshadow the pursuit of individual happiness? How many know that the hero in the Chinese equivalent of *Gulliver's Travels* was not alone, but accompanied in his adventures by a friend and a brother-in-law? Finally, how many of those here knew, prior to today, some other version of the flood myth and its totally different solution? Do we even know that the Sumerian and Babylonian versions of the myth, from which the Hebaric version was derived, differed from the latter in important aspects?

These are not mere exotica. They are expressions of other basic approaches to men, gods, and things. Few Americans know about such matters because Americans have been brought up so exclusively on Western literature that they are led to see the struggles problems of a Captain Ahab or an Elmer Gantry or an Achilles as pan-human. How can they feel otherwise? Their writers, critics and instructors are accustomed to speak of the human condition when, in fact, they are merely dealing with the condition of Western man.

One revolutionary idea I wish to propose is not merely the introduction of non-Western literature and art into our schools, museums and galleries. To a certain extent this is being done. What I envisage is that they will be introduced not as separate segments of the curricula or exhibits, but as part of the general program of instruction and research. They should be incorporated in our basic readers and nursery rhymes. At the high school and university levels, black literature or Japanese art should be taught not only in Black Programs or Japanese Studies. Instead they should be required, for example, by English departments, which teach Homer, Melville, Hemingway, and Joyce.

Another revolutionary idea I wish to propose is addressed both to our government and to our universities. In our universities we have departments of economics, government, and business management, but none of the family, except when it is subordinated to home economics or some other low prestige subject. Our government has Departments of Health, Education, and Welfare, the Treasury, and Justice, but none of the Family.

If the family is so important to us, why not create an independent and prestigious unit devoted to the family? Such a unit would examine not only the questions already posed in the preceding paragraphs, but also whether, as some journalists report, counterculture lifestyles (such as unisex marriage, cohabitation without marriage, and so forth) are truly correlated with a decline in competitiveness and individualism.

"If America can send men to the moon she can do anything" is an often-aired sentiment. In view of my analysis, such a sentiment is highly misleading. Sending men to the moon is a technical matter and therefore in the role domain. I have no problem in predicting even more spectacular achievements to come in that domain.

But in the affect domain where change of patterns of human

feelings is required, we have yet to make the first major breakthrough. I am proposing that we aim at such a breakthrough by rethinking the way we feel about ourselves as individuals, about each other, and about the rest of the world.

May I conclude with my encounter with some land snails in Brittany, France, some thirty-five years ago. I was a first-year graduate student at London and took my first spring vacation in France. At a spot where two small farms were divided by a low ridge, I saw several land snails, barely on one side of the ridge, burned to a crisp. The stumps on that side of the ridge were burned but those on the other side were not. Had the snails been able to move but a quarter of an inch farther from the burning side they would have saved their lives. Unfortunately, they failed to do so.

Are we land snails on a French farm or Americans of the twentieth century?

Note

1. The passage concerning Noah's self-eroticism is generally deleted or changed into more neutral statements in the modern versions of the Bible or the Torah. However, if we hold such neutral statements to be correct, it is puzzling why Noah should be so angry with Ham. There are other versions of what happened in the tent. One of them even had Ham committing sodomy on Noah.

References

Bane, Mary Jo. *Here to Stay*. New York: Basic Books, 1977.

Bronfenbrenner, Urie. "Nobody Home: The Erosion of the American Family." *Psychology Today* (May 1977):41–47.

Hsu, Francis L. K. *Americans and Chinese: Purpose and Fulfillment in Great Civilizations*. New York: Doubleday & Company, 1970.

Hsu, Francis L. K., ed. *Kinship and Community*. Chicago: Aldine Publishing Company, 1971.

Hsu, Francis L. K. *Iemoto: The Heart of Japan*. Cambridge, Mass.: Schenkman Publishing Company, 1975.

Litwak, Eugene. "Geographic Mobility and Extended Family Cohesion." *American Journal of Sociology* (1960):385–94. Reprinted in *Society and Self*. Edited by Bartlett H. Stoodley. New York: The Free Press, 1962.

Mead, Margaret. Speech given June 15, 1976, at St. John's Church, Washington, D. C., in "Kin and Communities: The Peopling of America," as part of the Bi-Centennial Celebration of the Smithsonian Institution. Reported by Mary Ellen Perry in *The Washington Star*, June 16, 1976.

Parsons, Talcott. "The Social Structure of the Family." *The Family: Its Function and Destiny*. Edited by Ruth Nanda Anshen. New York: Harper Bros., 1949.

Slater, Philip E. "Some Social Consequences of Temporary Systems." *The Temporary Society*. Edited by Warren G. Bennis and Philip E. Slater. New York: Harper & Row, 1966, pp. 77–96.

Slater, Philip E. *The Pursuit of Loneliness*. Boston, Mass.: Beacon Press, 1970.

Winch, Robert F. *The Modern Family*. 3rd ed. New York: Holt, Rinehart & Winston, 1971.

Part 2

WORKSHOPS AND COLLOQUIA

Family Photo Interpretation

PARTICIPANTS

Joan R. Challinor, Department of History, The American University
Jonathan Garlock, Department of History, University of Rochester
Judith Mara Gutman, City College of New York
Amy Kotkin, Folklife Program, Smithsonian Institution
Catherine Hanf Noren, Free-lance photographer
Amalie Rothschild, New York University, Independent movie maker
Jamil Simon, Independent movie maker
William Stapp, National Portrait Gallery, Smithsonian Institution
Elisabeth Weis, Department of Film, Brooklyn College

Challinor Good afternoon. I am Joan Challinor, the originator of this workshop, a historian and photographer. The relationship between photography and family history has, until very recently, been *terra incognita*. We are breaking new ground today. Although from some recent books I sense a dawning interest in the social history of photography, our bibliography is still a short one. I do not think we can rely on anything except our own perceptions this afternoon. Your presence here indicates that we, of the Kin and Communities symposium, think that you have done interesting and imaginative work in this new field.

The session is divided into several parts: still photography, movies about family relationships, the use of photographs in teaching community history, and family albums. For this discussion of images and their meanings, we have assembled a distinguished panel. Our first speaker, Judith Gutman, is a social historian associated with the Graduate School of the City College of New York. William Stapp is the curator of photographs at the Smithsonian's National Portrait Gallery. Two independent movie producers, Jamil Simon and Amalie Rothschild, will show portions of films they have made of their families. Elisabeth Weis, a professor of film at Brooklyn College, will comment on these movies. Catherine

Noren, a free-lance photographer, will then discuss the album she has published on the history of five generations of her family. Jonathan Garlock, a professor of history at the University of Rochester, and Amy Kotkin of the Smithsonian's Family Folklore Program, will conclude by sharing their insights into photograph albums.

To start us off in good fashion, I will call upon Judith Gutman to give us her views on the aesthetics of family photographs.

Gutman Thank you. I am going to read my presentation because I can order my thoughts best on paper. See what you think about this: photographs are subjective, exaggerated, and gross distortions. They do not really deal with the truth. They slice segments from the "truth" and then go about actively distorting whatever it is they abstract.

They manipulate and organize experience. Yet, I maintain, they are accurate, informative, and clean cut documents—clean as a whistle. More than any other documents, they can take you right into the middle of a period of time, giving you the most precise information about a society's past. The point is, they are moments in time, literal pictures from an extended life; and because they are, they pull us into that society's belief structure and show us a changing society in a particular period of social organization.

Photographs may be our most perfect cultural artifacts. The nineteenth century photograph certainly is. To see how that is so, we must look at the family photograph; not the photograph showing us event "a," "b," or "c" happening *to* a family, but a photograph in which the family is the active component and organizes the photograph's aesthetic movement.

In a family photograph, the photograph's movement circles through the photograph's elements, but stays within the frame. Like a story line that resolves itself with the same set of characters who take the reader through a set of events, the family photograph takes the viewer through a set of happenings and settles the action right back inside the frame. Nothing takes the viewer outside.

This view results from my having looked at thousands of photographs over the last decade. Further, the more I have looked at photographs, the more I have come to the conclusion that wedding and funeral photographs are community, not family, photographs. They are more concerned with community events than they are with family events. The movement in wedding and funeral photographs takes the viewer outside of the frame, while the family photograph creates such an intense internal force that no matter how much it travels and moves around, it always comes to rest right inside that same photograph.

In this photograph of sledding, taken by Byron at the turn of the century in Central Park, New York [figure 1], aesthetic and subject matter movement are combined into one statement. One of the necessary ingredients for a family photograph is for the action to stay inside the photo. It can build a lyrical swell of movement as it does in the photograph of the women pushing the sleds or it can build a quieter, whimsical movement as it does in this photograph by Vroman of a snowman at a dinner [figure 2]. But after the movement fills the field and moves from one person to the next, touching as many persons as possible, it must come to rest inside that frame and not lead the viewer outside. Naturally, the more enormously it builds its movement, the better a photograph it is.

In most family photos, this kind of inward propelling action is led by the mother, not by the sister, daughter, or wife, but by the mother. Sometimes she pushes a sled, and other times she holds various infants. She usually holds the baby, and even if the father and mother are both holding babies, the mother usually holds the baby more tightly, closely, or in some way more dramatically. If the mother and father are both standing, it is the mother's stance which is more central [figure 3]. The fold of her dress which gathers up the hang of a suit, or the tilt of a hat, may be the main focus. She is often dramatically poised in a profile position, the angular features of her profile propelling the photograph's movement. But however the photograph is organized, and whichever

1. *Central Park,* 1896. Photograph by Byron. Courtesy Museum of the City of New York, New York, N.Y.

2. *Snowman,* ca. January 1895. Courtesy History Division, Los Angeles County Museum, Los Angeles, Calif.

3. *Family Reunion*, 1890s. Courtesy Historical Collection, Title Insurance and Trust Company, San Diego, Calif.

objects enter the stream of that organization, the mother's look, clothes, hand, or face becomes the fulcrum for the photograph's movement.

From 1880 to 1919 or 1920 the family photograph thrived. This was also the period which can be described as the "heyday" of the studio photographer. Sometimes the studio photographer came out to your house and sometimes he set the scene in his studio. But no matter where he photographed, the studio photographer planned and organized subjects, highlighting what either he or his subjects wanted. The movement we see in the picture results from his ability to play one person or tangent against another, sometimes letting the movement slacken, only to work it up again and keep it going.

Garlock As a social historian, I am curious as to the notion of a purely aesthetically derived definition of family photographs. In a sense, you are assuming, correctly or incorrectly, that the persons in these photographs are members of the same family. I am not sure what the evidence for the assumption is, other than some visual clues. There is nothing to suggest that the women with the sleds are sisters, so why you call that a family photograph, except on the basis of this aesthetic definition, is something that concerns me.

Gutman What I was suggesting is that as long as the pictures were taken before 1920 I think I can establish certain guide rules, at least certain beginning guide rules, for saying that all of these become family photographs. Regardless of whether they were popular culture or studio photographs, the formal structure is enough to tell us what a family photograph is.

Stapp In my job at the National Portrait Gallery, I deal with many, many family photographs. I feel that you are defining a family photograph in a roundabout way. I still do not understand what you mean by family photographs in the first place.

Gutman I thought I was describing it in terms of the aesthetic organization.

Stapp That describes an art object.

Gutman It describes a cultural object. The people in the photograph are the units or elements or objects that together make it what it is.

Stapp It is an interesting proposition, and I would like to hear you develop this further. It does intrigue me. You have raised some questions in my mind.

Gutman Let me raise some more questions if I can—this time concerning snapshots. Where the "studio" photograph records the texture of time—a past with a present—the snapshot is based on the present. Moreover, it is based on the reality, not even the dream, of the present.

Unlike the posed studio photograph, snapshots are essentially static: you cannot dip back in time, there is no background, you cannot weave through wishes and dreams, there is no texture. The present looms as the most essential fact in a snapshot. The only way we can capture continuity is to look at one snapshot, then another, catch another view, look for still another, catch the person the next day, look at the subject under the stars, go back to the beach. In other words, snapshots concentrate on single dimensions of events. Our instinctive feeling, when we look at a snapshot, is to want to look at another one, and another, and another. We want, or need, to look at *many* snapshots to give us the texture of a single studio photograph.

Kotkin In her new book, *On Photography*, Susan Sontag made a statement about snapshots that I found apt—she stated that the photograph itself has the capacity to tell us a lot because of many forces, including consumerism. Film and photography are advertised now as a method by which you can take so many pictures in such rapid succession that you do not have to be able to capture the truth in any one. We are encouraged to consume and throw away. Personally, I do not think that is an inherent property of the photograph. I think that it is a product, first of all, of the way that these things are presented to us, and secondly, that we are still very impoverished in visual vocabulary. We do not read photographs even though the information is there. The snapshot and the photograph are not so differentiated as we sometimes assume, in terms of the amount of information and potential that it has. We are not trained, and nobody from camera and film companies is going to train us, because we might stop awhile and start looking and stop consuming.

Garlock I came to this workshop knowing very little about the interpretation of photographs but am very interested in it. It seems to me that the approach that Judith Gutman has outlined is really more applicable to photographs taken by conscious craftsmen or artists than to snapshots. I am a little uneasy about the way snapshots are usually dismissed in the same way that literary critics and historians have traditionally dismissed pop literature.

Stapp Snapshot photographs pose very complicated questions because snapshot photography is in reality a very sophisticated mode of seeing. It is sophisticated, but it is naive at the same time. What has happened in the past twenty years is that the snapshot has been the stimulus of a whole new school of art photography that has actually developed in reaction to what I would call the humanistic documentation, which was the mode of expression used in *The Family of Man*. The snapshot has been incorporated into a whole mode of vision that was initiated or first experimented with by people like Robert Frank and later Joel Meyerowitz, and a number of other art photographers. They are working within this framework and are developing it into a very specialized, sophisticated mode of seeing that requires its own vocabulary. We are just developing the vocabulary to look at it.

Challinor Thank you, Judith, for starting us off so well. We will now take a look at some movies about families, and I will ask Jamil Simon, a free-lance movie producer, to prepare us for seeing his movie.

Simon I would like to say just a few words about the film you are about to see, which is called *A Portrait of Nana*. The film was begun in 1971, and finally finished in 1973. It concerns my grandmother relating stories about her past and about the place where she grew up. It was important to us to do the film because of her migration. She grew up in Baghdad, and ended up in New York, and my film was an attempt on my part to regain a relationship to my background. My grandmother is an Arab-Jewish woman, who was probably one of the last people in the community of Jews to live in Baghdad. This community had been there for three thousand years. These Jews were forced to leave because of various historical forces. To a degree, this film is a portrait in the classical sense. It is certainly selective, and it is certainly a way of trying to pull the whole story together to make a coherent presentation of what she was like and what she felt. [*Movie is shown.*]

Garlock It is a very interesting experiment, and as a historian I was both interested in the film and concerned about some of the problems built into the family. I think that perhaps the real theme of the film is your grandmother's vitality. You have done a superb analysis of the kind of vitality that obviously attracted you to her as a person, and I would be surprised if anyone would not feel that she would be a really interesting person to meet and talk to. However, the problem is whether a film is an effective medium for the recalling of a grandmother's life. It is something that I am concerned about because I would say her story is interesting, but it ends up being somewhat verbal. There is not enough visual support for some of the claims she is making, and yet I am fascinated by the photographic evidence and the family history.

Gutman I think you are short-changing the significance of your film by calling it "simply a family document," as if it were only a personal memoir. It seems to me that if historians are going to accept oral history then we can regard this film as visual oral history. As such, the oral history, or film story, is greatly enhanced by the visual aspects you have portrayed.

Challinor On that positive note we will turn to the second movie, made by an independent movie producer, Amalie Rothschild. Amalie, will you come up and prepare us for your movie?

Rothschild I am trying to get a bearing on the focus that this working session is taking so that I can be a little clearer about how to introduce this film. There are several different groups here who have different points of view about the subject. I know for myself that I made this film for very personal reasons, some of which I became aware of in the process of making it, and some of which were already conscious at the beginning.

Initially the film began as a portrait of my grandmother, simply because I did not want her to die. My motivations seem to be pretty much the common ones that most of us have experienced: wanting to find out about our background, where we came from, how we became the people that we are, and how to search out our roots. I started this film in 1972. As I began to learn more about my grandmother and started making the film, she became very uncomfortable with the idea, and drew back from the project. I then turned to my mother, at first to find out about my grandmother, and in the process for the first time discovered my mother as a daughter. I also began to get a clear idea that the film I had wanted to make all along was really about my mother, whom I had not known how to reach, and to whom, through this film, I began to get really close. The film itself is an odyssey of that recognition and a record of the process of coming to terms with my female roots in my family in order to trace the values and the continuity between the generations as they were passed on to me. I am a film maker, and all my life I have thought of myself as a professional person. My mother is really the pivotal force in my life, as she is a professional artist.

I had, of course, a lot of family material to draw on and to use. I was attempting to use still photographs and old home movies to try to understand the subtext of the family relationships. Through an exploration of images I attempted to get at the real feelings of family members. The legitimization of the subject of family photographs, snapshots, and family albums is new to me. I did not come to this from that background at all, and I think that part of what I was, in fact, trying to do was to get behind the myths that these family photographs often portray for us. [*Movie is shown.*]

Weis As a teacher of film at Brooklyn College, I would like to put these films into a larger context. What you should know is that in the early 1970s there was a whole spate of films dealing with family history. I think the genre is still popular among independent film makers. Almost all of these films were made by people of the same age, their middle or late twenties, and a majority of these film makers are Jewish.

I do not think the age of the film makers was any accident. When you are of college age you rebel and you throw out everything you inherited. Then, after college, you start wanting to look back at your roots. You want to keep some of them and to throw others out. There is a very poignant moment in a movie called

"Joyce at Thirty-Four" in which the girl has married and is pregnant. She has the baby during the movie—in front of the camera, in fact. She proudly takes her daughter to her mother's house, and says, at one point, that "if my mother loved me as much as I love my daughter, she must have suffered a great deal." Suddenly she has become aware of her mother's perspective. I think this was going on in Amalie's film, too.

Gutman What I especially like about this movie is that Amalie had the nerve to deal with herself, and then to put that on film. What Amalie is admitting is that this film is in some ways a rite of passage. It is something that you go through before you make other films. Would you admit that, Amalie?

Rothschild Well, I did not realize it at the time, but I know it now.

Challinor Thank you for sharing your movie with us, Amalie. I am now going to call on Catherine Noren, a free-lance photographer whose book *The Camera of My Family* has recently been published.

Noren Like many of my contemporaries, I found the need for identification and for my roots and for finding my own past, but I found it long after I was well into the writing of the book. I had barely started on the project when I had a publisher for it, so I knew from the beginning it was for publication. That knowledge may have slowed down my emotional involvement with the material.

The Camera of My Family is a family album encompassing five generations of a German-Jewish family. The more than three hundred photographs and mementoes, together with their captions of family history and anecdote, form an intimate record of the passage of the family through the halcyon decades 1870–1920, through changes of fortune, escape from Hitler's Germany, the war, and their dispersal and resettlement in countries all over the world—but especially in America.

I was born in Germany, and I left there when I was an infant, before World War II. I come from a family that did not speak of its past. Many German Jews speak endlessly of their past, and many of them do not speak of it at all. I did not know my own history, and furthermore, I did not care. But I cared very much about the photographs I found, and I started with them, and through them I became intensely interested in my own past.

I started with the photographs, and for them I had to find a structure, a narrative. Obviously the narrative was the story of my family, but I had to find the format that would fit the photographs. It was like doing a comic book and then having to find the captions for it.

I had two very big problems. One was organizational; I have a huge family. On my mother's side alone, there are eighteen great uncles and aunts. My father's family was also large, and there was visual material for all of these relatives too. I had a hard time dealing with the sheer volume of material. I wrote to all the pictured relatives who were now dispersed all over the world, told them what I was doing, and I had a tremendous response from them.

I had a difficult time deciding whom to include, whom to exclude, and where to cut them off generationally. Anything that had to do with great grandparents or great-great grandparents I included because there was not very much about them and what did exist was useful in genealogical terms. I found that eventually I let the photographs themselves decide who was to be included. If I found an absolutely wonderful photograph, that person would be included, because I could not bear to leave out the photograph. It actually ended up working quite well, if not very symmetrically.

The second of my problems was that the photographs were static. Most of them were taken between 1900 and 1938, some before and some after, but those forty years are the main time frame. I had envisioned, when I started working on this project, a book in which the captions would simply describe the activities in the photographs. I found that I could not do that. The photographs were formal, and I had to find the caption material that would specify the time of the photograph, or something that was

4. *Strauss Family*, 1903. Courtesy Random House, Inc. From Catherine Hanf Noren, *The Camera of My Family*, Alfred A. Knopf, Inc., New York, N.Y., © 1973, 1974, 1976.

evocative of mood or circumstance. I tried to match them up so that within the book there are two running narratives, one told by the captions, the other by the photographs.

What I would like to do is to show you some of the photos. My concerns were with time, continuity, and change. I was always after the unfolding of a mystery, and the mystery was that these people had really existed. This was intensified for me because there was such secrecy about my own past. So making the book was a revelation. I was always trying to find the humanity; always trying to find the relationships between the people. This staunch Victorian family [figure 4] revealed to me their humanity, and I became very interested in them as a group of people.

I was interested in what Judith Gutman said about space and about the fact that in most of my old family photographs the women are posed in profile. This is a good example. I had thought a great deal about this pose, and the only thing that I could come up with is that perhaps it was to show their busts.

Garlock I would say that it is more a reflection of the fact that in the societal context the men were visibly to take precedence. Women were subordinated to them physically; they were in the background. They are looking away so that your attention is not drawn to them as it is to the men. It does not reflect the fact that the women were the center of the household.

Gutman Two things are happening. One is that the men are sitting and the women are standing, and that is typical up to the 1920s. Then, in the 1920s, you have a new style taking over. We see it in wedding photographs: the woman becomes more important for the aesthetic organization of the photograph. Men and women become aesthetic equals. Now, if we realize that we are talking about wedding photographs, photographs which I have dubbed "community" rather than family photographs, then we can begin to see the tremendous importance of such a change. The changed aesthetic style reveals a change in culture.

Garlock What seems to me crucial in this discussion is that the answer to some of the questions that have been raised must come from an explanation of other kinds of historical information. You cannot derive an explanation from the poses that you are observing in the photograph. You can make hypotheses, but to confirm anything you will have to do some other kinds of research.

Noren I not only found this a beautiful photograph, but I also found a point of identification with this little girl [figure 5] (who is my mother's cousin) because she looks like me. She not only went into the book, she became a character in it. I told her story. If it had not been for this photograph, she would not have appeared at all. Her story turned out very well: she represented a branch of the family that did get out of Germany.

There are five generations in this book, and in dealing with so

5. *Little Girl*, ca. 1917. Courtesy Random House, Inc. From Catherine Hanf Noren, *The Camera of My Family*, Alfred A. Knopf, Inc., New York, N.Y., © 1973, 1974, 1976.

6. *Four Generations*, 1900. Courtesy Random House, Inc. From Catherine Hanf Noren, *The Camera of My Family*, Alfred A. Knopf, Inc., New York, N.Y., © 1973, 1974, 1976.

7. *Picture at the Well*, ca. 1928. Courtesy Random House, Inc. From Catherine Hanf Noren, *The Camera of My Family*, Alfred A. Knopf, Inc., New York, N.Y., © 1973, 1974, 1976.

great a span of time there is no way that you could leave out this photograph [figure 6]. It is my great-great grandmother, my great grandmother, my great aunt, and her child. As I looked at this photograph again and again, I finally saw something going on between the two middle-aged women, and that made me much happier. There is some kind of collusion between them, some kind of awareness that they have of each other. Perhaps they set up this portrait. But there certainly is something going on between those two sets of eyes. The two of them created a tension, an awareness, that I tried to keep going all the way through the book.

We come now to the generation of my grandparents [figure 7].

These are their children, my mother and aunt and uncles. I think that this photograph in particular is very revealing of their relationship to each other. The father stands guard over the whole family, my grandfather is on the left, and the oldest son is on the right, as the other flank of the picture. The child, the only child, is on the well playing. My mother, the ingenue with the smiling face, must just have acquired a new boyfriend—why else would she be smiling so? My grandmother is the only person sitting. There is one person who is out of place, my other uncle. I have a distinct feeling he is uneasy with this, maybe because he is fifteen years old. Still, this, to me, seems a very integrated picture of a family, and an important one.

I was very interested to hear this afternoon that everybody has been documenting their grandmothers. Although I did not know this was usual, who the main character was to be was never a problem for me; it would be my grandmother. I knew the beginning and the end of the book almost immediately. My grandmother appears constantly throughout, and I included more photographs of her than of anyone else. I wanted to show the string continuing, and you can see this by the way she ages [figures 8a, b, c]. She is the bearer of time.

Challinor Thank you, Catherine. The next presentation will be that of Jonathan Garlock.

Garlock I feel a little strange coming toward the end of this session, although it is the most appropriate place for me. I did not bring any videotapes; I did not bring any film; I did not bring any slides. In a sense, I did not bring any images. I am not making films about my grandmother or about my family. I am not even a film maker, except incidentally. I am a historian. Very briefly, I got into community history through the back door. A friend of mine and I were teaching a course in immigration history. We decided that, instead of having students read secondary works on immigration by historians, we would send students out to look at the local immigrant community. We studied a neighborhood in Rochester which had gone through a complete ethnographic

8. a, b, c. *Meta Wallach*, 1903, 1939, 1976. Courtesy Random House, Inc. From Catherine Hanf Noren, *The Camera of My Family*, Alfred A. Knopf, Inc., New York, N.Y., © 1973, 1974, 1976.

transformation, from being entirely German and Irish to being entirely Italian, and is now entirely black and Hispanic.

In order to do community history you have to teach people skills, especially if you are trying to get them to do history through informal structures such as museums and neighborhood associations. This is our essential goal whilst we develop formal curricula. Our main concern is to teach the community to do its own history. This means helping people learn how to use traditional materials and documents. It is important to get them to look at many other things too—everything from photographs to buildings and artifacts.

We realized that we were dealing with the community as a physical and visual entity. It also occurred to us that we were trying to present history to the community in visual form. It seems to me that there are two kinds of repositories for images. We have, first, official repositories in our community—places like the George Eastman House or the Rochester Museum of Science Center. The second repository is the community itself.

We became interested in family albums in both the public repositories and the community. There are only about sixty family albums in the George Eastman House in Rochester. We did our own survey about albums, and I am going to share the results with you. We distributed questionnaires to the community at large. The group of people who responded may not be representative, but I think the information that we have gathered says a lot about the potential of using family images in the community.

Our first question was: Do you have family photographs, prints, or snapshots? Next: Do you have family slides? Do you have family home movies? About half of the people said that they had both photos and slides, and about half of them said that they had all three. We asked how many photographs they had, and almost all of them said that they had between one and five hundred. One couple said that they had over a thousand. We asked what historical period these photographs covered: before 1900; from 1900 to 1925; from 1925 to 1950; and from 1950 to the present day. A few had no pictures from before 1900, and a few had no pictures from before 1925, but most people had pictures spanning the whole time period.

We were curious to know whether the respondents or other people in their households knew who the people were in the old photographs. Most of them said that they did know who all of the people were in the old photographs, or that there was somebody in the house who could identify them. A few could only identify most of the people in their photographs. Many of the owners of the albums could identify what was going on in their pictures, both those in their albums and those in drawers and envelopes.

We have very clear evidence that most people do not keep all their photographs in albums, so that albums have clearly gone through some kind of a selection process. When you look at a family albums, a whole other range of images has been excluded.

Challinor Jonathan, have you done any work at all with families, or asked them, in their own judgment, what they have chosen to put in their albums, and what they have left out?

Garlock No, we have not done that much work with them yet. We wanted first to discover the range of things covered in the photographs that people had.

More than 90 percent of the respondents said that they had pictures of relatives, family members as babies, friends, family vacations, and trips. Between 80 and 90 percent of those asked said that they had pictures of graduations, weddings, scenery, holiday events and personal possessions. Many people have commented how important automobiles were to them. Between 50 and 80 percent of the people said that they had pictures of birthdays and buildings. Family members at work, family reunions, and children's first achievements, were also included.

By contrast, people had few pictures of confirmations, bar mitzvahs, animals other than pets, athletic events, and pictures taken from television. I think only one or two people had ever taken a photograph of anything on television.

I think all of that simply reveals that there is a tremendous amount of visual information in terms of family images owned by the community. One of our real concerns in this project is to get out into the community and work with people and the images they own.

Challinor We do have an expert on family albums with us today: Amy Kotkin.

Kotkin Like Judith Gutman, I have written out my presentation, and I would like to give it in that form.[1]

Though amply warned that the family was a doomed, decaying institution, members of the newly created Family Folklife Program at the Smithsonian began in 1974 interviewing Washington, D.C., area residents about the stories, expressions, and traditions that encapsulate their families' past experiences and characterize their relationships in the present.

From 1974 to 1976, the Family Folklife Program interviewed over five thousand local residents and visitors to the nation's capital. Virtually everyone contributed a narrative or tradition unique to his or her family. Beyond this, our informants described a variety of other means by which their families preserved shared experiences. These included home movies, photos, photo albums, and all forms of needlework.

Our consideration of home photography as a form of family folklore began in 1974 when a young woman who had heard about the project shared her personal photo album with us. Nancy Brown's (the name is not hers) album had been made for her by her mother as a wedding present and contained not only a visual history of her own life but of her parents, grandparents, and great-grandparents as well.

As we spoke with her, we found that there was a strong relationship between her photos and the stories that were told regularly in her family. But while Nancy's photographs were almost invariably happy, many of the stories they rekindled were not.

Turning to a jovial photo of her Aunt Rose on an American beach, Nancy recounted a harrowing and oft-repeated tale of that aunt's escape from Russia. A proud photo of Nancy's father in his

World War II army uniform was counterpointed with a tragic tale of how he had shot a little boy in Germany, mistaking him for an enemy soldier. Only by eliciting the stories brought to mind by family photographs could we begin to understand how visual images relate to a family's verbal lore.

Over the next two years, hundreds of families responded to ads we placed in Washington, D.C., newspapers and lent their photos and photo albums to us for research. Looking at discrete images, we found that Nancy Brown's pictures had their counterparts in almost all the collections we saw. Common themes (such as holiday celebrations or graduations) and common poses (such as families grouped informally on the front porches of their homes) appeared over and over again. On an immediate level, they represent shared notions of appropriate moments to photograph. New York psychologist Stanley Milgram addressed himself to this phenomenon in noting that while we are free to photograph anything we want, we in fact do not. "Photography," he says, "extends two psychological boundaries, perception and memory. . . . It is essentially a future-oriented art."[2] We tend to take photos according to how we want to preserve, remember, and be remembered. Expressing our values and ideals, family photos represent stylized reality.

On at least three levels, photography has become an important expression of a family's folklore. Viewed over time, photographs evoke stories and expressions, and may even serve as the basis for family legends. As part of our material culture, their similarities in pose and setting suggest that they derive from widely shared values and aesthetics. Finally, photographs not only capture the common folkloric events in the family, such as weddings, birthdays, and holidays, but become part of the rituals they record. Today, the act of picture-taking itself is a central part of holiday celebrations. The album represents an organizing principle above and beyond a simple collection of photographs.

Family albums are certainly the most common and in many cases the only document of a family's history in America today.

Yet, though we commit ourselves to posterity increasingly through visual images, we remain tremendously uncritical of those images. We have yet to develop an adequate vocabulary for "reading" photographs and for recognizing that their research value lies not in their proclivity to detail life as it is, but in their tendecy to express our ideals and beliefs. For the student of contemporary folklore, photography is a superb example of how modern technology, so often blamed for the decline of folk cultures, has provided yet another language for the creation and transmission of folklore.

I think what we need to do, really, is to create or establish a critical framework by which to judge albums. We know that photographic images themselves are selections. We have established that very clearly today. What then do we say of the album where a process of selection has gone on and another process of editing, of juxtaposition, has been imposed. You are two stages, at least, removed from reality, and yet the photographic images, as Susan Sontag and other people have pointed out, have such unquestioned credibility in our own lives that we tend to be very uncritical of those images. We tend to accept, even though we know better, the album as an accurate reflection of family life.

The way I like to think of it is that our culture provides us with a tremendous number of modes of communication. Each one of those modes of communication really becomes a vehicle by which our folklore and our history are transmitted from one generation to the next, and yet each one of those modes transmits a somewhat different message. That is why it is absolutely necessary if we are going to be able to view photograph albums as historical documentation (and we have to because it is so often the only record), to put it in a context of asking very specific questions. Who made the album? When was it made? Why was it made? What can we say about the way images are arranged in terms of pose and setting, and the kinds of things that people want to convey with their albums?

Secondly, we need to know things like what kind of emotional attachment is there to the album? How much do the family members feel that they have learned about our cultural history and their personal family histories from looking through the albums? We need to know the context in which it is used to assign the album a rightful place in our study of cultural history, to know that it is one element, but not the total picture.

Challinor We have covered an enormous amount of territory. I want to thank you all for coming and for asking so many provocative questions. The task of interpreting photographic images is just beginning. The greatest courage will be necessary to admit we understand, as yet, very little. I believe all the panelists this afternoon have shown the required courage. Thank you for your contributions.

Notes

1. A longer version of this paper was published in *Exposure: Journal of the Society for Photographic Education* 16 (March, 1978):4–8.

2. Stanley Milgram, "The Image-Freezing Machine," *Psychology Today* (January 1977):48.

Collecting Oral History

PARTICIPANTS

Robert Byington, Folklife Program, Smithsonian Institution

E. Culpepper Clark, Department of Speech, College of Arts and Science, University of Alabama

Susan Kalcik, Folklife Program, Smithsonian Institution

Robert McCarl, Folklife Program, Smithsonian Institution

Beverly Robinson, Department of Folklore and Folklife, University of Pennsylvania

Ralph Rinzler, Folklife Program, Smithsonian Institution

Steven Zeitlin, Folklife Program, Smithsonian Institution

Rinzler Good morning. I am Ralph Rinzler, a member of the Smithsonian's Folklife Program, and co-chairman for this morning's session. We are here to discuss all aspects of the recording of oral history: its uses, its advantages and limitations, and the unique insights it can give, as well as moral and even technical aspects. Since the Smithsonian Folklife Program has profited greatly from various forms of oral history during its projects, several of my colleagues are on the panel today: our co-chairman Ralph Rinzler, Susan Kalcik, Steven Zeitlin, and Robert McCarl. We also welcome two panelists from outside the Folklife Program: Professor Culpepper Clark of the University of Alabama and Beverely Robinson from the Department of Folklife and Folklore at the University of Pennsylvania. They will speak about their experiences with oral history, their methods, the problems they have encountered, and the various uses to which they have put their material. They will also discuss some of the broader implications of the field of oral history.

Let me call on Cully Clark to begin with a few words on the importance of oral history.

Clark If, as Aristotle defined it, rhetoric is "the available means of persuasion," then history is rhetoric. Its purpose is to persuade the present and future by arguing a view of the past. Be it shaped by scientific positivism or relativism, empiricism or analytical philosophy, be it determined by economic forces or the ideology of Whigs and Tories, history is argumentative. Not only do historians seek to persuade, but those who make history also have a rhetorical perspective, preserving through artifacts, the written record, or oral tradition that which they wish subsequent generations to remember.

Beginning with Bancroft in the Jacksonian era, American historians placed greater and greater reliance on tangible (written) evidence as they sought to become more and more scientific. In the process they left neglected those voices of the past whose plea for a future hearing was and is necessarily cast in an oral medium. Such a focus has left historians open to the charge that they serve as the agents of "Great White Men": that they neglect perspectives which come from the consciousness and experiences of ethnic minorities, members of regional subcultures, women, and working people—people who have written very little about themselves.

It is no indictment to say that history is rhetoric, only that it is poor rhetoric. Aristotle believed the purpose of rhetoric was to discern the "genuine" from the "spurious," the "true" from the "sham." The function of rhetoric, he argued, was "not [absolutely] to persuade, but to discover the available means of persuasion in a given case." Thus, if the historian ignores the losers to pursue the winners, the inarticulate in favor of the articulate, the non-elite in deferences to the elite, then in what Aristotle called "the given case," the point the historian purports to study, he or she has failed to discover all the available means of persuasion.

Aristotle did not mean to charge subsequent generations of scholars with more than they were capable. He did not intend that rhetoric should attain the dialectical certainty of the syllogism, only that rhetoric be rigorous, that it seek to approximate truth. Turning to analogy Aristotle explained, "Thus the aim of medicine is not, strictly speaking, to restore a sick man to perfect health, but to bring him as near to health as the case admits. . . ." For the historian to ignore oral data because it is not as manageable as written data is like the physician ignoring a patient's complaint because it did not fit a textbook explanation. Under such conditions the physician could not bring the patient "as near to health as the case admit[ted]." Indeed, he would not even know the case.

Were Aristotle here today, he might well say: "Historian, heal thyself."

Zeitlin The disciplines of folklore and oral history are intimately bound up with one another. The differences between them are ones of emphasis. If we take any given reminiscence, the historian will emphasize those parts of it which can be substantiated as factual, while the folklorist will stress those parts which are embodied in traditional forms such as stories, folktales, anecdotes, expressions, recipes, jokes, and proverbs. Folklore subsumes both factual and fictional material in its expressive forms.

When I think about the relationship between folklore and oral history, two examples come to mind. The first concerns a great-great grandfather, who, as Susan Meehan put it, "did *not* fight in the Civil War." His mother bought him out. For $300 she found someone to take his place. This was such an embarrassment for the poor man that on Veterans' Day he stayed at home, closed the shutters and locked the door to hide his shame.

I can remember, on the other hand, speaking with a gentleman in Portland, Oregon, who seemed to tell quite the opposite story. His great-great-grandfather had not only fought in the Civil War, but had apparently been wounded so that he was remembered as having walked with a limp for most of his adult life. In fact, he started a tradition of military service in the family. His grandson had fought in World War I, his great-grandson in World War II, and his great-great-grandson, with whom I spoke, in Vietnam. All had been decorated soldiers. Well, after *Roots,* this young man began to do some research on the history of his family. Lo and behold! What did he discover? His great-great-grandfather had been bought out by his mother for $300—just like the great-great-grandfather in the earlier story! Rather than close the shutters on Veterans' Day, he simply decided to walk with a limp and pass down heroic stories.

The military history of that family is incomprehensible without the knowledge of a family story—and an inaccurate one at that. It suggests a way in which family stories can be critical for the historian. A family often acts on the basis of information passed down in stories, legends, expressions, and proverbs. The information may or may not be truthful, but the historian cannot afford to disregard it. Often what a family believes to be true is as important as the truth itself, for the family acts on what it believes.

McCarl As a folklorist, I approach the study of occupational groups in an ethnographic manner, attempting to understand how workers themselves perceive the form and content of interrelationships and interactions. Focusing on the forms of communication within the occupational setting, I attempt to understand how communication influences and is at the same time influenced by the work environment.

Experience in various settings indicates that occupational groups tend to generate unique communication forms or styles based upon the work process itself. This process is comprised of techniques that result when people manipulate tools and machines in prescribed ways to make a specific product or provide a service. The shaping principle of sheet welding, for instance, is the joining of two metal pieces by melting the two rivets together. The associated techniques include layout, shearing, and various types and styles of welding and grinding, all of which have varying levels of complexity.

In addition, members of occupational groups also communicate through customary behavior, for example, apprenticeship initiation, and through defensive, or what social anthropologists call "alienated," mechanisms of pranks and sabotage that require techniques developed to fight back at highly rationalized or compartmentalized work on all sides of the blue, white, and pink collar line.

Oral expression itself ranges from lengthy, pedagogical narratives about occupational experiences to legends about particular characters, anecdotes and jokes told in passing, and even nicknames and jargon developed for the articulation and accomplishment of the work load. The key to understanding and recording this material lies in perceiving oral expression as just one aspect of occupational interaction, an aspect that can only be understood within the larger work culture itself.

Robinson I would like to speak briefly about the working concepts that I use in the field. These concepts are concerned with community, and with the idea that there are shared sentiments that bring people together. With this idea in mind, my fieldwork focuses on examining various folkloric elements in a given society with the expressed intention of attempting to discover how these elements mesh into the overall construct of community. It means going beyond the typical documentation and preconceptions that so many of us in fieldwork share.

For example, we can go to a cane maker, or a walking-stick maker as they are generally called, and take pictures of the artisan and of his work. We can record how long he has been making canes, what type of wood he is using, and so forth. What, however, does cane-making mean to the artisan? What does it mean to the people who use his canes? A self-taught cane-maker from Louisiana once told me that his canes were made out of hickory, and that the hickory wood always comes from the root of the tree. Why, I asked, does he always use the root? If you use the root of the tree, he said, it gives you your design, and you do not have to sit up and think, well, I want this particular design. He also makes his canes for elderly people in the community and believes that when you have walked above ground on two legs, then your third leg deserves to be from the root, underground.

Hence, for the fieldworker, something more has evolved than just an object–a philosophy regarding the object, its users, and the artisan.

Question In cultures that use writing, it seems to me that written sources tend to glamorize experiences.

Kalcik Yes. I think that is because the writing was intended for public consumption. So, for example, immigrant novels written around the turn of the century are usually success stories of one sort or another. They are highly polished, and therefore give an unbalanced picture.

Question When you say that history is rhetoric, you are echoing the Soviet and Chinese approach to history. Can we afford that? What is the analytically correct and objective way of understanding this material?

Clark A recognition that we operate from a present perspective to expose and explore reality out of our past is part of the persuasive element of which I am speaking. For example, there was black history before we discovered blacks in the struggles of the 1950s. There was women's history before we discovered women in the 1960s. Out of these present realities and needs to find and discover our past, we tend at any given time to persuade ourselves that certain aspects are more important than others. History takes on an argumentative perspective, and I think this is quite legitimate. History is fluid. It changes through time, but it can still be honest and rigorous. As I said, the purpose of rhetoric is to discern, as best we can, the truth. Or, as Aristotle would have said, to approximate truth in a very rigorous, scientific fashion. I did not mean we should abandon ourselves to the passions of persuasion, or to suggest that our history should adopt any particular focus. As long as it is fluid in adopting perspectives out of the present, then history will remain a living science, and a rigorous one.

Question There are really two streams of oral history right now. One is the attempt to record the history of ordinary men and women; the other is the attempt to record the history of people like Supreme Court justices, congressmen, senators, and business leaders. I think our discussion so far has quite rightly focused on one direction of oral history, the recovery of experiences shared by the inarticulate and the common people. I think it important to mention briefly that oral history and oral tradition are also extremely important for understanding the history of the elite and for understanding the history of institutions that guide and shape our lives.

Rinzler This is an extremely important point of view which a number of us here share. Even during the Folklife Festival, we had contention over this, because some of my colleagues felt that much "folklore" dealt only with the peasantry. We have to abandon the idea that folklore concerns only working class or peasant culture, or whatever term you may care to use. During the Folklife Festival we became aware of the necessity of presenting the traditions of the upper class, even, let us say, the aristocracy. We did not do this until we reached the Washington suburbs in the State of Maryland. Here we realized that among the most startling examples of folklore were fox hunting and horse racing, both of which require a great deal of money. Down came Mrs. Dupont and a number of her neighbors. They made it very clear to us that the people who were hunting the fox had a language, a way of dressing, a way of relating to each other, and a hierarchical structure within the hunt itself, which dated back hundreds of years. This was an example of folklore that was fully aristocratic both in its origins and in its continuing maintenance.

Question The tape recorder has been around for about twenty-five years now, and many, many people have used it. I wonder if any scholars are researching collections of old tapes as they do collections of old photographs.

Rinzler Even before there were tape recordings, disc recordings were available for many years, and they have proved very interesting. Many radio transcriptions made during the war, as well as interviews with and performances by different ethnic and cultural groups, have yielded tremendous amounts of data. The

Library of Congress American Folklife Center recently held a symposium on ethnic recordings. These recordings were made primarily by commercial recording companies, but recently scholars have come to regard them seriously as important sources of data. These recordings were made in an era before scholars began to record folklore. This is just one example of the recent investigation of old recordings; there are many more.

Question I wonder if any member of the panel has had an experience in which the subjects of the inquiries have questioned the very process of collecting oral history?

McCarl You have to take the people you hope to interview one at a time and explain clearly to them what it is you are planning to do. You should say, "This is what I am doing, and this is why I am doing it." Sometimes the subject will refuse to be interviewed, and sometimes he or she will agree. To start out with any predetermined methodology is a mistake.

Question Have you been able to trace occupations over time in your research?

McCarl Yes. In America there is still a tremendous amount of generational passing on of occupations, particularly among the elite and in the professional occupations. We learned this through the research done for the Folklife Festival.

Rinzler We will now move into the area of morality. We began with a very simple thought. If you are collecting material from individuals, you must be responsible to those people, whoever they may be. The way you behave, and the way you understand the behavioral patterns and the particular moral code of the people with whom you are working, is crucial. The significance of that goes beyond what you are able to accomplish, or what is fair, and relates to how you portray to the world the people whom you are studying. Any researcher who may come after you will be very much affected by the way you have handled the confidences that were offered you.

Clark The ethical problems of the oral historian differ only in degree from those of historians employing more traditional methodologies. The oral historian's central problem is that he or she is an intruder upon people's history and oral traditions. The intrusion is made obvious at the point where oral data are transformed into a written form.

The only difference between written data and oral data, as the historian uses it, lies in the intention of the original author or authors. A letter or diary may be an intentional act of preservation by its author, a commitment to leave something in writing. In oral history, the historian initiates the act of preservation, breaking into a chain of living testimony or into the memory of a witness for the purpose of recording.

No American writer was ever more conscious of the ethical dimensions of this intrusion than was James Agee. When he came South in the summer of 1936 to do an article on cotton tenantry, he so identified with the families he was observing as to create an intellectual hell for himself over the prospect of revealing their wretched lives to the literate public. To read Agee's *Let Us Now Praise Famous Men* is to understand what Stephen Spender meant when he called it "a sustained exercise in empathy." Every oral historian should read Agee to heighten his or her awareness of this element of intrusion, but having read Agee, the historian should also beware of the trap it created for the author, "a kind of intellectual paralysis," as a friend of Agee's so aptly put it. Once the historian has confronted a subject and grappled with the ethical dimensions of revealing it, she or he must get on with the business of reporting it fully and accurately.

Kalcik The first thing that you have to remember is honesty. You must be totally and completely honest about the project, about its purpose, and about the uses to which it will be put. I am speaking of a very active kind of honesty, because it has been my experience that many people are all too willing to tell me a great deal about themselves without really quite knowing who I am or what I am doing.

Secondly, I think that respect is incredibly important in the kind of work that we do: respect for the rights and wishes of the individual and of the community. Very often that means that if people do not want the material used in the ways in which you would like to use it, you do not use it, and that is that!

Furthermore, I feel very strongly about returning the materials to the community. I am very concerned to make sure that there is community access to the materials collected and that materials or archives be indexed in such a way that people can use them easily.

There are many ethical and moral problems in dealing with ethnics, and there are many reasons why one must tread carefully in ethnic communities. Sometimes you are dealing with recent immigrants who have very real fears about their situation in America. Perhaps their citizenship seems to them to be at stake. Sometimes you are dealing with illegal aliens, and even if they arrived in this country fifty years ago, they may be unwilling to talk to you. In that kind of situation you must push.

Zeitlin I want to talk about the guidelines the Folklife Program uses in collecting folklore. In just an hour or two of interview time we cover perhaps a few hundred years of family time. This observation indicates that folklore tends to cluster in different nexuses of family life. Not every event is covered chronologically. By interviewing many different families, we have been able to obtain a sense of the nexuses around which folklore tends to cluster. These focal areas of folklore include, for example, the personalities of individuals and the kind of food that a family eats. A great deal of folklore concerns food and dining customs. In collecting family folklore, we find that any given family will have an individual, single nexus. One of our interviewers was unable to gather information from an interview, until he discovered that the Friday night poker game was a rich source of folklore in that family. In addition, whatever occasion is at the heart of a family's life—the family reunion, the dinner, the picnic, the drinking session—can also be used as an occasion for collecting folklore.

McCarl The only moral perspective from which a researcher can work in an occupational context is that of the sensitive and perceptive outsider. No matter how credentialed or accepted he or she may be by the group, in the world of other people's work, whether it is that of a house worker or a tool and dye maker, the investigator is an outsider.

A number of years ago, Saul Tax pointed out that one way in which social scientists and humanists could begin to dig themselves out of their admittedly culturally exploitative role, was to use their expertise, training, and, I think, valuable insight to aid those whom they are studying. People in a community should be taught not only to perceive but also to use the information the researchers have collected. This approach requires that we articulate daily the motives, definitions, and results of our work.

If, for example, I was attempting to record the occupational narrative of cement workers in the Lehigh Valley of Pennsylvania, which I did last year, I would first have to understand the rich ethnic, cultural, and historical background of that area through field and literary research. Secondly, I would have to approach a group of cement workers through their union, which is, in many cases, the only organized voice of the work group. I would have to explain to these people my view of work culture, technique, and oral expression.

This explanatory function would be an ongoing activity as I met new people, and explained my purpose in gathering information. The culmination of the effort, and, I think perhaps the most important aspect of ethnographic field work, would be in discovering an appropriate method for reporting my findings. This method should be, firstly, consistent with an objective and honest position in the community; secondly, should be comprehensible to the cement workers themselves; and, thirdly, should be given a final form that could be used by them as they saw fit.

Robinson Before conducting an interview, I make a specific point of letting people know something about me, the researcher and—the person. It is particularly important for them to understand my reason for doing the research and what I intend to do with the data after I have left. Whenever possible, a copy of my final work is sent to the people who have made the research possible; and I always ask whether they would like a copy to be put in their local library. If I get permission to take pictures, I try to send a copy of the picture. If there are no pictures, then a handwritten letter of thanks is always sent.

Also, it has been my experience that many people have an idealized conception of the researcher as a scholarly genius who thinks he or she knows it all. To dispel this myth, I try to assume a student's position, thereby offering them the position of teacher. Any suggestions or comments I make are presented as an interchange, and are not delivered from the position of "I know." This methodology has created a congenial and productive research environment.

Question I would like to ask about the implications of utilizing research. It seems to me that there is a whole new range of ethical and moral implications that have to be addressed both for scholarly uses and for transforming research into something that is acted upon in the public domain.

Byington All scholarship and all use of evidence depends on the original intention of the author or authors of a document. I think that any time you are collecting oral data, it must be considered a joint intellectual project. The person being interviewed has to agree in advance how it will be used. There are many potential uses for that information. As long as one comes to an agreement with those being interviewed, not much intellectual difficulty remains, provided one follows the canons of common sense.

Question How do you feel about the morality of the television series on six families?

Zeitlin Perhaps an even more exaggerated example is the Loud family. It seems to me that in a case like this, the people are getting fame in return for being exposed. I do not know, however, to what degree this is the case in ethnic communities. In much of the research that we do with families, people think that to have material about them published offers them a little fame. We have such an anonymous culture that people place an enormous value on fame, and are willing to pay an enormous price for that in terms of their own self respect. In order to escape from their anonymity, they seem willing to do almost anything.

Kalcik I think you have touched on a really tricky issue, because in many cases the person who is doing the research will understand the implications far better than the person who is giving the information. In a way, people are relying on the goodwill of the researcher.

Zeitlin Think of the motives of film makers. You can be certain that if a film maker wants to make a film about you, the chances of his making a film that shows the value and beauty of your traditions are very slim. The journalistic approach to families is essentially an exposé. At the moment this kind of journalism, based on the quest for the sensational, is in vogue in our culture.

Question I would like to offer a critique of the approach to oral history taken by members of the panel. Unless you are very aggressive, ask complex and embarrassing questions, make people feel uncomfortable, and touch on things that may be a part of what they consider their private lives, you will be given a distorted, misleading, glossed-over impression of what actually happened.

Kalcik What kind of picture will you have from the answers to these uncomfortable questions? Do you think you will be given honest answers to them?

Question Well, if you ask enough questions, even if they are not giving you an honest answer to a single question, you are given a picture that you would never see unless you ask those kinds of questions.

Kalcik I do not agree. I think you can learn a great deal by asking people simply to tell you the story of their lives. I am not sure that probing questions are necessarily the way to discover the truth. I think that if people want to evade an issue, they will evade it, even if you ask a direct question. If you work indirectly, you are more likely perhaps to be told more, at least in certain cases. Each case must be approached on its own merits.

Robinson Sometimes it becomes necessary to probe, but there is a way to ask anything. I have found that people will tell you what they want you to know. But there is always a way to ask questions, even when you are violating privacy or moving into a taboo area.

Question Will you ask these questions in such a way that people do not realize that you are questioning them?

Robinson Well, let me give you one example. The cane maker I was dealing with in Louisiana had at one time suffered a very bad experience. This experience related to his whole involvement with cane-making. I said to him that I realized that this was probably not a very pleasant subject, but I would like to ask him about it. I went right ahead and asked my question. That preface to the question prepared him and he opened up. He said, "You know, I have not talked about this to anyone else besides my wife, but I am glad that you brought it up." Later, I asked him if his cooperative answer was made easier by the way that I asked the question, and he said, "Yes."

Still, regardless of how you ask them, *people will only tell you what they want you to know.*

McCarl If you were approaching oral tradition from a group point of view and trying to get a contextual perspective, there would be an inherent internal check on your information. It seems to me that in cases when you are trying to obtain a tremendous amount of information from an individual, then your questions might have to be more aggressive and argumentative than when, for example, you were dealing with a person as part of a work group.

Question If you set yourself up as an expert on what will and will not be published, do you have a moral obligation in some cases to say that I will not allow this to be released?

Rinzler Part of this could easily depend upon the security of an archive. I know of one researcher who gathered data for five years among the Amish. This information is still under lock and key at Yale University; no one is permitted to use it.

Robinson I feel personally that my word is my vow. When I tell someone that I am going to do a particular thing with the data, I will stick to that. To consider other implications, I am not sure whether the focus on a community means that people spend more time within their respective ethnic enclaves, or whether they get a much wider understanding when they want to deal with other ethnic groups. What I would like to see happen is for people who are being educated to become aware of others, and to return to their enclaves as part of a process of healthy revitalization.

Rinzler The third area of discussion is techniques for recording oral tradition.

Clark I will address the issue of interviewing techniques. For all its value, oral history carries with it the potential for serious abuse. A historian must beware of substituting fascinating vignettes captured from a spellbinding raconteur for the hard data essential to detached historical judgment. It is easy to pile up mountains of tape. It is far more difficult to obtain incisive information which has eluded the historian and to make it readily available.

To avoid the pitfalls of tape-recorded research, the historian must do all the work required in more traditional investigation before he can undertake the task of interviewing. Although no figure is absolute, one estimate suggests that for each hour of tape interview, the oral historian has probably invested 120 hours in preparation and follow-up. The point to be remembered is that oral history should be considered a supplement to more traditional methods of investigation. So much preparation, however, can be hazardous from the standpoint of interviewing technique. An interview is by its nature a joint intellectual product, emerging out of the interaction between interviewer and interviewee. The interviewer may often know more about the subject than the person being interviewed and so dominate or bias the product.

Learning and practicing the skills of informational interviewing can help avoid some of the problems. The most difficult problem for the beginning interviewer is learning to ask open ended questions that do not call for or lead to a specific answer, or call for a specific choice among alternatives. Let me give you a simple example here. The question, "Were you angry or dejected at that turn of events," dictates a choice between stipulated alternatives, anger or dejection. How much better to ask, "What were your feelings at that turn of events?" The respondent now has a whole range of possible answers.

There are, to be sure, differing schools of thought as to what should be the relationship between interviewer and interviewee. A recent survey of projects supported by the Rockefeller Foundation revealed an array of approaches, ranging from the program at Duke University, where the questioner had the upper hand (a kind of investigative journalism), to the Appalachian Oral History Project, where the issue raised was how the interview helped the person being interviewed. Did it give him a sense of his own importance? No matter what the focus, the end aimed at should be an interview which takes places in an atmosphere of controlled freedom. The questioner should control the subject matter, always being flexible enough to move in unexpected directions, while the answerer should perceive a complete freedom to respond within the given subject.

Kalcik I would like to talk first about the settings of interviews, because I think settings are very significant. Ethnicity exists in both public and private forms. If I am interviewing people at a performance, at an event, or even in a studio, I tend to be given a fairly public statement on ethnicity. To tape the private side of ethnicity, I choose the home setting or the workshop. These are settings where the people are likely to be most comfortable, most at ease, most private, and most willing to deal with you as a friend. Often you must put in a year before a person is willing to reveal the private side of his life to you. Sometimes it takes no time at all, and people will share their private lives with me almost immediately.

You should also keep your equipment in tune with the setting. In a home interview I use a little Sony recorder that has a built-in microphone; I never use an external microphone. Except for a notebook, that small recorder is the only equipment I use.

Zeitlin How can you best interview your family or do research in family folklore? The best place to start is not with your oldest relative, but with yourself. Sit down and try to figure out how much you know about your family, so you can use it as a starting point in your interview. We find that the best interviewer is the best informed interviewer. By interviewing yourself, you can gain a sense not only of what areas of family life to ask about, but also what kinds of social situations are likely to be loci of family folklore. One folklorist, for example, interviewed her grandmother in a setting where she remembered hearing stories from her grandmother. She set up the situation deliberately, brought the grandmother into that situation, and thereby recreated the kind of rapport that they had when she was younger.

You can also try to combine group interviews with individual interviews. We have, for example, a picture of a happy, smiling soldier, and a tragic story behind it of the father who accidentally shot a child during the war. In public the father always told a different story, of a hand grenade that fell right by him, but which turned out to be a dud and did not explode. In this case we discovered two stories, the public story that the father always told, and the private story that turned out to be the less pleasant side of the truth.

An individual interview, or private interview, may be able to reach the deeper level, whereas the public story may be better elicited in a group interview. A group interview is also effective because you can create a sense of cohesion among the people involved, each person interacting with the others. Perhaps the best approach is to begin with a group interview and then to proceed to a series of private interviews.

McCarl I have done some photography and made videotapes in occupational settings, both in the field and out on the Mall. The problems in dealing with occupational groups are rather special. Due to the unique constraints that are put on field workers in any work situation, the recording of oral material is extraordinarily difficult in the field of occupational culture. Industrial noise, hazards, security regulations, Office of Safety and Health Administration standards, fears of exploitation which are common to labor and management, and the general reticence on the part of workers to discuss their work while they are on the job, militate against the successful use of a tape recorder or camera in the work place. Most often, therefore, the field worker finds him or herself in a situation of attempting to record material out of its natural occupational context, in the workers' home, or at a place where people congregate socially, the union hall or a bar.

The demands of recording in these environments have provided me with the following technical considerations. First of all, you should work through some kind of organized activity, whether it be a bowling game, a weekend get-together, a backyard barbecue, or a union meeting. You must try to make people feel comfortable when they talk about their work, and the context of an already familiar group can be extremely conducive to the obtaining of oral material. Detail your purposes in conducting the research, and make sure that the people involved understand the ultimate intent of your collecting project. You will eventually need written permission from them before you can use this material in publications and films. Use the tape recorder as a tool by letting it record all the verbal interchanges, while you concentrate on making notes that will aid you in understanding and reconstructing the actual story-telling situation. You should take careful note of facial expressions, gestures, things that were acted out, and so on. This gives you an idea of the context in which the material was recorded. Transcribe your tapes as soon as possible, and include this other information marginally in your transcriptions.

Visit the work area if you can, even if you have to take an official plant tour. When in the field, I usually try to eat lunch with the workers, since this is a less structured and therefore more open time. An inside view of the plant will also provide you with some idea of the work processes that shape the occupational oral material that you have collected. Enlist the aid of an insider, someone who knows the trade or group that you are attempting to investigate. Often a retired person has the time and access to make contacts, and sometimes even to record material which is simply unavailable to an outsider. Keep your informants abreast of your progress and of the use you are making of your material. Have them check the transcripts for errors or sensitive areas and incorporate their ideas or concerns in your treatment.

Finally, it is extremely important that we begin to develop methods for the recording of word processes and techniques as they are practiced on the job. This is virtually impossible at the present time, for the reasons which I have already cited. It will never come about unless the work community itself is involved in the documentation process as an active and full partner.

Robinson The major tools that I use are currently a portable cassette recorder and a 35-millimeter camera. Often I use a pair of microphones, particularly when I am doing interviews. I find that a small pair of microphones is fine for people who, like me, prefer not to carry pieces of heavy equipment, such as a large reel-to-reel recorder, on initial interviews. I understand that you can now buy lapel-microphones with cords which stretch as far as twenty feet, so people can move around while you are recording. Be sure to check your equipment before you go out. Know how to work your equipment and be an authority on it.

Whenever possible, I make prior contact with the various community members, letting them know that I am coming and what type of equipment I am bringing with me. Once I arrive within the community, I never bring out my equipment immediately. Usually, after the introductions are made, I sit down and talk to people. Invariably, someone will ask me, "Where is your tape or your camera?" I consider that my cue to begin bringing out my equipment for technical documentation. I found that within the Afro-American community, if you ask permission to record or photograph, people are fairly straightforward; it is either yes or no. You should, however, go further, and note the innuendoes via eye communication or hand gestures in their answer. For example, the whole body kinesis can be a key factor in letting a researcher know how much technical time he or she is being allowed. For those who are leary of being recorded or photographed, it is usually merely a matter of briefly explaining the equipment to them. I find it helpful to take samples of my work to demonstrate my ability.

Once people begin to feel reasonably comfortable about the technical equipment and about me, then I am in a position to negotiate for what I call "more sophisticated technical documentation." Normally this takes place at a later date, using such equipment as the reel-to-reel recorder and the movie camera. By setting a later date for more sophisticated technical documentation, I give people time to digest my explanation, and to prepare myself physically and mentally for something in which they want to be involved.

Kalcik One must always remember to show genuine respect for people's knowledge and for their intelligence. People are aware of the worth of what they have, and, in my experience, they are very, very clear of the value of their own experiences. The researcher, who is in a sense profiting from these people's goodwill and experiences, must treat them with the respect they undoubtedly deserve.

Rinzler Thank you, Susan, and thank you, all the participants.

Family Documents

PARTICIPANTS

Allen F. Davis, Department of History, Temple University
Richard S. Lackey, President, Mississippi Genealogical Society
Bill R. Linder, Director of Central Reference, National Archives
Sylvia Wright Mitarachi, Author, Hamden, Connecticut
James Walker, National Archives

Linder I am Bill Linder, director of Central Reference at the National Archives. We are here today to discuss a subject with which we at the Archives are very familiar: documents. With me today are Sylvia Wright Mitarachi, an author from Hamden, Connecticut; Richard Lackey, the president of the Mississippi Genealogical Society; James Walker, a specialist in genealogy at the National Archives; and Allen Davis, a professor of history at Temple University.

You will not be surprised to hear that today more people than ever before are searching for their family history and genealogy. From Maine to California it is the "in" thing to do. The question most often asked is, where do we start? We answer, you begin at home. You make a search for those documents in your possession that you have around the house. Then you move outside. You interview your family's relatives; then you proceed on to the depositories, the libraries, the county courthouses, the state archives, and the National Archives.

As we begin to put together a family history and genealogy, to get at the real story of the family, documentation of family information can make a great deal of difference. As a youngster I was told that my family was of German descent, and that great-grandfather came from Germany. Well, when it came to the documentation, I found in the census that great-grandfather was born in Mississippi; another census says that his father was born in Georgia; and yet another census says that my great-great-great grandfather was born in South Carolina.

But, lo and behold, a document dating from almost 250 years ago actually establishes the German origins of one branch of my family. Old Ludwig Linder appeared before the council in Charleston, South Carolina, and stated that he had come over in the year 1735 from Germany, and was applying for the land due to him as an immigrant. That document made a great difference to my family tradition. Today, we are going to talk about documents that can make a difference in your search for family history and genealogy.

Mitarachi I am working on a biography of a nineteenth-century woman, with some side glances at her mother and sisters. My subject, Melusina Fay Peirce, born in 1836, a writer and feminist, was one of the many women who burst into militancy in the period of the sixties and seventies.

Like many other women of the period, she was driven by the three R's of religion, reform, and rights. Her reform interests centered in cooperation, and she organized a shortlived cooperative housekeeping society in Cambridge, Massachusetts. Among her writings is a novel called *New York: A Symphonic Study:* In Three Parts: (1) The Terrestrial Discord (2) The Celestial Concord and (3) [She had an orderly mind] The Discord vs. The Concord. She was also, for thirteen years until ended by divorce, the wife of the philosopher, Charles Sanders Peirce, and as such lived in the circle that included the James family, the Lowells, and the group of scientists including Alexander Dallas Bache and her father-in-law, Benjamin Peirce, who had so many important contacts with the Smithsonian Institution.

The usual way a study like mine gets started is something like this: Perhaps I have been working towards a Ph.D. in American social and intellectual life in the nineteenth century, and I need a dissertation subject. Something about the influence of their religion on women in this period? Or a certain reform movement? Or perhaps a thesis with one of those impressive sociological double titles, for instance, "Sisterly Dissension: A Study of Kinship Rivalries in a Middle-Class New England Household." Darting around among possibilities and the literature of the time, I come upon a reference or two to Melusina Fay Peirce; my interest is piqued; and I decide that a study of her life will serve my purpose.

But, as my title indicates, this was not how it happened. My first confrontation with the person I must unavoidably refer to hereafter as Aunt Zina came many years ago. I returned home from college full of a number of new and revolutionary ideas about what was wrong with everything, including my family, and I began to try to enlighten my mother who, I assumed, had never heard of these ideas. My mother took me up to our Cambridge attic and showed me a small corrugated trunk—Aunt Zina's. It was different from other trunks in the attic. My grandmother's contained dresses with lace carefully wrapped in tissue paper, feathered hats, necklaces, and smelled of Parma violets. Aunt Zina's trunk was full of manuscripts, galley proofs much scrawled over, and newspaper clippings. In showing me Aunt Zina's trunk, my mother was pointing out that I was not the first person in the family who had had "ideas"—very annoying, of course, particularly since it emphasized that I was not simply myself. I was also a member of a family.

The scholar (which I am not in any professional sense) approaches his or her material with an appraising but reverend scrutiny. He has had to search it out. We assume that he cherishes it. Choosing to work from your own family papers is something else. As a family member you have grown up at once deeply involved and slightly bored. Between the family member and the family papers rises that wall of anecdotes, tracings of kinships, routine recitals of eccentricities, which you have learned to listen to with a quarter of an ear. Whatever you feel, it is not likely to be reverence. In my family we grew up referring to our most reverend ancestor as "the old Bish."

As a family member you love and hate your material. Love—after all, this is your family. Hate—because it puts a burden on you. Something must be done about the papers in the attic, but they are a threat: if you become involved with them, they may prevent you from leading your own life. (This is one way in which the family papers are just like the family.)

One feels about them as one does about the family—ambivalent. I sensed, from reading a few letters and manuscripts, that Aunt Zina might be interesting. After all, everyone in the family always referred to her as a "remarkable woman."

Yet there was something ritual about this "remarkable woman" label. I have noticed that any woman who made people uncomfortable in the nineteenth century was called either a character or a remarkable woman, just as anyone who, at that time, had "ideas" is now described as "ahead of her time," although her time was bursting with ideas.

So, unlike the scholar, I began by being not quite sure of the value of my material. Maybe I just thought it was interesting because Aunt Zina was my great aunt. Maybe Aunt Zina's were a dime a dozen a hundred years ago.

At this point there arrived—a scholar, who had, as scholars will, smelled out the family papers and wanted to have a look at them.

Now some of my best friends are scholars. But when they appear to examine the family papers, they seem intrusive. They refer to elderly dignified great aunts by their first names—even by nicknames—lèse-majesté at the least. If the scholar is a woman of a certain generation, she refers to them all by their last names. That is, she calls Aunt Zina "Peirce," as if Aunt Zina were a member of a girls' field hockey team. I realize that I should not criticize this habit because it comes under the head of equal rights, yet I am used to "Peirce" being the philosopher. Should you refer to Shakespeare's wife as "Shakespeare"?

The scholar is also fussy, and this is instructive. "Who," he asks, "is Maria Fay—Miss Fay or Mrs. Fay?" "Miss Fay," I answer. "How do you know?" is the next and reasonable question. A poser. How *do* I know? I have always simply understood that she was everyone's favorite maiden aunt. In other words, I just know.

This is not good enough for the scholar, and of course the scholar is right. You should not take any family facts and stories for granted.

But I *do* know—certain things. As far as one's family is concerned, one has a context, or perhaps one is part of a context.

In preparing this talk, I have found myself forced into wondering if there is any special value to this family context?

For one thing, there is a certain intimacy. The grandmother and the great aunts walked in the same rooms, sat in the same chairs, even wore the same bracelets, and in the case of Aunt Zina made rice croquettes from the same recipe, though I must add that I will never do it again—it was complicated, messy, and time-consuming.

There is a persistence of a certain family cadence. I noticed in Aunt Zina's letters that, a hundred years ago, among repeated family expressions was "Be that as it may." It was a shock the other day to hear my fourteen-year-old son say to me firmly in a new deep voice, "Mom, be that as it may." Thus I discovered that I was a conduit.

This intimacy makes it possible for me to feel Aunt Zina as almost a contemporary, and I am startled to realize that she was living during the Civil War, wore a crinoline, and believed in the curse of Eve.

I also find that, as a family member, I am particularly alert to what if I were a sociologist I might describe as family self-identification. Today our emphasis is on *personal* identity, which is usually perceived as elusive but there, already formed but hidden somewhere to be discovered. I think members of nineteenth and early twentieth century families were more likely to consider their identities as at least partly familial.

Zina was a product of two family strains—Hopkins and Fay. Everyone was clear they were very different. The Hopkinses believed that they belonged to a really remarkable family; they were supremely self-confident; they believed they could do anything. The Fays were diffident, subject to depression, or what was called at the time hypochondria. The family quotation was that the Fays "always saw lions in the path." Faults, bad habits, long noses, talents for music, fine hair could all be pinned down as family characteristics. Family qualities were also a way to assert one's superiority over another family: "As for Z[ina]," wrote Charles Peirce's mother in 1867, "we hardly know what she does, but she seems always too busy to come to see us. The Fays are not a warm-hearted race."[1] To be superior to a lesser family was a way to identify yourself and without being personally immodest, which was not acceptable to the period.

These family self-identifications are tempting—easier to deal with than our present digging for personal identity. When I visited the Peirce Editions Project, where a group of scholars is preparing a definitive edition of Peirce's work, I found that the first thing they wanted to tell me was that they did not really like Zina. They were on the Peirce side. Of course I did not visibly bristle, but I found their attitude rather unscholarly—as well as, of course, wrong.

Working with family papers, one finds time curiously and provocatively jostled. I look back, from my present great chronological age and high degree sophistication and see—back there as at the end of a funneling tunnel—a small crinolined girl—sixteen years old—a great aunt, or a grandmother. I am much older than she, old enough to be her grandmother. I wonder what she will become.

But I am part of what she became. What can one make of this eerie relationship? Perhaps a book.

I want to end by mentioning another character, who is real, but whom I take as a prototype. This is Aunt Lizzie, who was the maiden aunt of Charles Sanders Peirce.

Aunt Lizzie, typically, lives with and looks after her aging mother. Every few days she writes to tell the Salem cousins everything that is going on. Every detail in the lives of the family members is important. Aunt Lizzie, with a quick eye, a malicious tongue, and the stamina to write long letters, is worth her weight in gold.

Aunt Lizzie's sort of letters are less likely to have been kept than others. What *was* kept was Aunt Maria's letters about her visit to Paris under the Second Empire, or Aunt Pauline's trip on a raft to the headwaters of the Amazon where Uncle Arthur got bitten by a vampire bat. These (I am not making them up) were kept because they chronicled *unusual* days. They were read aloud to friends as the equivalent of "I'd like to show you my slides." The quotidian was considered less interesting.

Aunt Lizzie's chronicled the everyday: the awful way prices had risen with the war (coffee thirty-seven cents a pound—two exclamation marks);[2] exactly what it felt like to be treated with ether: "first the choking feeling—then the dying sensation";[3] and her thoughts about what Zina, who "is no saint and never was and never will be in this world," would do when she got to heaven and tried to open a cooperative store there.[4]

Happily, Aunt Lizzie is in a file at Harvard, for she, and many other women who scribbled away about daily events, are coming into their own in the new discipline of women's history, which is concerned with unknown lives.

Several times in the past I thought of writing something about Aunt Zina and then rejected the idea. Could one, was the question, write a book about someone who was not successful in her life?

Two or three years ago when I finished another book and looked at Aunt Zina again, I saw that times had changed. Everyone was digging into manuscript collections and had her (or even his) own pet nineteenth-century feminist. The dusty letters in the attic had become precious. I could not resist seizing this opportunity to be fashionable. In fact, I told myself, I had better hurry up.

I had changed too. If I had read them for the first time twenty years ago, I think I might have found Aunt Lizzie's letters fun, but a little trivial. Now triviality is irrelevant. So is success.

Of course, the reason we have become so much more interested in the everyday details of past lives—in the studying and plotting of hitherto ignored relationships between sisters, friends, women and their doctors—is because we want to find out more about women. But I think there is something more. There is an enormous appeal to this rich texture of family relationships, humming with loves, hates, with different variations on the same theme. It is something we are missing and perhaps want back.

Linder Having come into possession of my grandmother's papers, I understand precisely what Sylvia means. You have an obligation to them, and you love those papers, but if you let them, they can consume your life.

Talking to us now about key documents in state and local custody useful for family history will be Richard S. Lackey.

Lackey Many people approach state and local records as unrelated subjects. You might think that I have two subjects here: key state documents and key local documents. In fact, we are talking about records which complement each other. In using these records, I think we have to consider them as such.

Mr. Linder mentioned that, many times, the question is where to start. Begin by interviewing those who know about the family. Also, obtain any home records that you may have, such as manuscripts or family Bibles. At this point, how do you know that the detailed information you have discovered is accurate? You will have to go to the local, state, federal, and other official documents to verify and to prove the facts you have. The value of any particular record to you will depend on what you already know when you consult the record. In other words, if you find an isolated fact, unless you already have pertinent information, that one fact may not mean very much to you.

No one can possibly live long enough to look at all of the available documents about any family. We must try to select key documents that are helpful and that we hope might contain the desired information.

We have at our disposal all the records in state archives buildings throughout the country. First of all, we need to recognize that these records are entirely different in each area. Records differ in the amount of information that they contain. For example, an application for a marriage license in Illinois may include information entirely different from that which would be found in a marriage application in California. Moreover, the competeness of the records varies from place to place, depending upon what records were initially kept and what documents have since been destroyed.

The location of original local records is likewise difficult to pinpoint, because so many of the state archives throughout the country collect their state's local records. Such records may or may not be in the county courthouse or other local depositories. Among the key state and local records are those pertaining to birth, death, marriage, and divorce. The United States superintendent of documents has three publications that indicate the availability of these vital records: where to write for birth and death records, which is publication number 630-A1; where to write for marriage records, which is publication number 630-B; and where to write for divorce records, which is number 630-C.

Certainly, when we use these vital records, we can identify members of the family and learn what marriages and divorces have taken place. This information can aid greatly in the use of other documents. For example, if you start working with census records before you obtain certain marriage, birth, and death records in a family, you may overlook certain marriages or fail to recognize the surnames of ancestors. You may find yourself rereading the same census several times, carrying out research that could have been consolidated had you known exactly what you were looking for. Thus the sequence of research is extremely important.

Not only the federal government, but also the state governments, took census enumerations from time to time. State census reports can be used in connection with the federal census to gather composite information about a family, even though the names of all of the children may not be listed. After consulting the federal census of 1790, for example, you might find a 1795 census of one of the states. Then, after looking at the federal census of 1800, you may get an 1802 state census. Even within a single state there is no uniformity about state census records. In many states, the legislature would simply order, beginning January 1, 1801, that there should be a census made of the residents of a particular county, or maybe of four or five counties. It is simply a matter of local usage and of what records have survived.

Census records should be examined in connection with tax lists. Tax records are often more reliable indicators of names than are census records. If a man is talking to a census enumerator, he might tell him that his name is W. J. Smith, or he might tell him his name is Bill Smith. When he talks to the tax assessor, he wants his name on the tax roll to be William Johnson Smith. Many times a tax record will be the only available document with the full name spelled out. You may find that he hedged a little on the property that he reported to the tax assessor, and the amount does not correspond exactly with the amount of land that you may find the deed records, but his name will generally be correct.

Land records make up a considerable proportion of those documents which may be helpful to researchers. For public land states, the original records which transferred the land from the government to the individual are held by the federal government. For the non-public land states, the original disposition of the land was a state matter, as in all thirteen original colonies and many of the other states. Supplementing these state records are the local land records recording subsequent transactions in land.

Another key record is the state military list. There are, for example, militia lists for all the original colonies. Many records of the Confederacy are also deposited in the states. Even though the

National Archives has many of them, it is best to check Confederate records with the states first, because not all of them are in the National Archives' collection.

Court records of various kinds are also important to researchers. When considering court records, I am often reminded of a lady who had compiled a book on Mississippi court records and was telling a friend how these records might be helpful to other people. The friend responded that, well, she would have no use for it, as her family were nice people and did not get into the court records. Yet almost everybody got into the court records at one time or another, if only because they had an assignment to work on a state road or perhaps served on a jury.

Official records can verify many of the things that you would learn by talking with people or by exploring home sources. Consultation of state and local records is one way to answer questions regarding your family history.

Walker I am going to talk about some of the federal records available to researchers in family history.

The National Archives has passenger lists documenting the arrival of immigrants in the various East Coast and Gulf Coast ports from 1820 onwards. The West Coast port records have been destroyed, as have been some of the records for the different ports for different time periods. The early passenger lists contained very little information other than the name of the passenger, his age, sex, occupation, place of birth, country of origin, and ultimate destination.

Especially from 1906 onwards, the later passenger lists began to include much more detailed information. These more detailed records are at present in the custody of the Immigration and Naturalization Service. There is a fifty-year restriction on immigration records. Only if the person arrived more than fifty years ago can you look at the passenger list.

Most of the passenger lists are indexed. But the indexes are usually organized by port, year, and name of vessel. This means that you will need precise information about an ancestor's arrivals to locate his records. Moreover, the indexes to the lists for the twentieth century are generally restricted because there are cumulative indexes which cover records as late as 1945. As a result of this, they cannot be made available for public examination.

Among the most useful series of records are the federal census schedules. For the censuses of 1790 to 1900 a researcher can consult the census-takers' reports on individual households. There is a great deal of variation in both the quantity and the quality of information available in the census reports. The earliest censuses are not quite as useful as are the later censuses, because prior to 1850 only the head of the household is identified by name. Later census reports not only identify members of a household but also include such information as date and place of birth, place of birth of parents, literacy, occupation, and the value of real estate. Different questions were asked, however, in each census year .The census of 1890 was almost entirely destroyed by fire. Indexes are available only for the censuses of 1880 and 1900.

Another source would be records relating to federal military service. A typical record for wartime service contains one or more cards on which there is a varying amount of information. Because the federal government was basically only interested in bodies, how many there were who could bear arms and could defend their country, not much personal information was included.

In addition to those who were inducted into the service or who volunteered strictly for an emergency, usually a war, there were many individuals who served in the regular federal military service, in the U.S. Army, the U.S. Navy, and the U.S. Marine Corps. In almost every instance an enlisted man began his service by signing a contract called, in this case, an enlistment paper. The information contained on those papers varies. Beginning in 1884, the U.S. Army required that a person be given a thorough physical examination, and the recruit was required to give information concerning the health status of his family. Thus, they might ask questions that are very important to the genealogist: Are your parents living? Where? Is your father living? How old is your father?

What is his occupation? Where does your mother live? How old? What is her occupation? Beginning in 1893, enlistment papers also included marital status, and the name and address of the person to be notified in case of an emergency. In addition, information may also be available regarding an enlisted man's service and his manner of discharge.

Officers' records are always separated from enlisted men's records. For a minor officer there may be only a few papers, whereas for a major officer, such as General Benjamin Harrison, there may be a file that is too bulky to handle. In every case, there are always three items in a file: a tender of a commission, a letter of acceptance of the appointment, and then something to indicate how the service under that commission was terminated.

The most informative files are those relating to the award of a pension based on federal military service. In some instances, two people, the soldier and his widow, were involved. Pension files vary greatly in content, depending on their date, the difficulty of getting the pension, and the number of claimants. The process always began with an application. Supporting evidence is always found in the file; proof of service, for example, had to be furnished from some federal authority. Proof of marriage was also required from a widow. In every case, there is a document in the file which summarizes the contents of the file and the result of the application. If denied, why? If approved, why? If approved, for how much? If a new claim was submitted, for what reason?

Additional records that may be of some use are such series as the records of U.S. Soldiers' Homes. Of course, one of the largest groups of records we have are the innumerable claims series in the National Archives. These claims were submitted for various purposes by various individuals.

Another major group of records is the Federal Land Series, which relates to claims for federal lands by individuals. These are the original claims. Once the claims had been satisfied, no additional information was given in the federal records. In various parts of the United States, other than the thirteen original colonies, Texas, and Hawaii, land was made available for purchase for cash or on credit. Land was also given away in return for military service, and for such other purposes as to encourage settlement, to attract industry, and to assure protection of the country. Therefore the content of the land records varies a great deal. Under the Federal Homestead Act of 1862 (a law that was only taken off the books in 1976, any veteran could have gotten 160 acres of free land. Under the original Homestead Act, veteran status was not a requirement. The government only stopped giving away land in Alaska in 1970, when it decided to put through the pipeline. Just imagine what the land is worth now.

Federal court records relate to the involvement of individuals with various federal courts. In many instances the original court records are still in the courts. Some court records have recently been transferred to one of the eleven Federal Archives and Records Service branches which are located throughout the United States.

Included in the federal court records are innumerable files of documents relating to the process of becoming a naturalized citizen. Naturalization records are, however, often difficult to locate. It is generally considered that most people arriving in this country attempted to obtain citizenship through the prescribed method, by filing a declaration of intent, waiting three or five years, and then petitioning for naturalization. Yet I would estimate that 90 percent did not follow this procedure. Moreover, the records are hard to find, since naturalization could be attempted at so many different places. Only since 1900 is there a complete list of persons who entered the country and of their citizenship status.

Also included in court records are claims by individuals, suits, and jury lists. I consider the federal court records to be one of the more valuable sources of information about residents of a particular locality. I am willing to bet that if I could get the records of a district court which began operation at the time of settlement, I could identify, from those court records, every resident within fifty miles of that court during the first ten years in which that court operated. People were either employees of the court, were ordered by the court to do a certain thing, or were identified in the court papers in one manner or another. They may have been plaintiffs, defendants, or witnesses. They may also have been listed in the militia rolls. Many of the ship passenger lists, which do not exist as part of the regular federal ship passenger lists, turn up in Admiralty court records because the crew, the captain, the owners of or the consignees of cargo on a vessel sued. The resulting lawsuit would be heard by an admiralty court.

The National Archives has many other series of unusual records pertaining to a limited number of people. These include, for example, records relating to the American Indians, and seamen's protection certificates, the documents issued to seamen to protect them while traveling outside the United States. We have records of applications and licenses of every kind and description ever filed with a federal agency. We are also, of course, the depository which receives your federal income tax forms, but those we throw away after a certain number of years.

Linder Thank you, Jim. To round off this afternoon's discussion, let me call on Allen Davis of Temple University to tell us how to use our documents to create a family history.

Davis Margaret Mead suggested a few years ago that as a bicentennial project we should all write our family histories, and I completely agree. We have talked about documents today. Every historian knows that, whatever his subject, he is never going to find as many documents as he would like. Even when writing about the most famous people in the world, there are always gaps. I remember trying to find out what President Woodrow Wilson did on a particular day, and was shocked to discover that, among the thousands of documents in the file for that one day, not one supplied the information I sought. That will often be your experience when you search for documents about your own family's past.

You may be disappointed by the sparse amount of information available. That does not mean, however, that you cannot write your family history. I think that too many genealogists and family researchers leave their material in its raw state. They take a lot of notes about their family, and they fill out a lot of charts. Then they never get around to thinking enough about those documents and notes to translate them into a history of their family that has some meaning.

Charles Beard once said that you can divide history into three stages. History, he says, is an event as it happens: a fire breaks out, a revolution occurs, a war begins. That is an event. Then there is history as records: how people describe that event. These are the documents that come down to us. Often the record of the event is a very sparse one, or different accounts of the same event may be contradictory. The third part of history is history as it is written. The historian, including the family historian, must take these documents and make some sense out of them.

Charles Beard also said that you should not worry too much about being objective, because objective history is history without any object. That does not mean that you should not carefully analyze your documents to ensure their accuracy. It does mean that you may have to use your imagination to understand your family's past. In other words, to construct your family history, you need, like any good historian, to have a thesis. History requires a point of view. What kind of a point of view do you have towards your family? Too many family histories are written as if the people in that family were all paragons of virtue who did no wrong. I would urge you to think about your family as if you were not a member of it; to think about its limitations and weaknesses as well as its strengths.

You might think about trying to recover some of the events that I try to get my students to recover. Concepts like the American Dream can also be worked in. Almost all of our ancestors, at one time or another, crossed the ocean to this continent. Almost everyone who came, with the exception of the black slaves, came voluntarily and came with a kind of dream about what this country would be like. Their dream was that America would in every way be a better place than their homelands. As a family historian you might consider whether your family profited from the American Dream, or were victims of various things that happened to them once they reached America? Were your ancestors successes or failures? Or, as most of us would discover, were there some successes and some failures?

Geographic mobility is another matter that you might think about when doing a family history. What did that mean? It means a great deal now for families to move from one place to another. Can you imagine the feelings of families saying goodbye to relatives coming to America in the nineteenth century in the full expectation that they were never going to see those family members again? Today we say goodbye to our young people as they whip off to California or some other place, but we fully expect to see them again, to have them back. Probably we never will have them back in any real sense, but we will at least see them again. The settlers leaving Vermont, or Massachusetts, or Wisconsin, in the 1850s, in all likelihood never did go back, never did return in any sense or see the people that they left behind again.

Try to reconstruct in written form a family history that goes beyond the mere listing of births, deaths, marriages, and even moves. As a family historian you can begin the process of discovering what Peter Laslett, a British social historian, calls "the world we have lost." We all live in a world that is very different from the world even of the 1890s. But if you go back just a few more years, you get into a world that is in some ways unrecognizable when compared with the world of the 1970s.

One of the most fascinating documents that can project you into your family's past is the inventory of an estate. I once found one for an ancestor of mine, a sheep farmer from Vermont, who died in 1837. The list of his possessions began with his land and his three pews in the Congregational Church, and then his horse (a valuable possession in those days). The inventory included everything from broken kettles to a worn pair of grey pantaloons.

As I read through the document I tried to imagine the things he did not have, and to imagine how he must have lived without those particular items. To begin to see the difference between living today and living then, imagine the difference between the estate list of an ancestor and the list of your possessions today.

It is an exhilarating experience to discover your own family in a real, official document. It was working in the National Archives one day when a young man let out what sounded like a war whoop. Like several other people, I went to see what he had discovered. He had found his great-grandfather's name listed in a census report.

Yet on a census return we simply get a few scribbled facts, not a real person. Your task as a historian, as distinct from a genealogist, is to breathe life into those few facts, and to appreciate and understand what it must have been like to have lived in 1880, or 1840, or 1810. How did those people live then? If you know or discover that you are Irish, but cannot discover your real ancestor who came from Ireland to America, you can certainly read about the Irish experience of immigration, and understand that your ancestor shared some of that same experience. If you cannot find the exact person, you can recover some of the historical experience. By using your imagination, you can write a family history that is more than just a bare bones record for those who will come after.

Some of us are able to trace our families back farther than others. But if you can trace your history back a long way, do not be too pround. You too still end somewhere in the great unknown.

Notes

1. Quotation from the Charles Sanders Peirce Papers, by courtesy of the Houghton Library, Harvard University.

2. *Ibid.*

3. *Ibid.*

4. *Ibid.*

Whither Families?

PARTICIPANTS

Wilton S. Dillon, Office of Smithsonian Symposia and Seminars, Smithsonian Institution, Washington, D.C.

Jared Hoffman, *Children's Express*

Francis L. K. Hsu, Department of Anthropology, Northwestern University

A. Sidney Johnson III, Family Impact Seminar, George Washington University

Rosabeth Moss Kanter, Department of Sociology, Yale University

Margaret Mead, American Museum of Natural History

Dillon As the originator of this symposium, it gives me a great deal of pleasure to introduce the participants in this afternoon's discussion. Sidney Johnson, the moderator for this afternoon, is very much a practitioner of the art of the possible, in other words, the art of politics. He is the former staff director for the United States Senate Subcommittee on Children and Youth, and left the Senate to set up the Family Impact Seminar. Francis Hsu is a psychological anthropologist from Northwestern University, and Rosabeth Kanter is a sociologist from Yale University, specializing in the conflicting demands of work and the family. Jared Hoffman is a reporter for the *Children's Express*. Margaret Mead belongs to the whole world.

Johnson I should like to thank all the participants for coming here today. Dr. Mead has graciously agreed to be the emphasizer and summarizer of the entire effort. Perhaps at this point she will make a few comments to start us off.

Mead I am fascinated by the complete absence of communities in these discussions. After all, "communities" forms one-half of the title of this symposium. Nobody has yet talked about the community, or about the terrible constraint of housing and location, which is one of the principal reasons why families are having such a hard time today. There is no place and no way in which the structure of the community holds people together. It is impossible for them to live near their friends, or those relatives they like. Almost everybody likes some of their relatives, provided they do not have to live with them. A hundred years ago the grandmother in an American family did not live in the house; she lived next door. In this discussion the community arrangements which allowed her to live near, but separate, have been totally left out.

We will have to consider the way our communities are constructed, the propinquity of home to work, and where schools are located. Unless small children, and grandparents who no longer drive cars, can walk, we cannot make a diverse community; we will not have communities where there are relatives and friends who care about each other. Our young families are in such trouble because we have isolated them and have withdrawn all support. Now, the kinds of support that were and are being discussed in the Department of Health, Education, and Welfare, are services that are supplementary to what the family should be able to produce.

Good town planning and housing are of the utmost importance. Also important are the locations of elementary schools, good housing for older people, and opportunities for people to live near their friends and relatives. All this can be done through proper town planning. We know how it can be made to work. We have the legislation which can make new towns within towns possible. But there is no sign that this is being done at the present. Instead, since World War II we have built up segregated, stratified developments and suburbs. These living conditions prevent families from developing healthy emotional life; they restrict closeness to a very small circle, and hinder mutual caring. People can learn to enjoy family life and to pay attention to it only when they can live without the kinds of anxiety and isolation we have imposed on young families all over this country since World War II.

Hsu I think it important to point out that we must understand whether we are talking about palliatives or more fundamental measures. You are saying, Margaret, that there need to be sidewalks, there need to be places where people who want to live together can live together. Those are external measures. First of all, people have to want to live together. Unless you have some genuine affective feeling for your ancestors, collecting their genealogy will not do any good. Without those feelings genealogies will be no more than stamp collections.

You will have to decide what to do about your feelings of exclusiveness. Do you want to live together with other people? Do you want to share with other people? How can we get that feeling for sharing? Legislation will not bring about this kind of sharing. Merely providing housing or sidewalks will not cause people to come together. I do not mean to say that there is one panacea to solve all problems; to live is to have problems, all of which are totally solved only when we are dead and buried.

Mead That is just not true. When their children go to the same elementary school, people meet and relate to each other. The whole quality of life changes when grandparents can live within walking distance of their grandchildren. Peace means living where people can listen to and enjoy the sound of children's voices. Where there are sidewalks, children themselves can go from place to place; they can be loved and learn to love. Otherwise, they may want to love people until the cows come home, but without sidewalks, how can they make contact with other people?

Kanter This symposium may do a great deal for many people. Movement within neighborhoods is important, Margaret, but a great problem is the geographic mobility in search of economic opportunity. We have a system with appallingly little national economic planning. Some regions go bust; others go boom. Then people have to move in search of jobs. We are letting New York go under; meanwhile the sunbelt is swamped with more people than can possibly find work. We may become age segregated, both regionally and in terms of urban housing. Older people live in Florida and Arizona, and younger people live in industrial areas where there are still jobs.

My second problem is the corporate issue. For reasons best known to the company, the corporate executive, in order to keep his job, must often move geographically. The company thinks it is training; in truth it is one of the crazinesses of corporate life. Much of it has to do with inducing loyalty; it is creating people whose primary community is then the company, rather than the place where they live. The company becomes their only life continuity. There are signs that young people will no longer stand for it. Transfer policies certainly do disrupt the family. They also inflict great stress on whichever spouse is dragged along. The principal breadwinner spouse has the company and the organization, but the other spouse faces the problem of reestablishing roots in a new community. We ought to see some changes there. There are several different stupidities in our current economic life which contribute to mobility both in search of a job and in order to keep it.

Mead You do not have to break up the family when you move, you know. If you are brought up to believe that one's family can live comfortably and well in different places, moving will not necessarily disrupt it. Whole groups of people in this world move a great deal, but they understand the various communities into which they move. The oil company kids understand the way of life that oil company kids lead; they marry into other oil company families, Anglo-Persian marrying Aramco. It is equally true that in some of the scientific and professional labs, in the Foreign Service, and in many parts of the armed services, you move to another community that provides you with a known structure. Army brats know where they are going to be allowed to play tennis and where they are not going to be allowed to play tennis. They know this the day they move in. Moving need not harm you if you structure your communities so that people can relate to them—we moved four times a year when I was a child, and I can live anywhere and enjoy it. It is only because we believe that moving hurts you that it does so much harm. We ignore the way in which families can hold together if they have to move.

Hsu I think, Margaret, that you personalize too much. How many Margaret Meads are there in the world? The fact that you can move from one place to another and still make it, does not mean that the majority of us can make it. We are not Margaret Meads.

Mead Well, I have studied these people, you know.

Hsu Well, I have studied them too.

Mead I have studied these groups; I have studied the kids in Aramco; I have studied the Foreign Service kids. I am sorry I mentioned my own family, but it is fashionable at this symposium.

Johnson I am going to have to ask the panel to step outside and settle the question. We could discuss many more questions, but perhaps Dr. Mead will agree to summarize this panel's discussion.

Mead Frankly, I do not think that government can do anything to make people change their feelings, but it can stop passing legislation that in effect prevents families from having good feelings. Some laws work out to separate generations so that they cannot learn to care about and love one another. So, in this symposium, we have made recommendations as to what we can do. Now, the recommendations we have heard deal with both external and internal behavior. When Dr. Hsu recommends that a wider range of literature be taught at school, he hopes that changes in external behavior will produce some internal changes.

This panel has addressed itself to ways of strengthening the family. It has recognized that the family today is in no great danger. In spite of all the difficulties, we will still have families, and children will be reared in them. The problem is, what are we doing to the people in families today? How many of them are suffering? How many of them break up? How many of them are unable to sustain deeply meaningful relationships? Here, we have considered steps that can be taken by the federal government, by local government, by school systems, by architects and by town planners—steps directed toward removing the obstacles to a good family life.

We need to look at the whole nation as we plan. Replanning industry and siting communities near each other is one of the things that we can ask for. At present we kill off a whole area by deciding to close a plant, say a Navy yard, on a statistical basis without looking at what happens to the people who were building and working there. Or, we make provisions for water projects or for industrial plants with no reference to what happens to the people involved. Ultimately, we have an excess of people in a depressed area.

We need to create opportunities and frameworks for people in which they can live and behave like whole persons. We need both impact statements for the family and planning for the whole country, in many cases for the entire continent. We must plan a structure which makes it possible for people to continue living near their neighbors if that is what they want; the structure should not disperse them in all directions when they want to remain together. I think that children are the most useful foci that we have for activating good communities, and we should value highly children's ability to enliven their communities.

At present, I think it is even more important to look at the whole life cycle and to realize that sacrificing one group of people for another, even parents for children, is not a good idea. The story of the fifties is that people moved to the suburbs for their children's sake; the fathers commuted and died of heart attacks ten years earlier than their wives. Those children whose parents made the biggest sacrifices in the fifties most disliked the style of life in which they were brought up. They were given a large number of material things which many of them wholly repudiated later.

One of the interesting things in this symposium has been the emphasis on lineage, and the recognition that you do not inherit from Ham or from any other mythical ancestor, and you do not inherit from a whole race. You inherit from eight great grandparents, four grandparents, two parents, and you can add them up. In our contemporary discussions about genetics, we have forgotten that there are lineages, and that people inherit their characteristics from their family lines, rather than from races or mixtures of races. In this symposium we have attempted to emphasize the relationship between genealogy, interest in one's past, and respect for one's true ancestors. All of these concerns should contribute to a sense of identity in the present and to community planning for the future.

Finally, I think we can go beyond the idea that everyone must live in a family all the time. Throughout American history large numbers of people were not married for much of the time. Since many people died early, widows and widowers were common, and a great many women never married at all. Only in the fifties did we adopt the bizarre notion that everybody must be married, as it were, from the cradle to the grave.

We must build communities with room for single people: people who have been married, people who have never been married, people who do not want to get married. But all these people should live close to children. When we segregate single people, when we segregate grandparents, when we segregate adults from children, they all become self-centered. The grandparents work against the very school bonds that they once worked for when they were members of the P.T.A. This again is a function of the way we handle retirement, the way we handle federal help to housing, the way we plan our entire communities. Whenever we insist that only old forms of living and communication are valid, and do not experiment with new ones, our society is already in trouble. We need new ways to bring together kin and community.

Johnson My thanks to you, Dr. Mead, and to all the panelists, for an exciting afternoon.

Epilogue

JOAN R. CHALLINOR
Lecturer in American History, American University, Washington, D.C.

The historian Daniel Scott Smith, writing in 1973, described the American family as "the most impenetrable social institution." This description, perhaps accurate in 1973, is no longer true. Scholars have made a strong start in understanding not only contemporary families, but also those of past times. Yet a considerable task lies ahead. What direction should the study of the family take? In which areas will returns be most valuable? What type of study will yield the greatest insights? How can both groups and individuals be given equal attention? What combination of disciplines will make the family less impenetrable? Although only a few directions can be suggested in this short essay, they are proposed with confidence and some urgency.

Future studies of the family must continue to see the institution in its historical perspective. The American family is deeply rooted in its past. Since family values, roles, the very structure itself, change over time, our present vision offers only a glimpse of a continuing process. Gloomy assessments of the state of the modern family are often made without reference to families of other times. The strengths of present families are often overlooked in unflattering comparisons with veritable fantasies of the past. We are left with what has been termed the "golden glow of yesterday." According to this view, all of life, families included, was more satisfying in centuries other than our own. This evaluation falsely idealizes rural life as well as family life, slighting the durability and resilence of the American family and impeding the task of understanding its structure. Without a long-term perspective, efforts to comprehend the family will at best be superficial. It then becomes difficult to decide which features of family life are most enduring, have in the past given strength to families, and are therefore most worthy of conservation and encouragement.

The changing nature of the American family must be recognized and dealt with. Dr. Theodore Lidz, writing in 1963, described with great precision the inability of the family to return to outmoded forms:

> The old extended family cannot be reconstituted, nor would it be suited to contemporary needs. Although, with sufficient time, a new and more stable pattern may evolve, the scientific era permits little respite from change. In a scientific era, the family requires intensive study by behavioral scientists to ascertain what is essential to the family everywhere . . . so that in a changing society, that will require future changes in the family, the requisites can be maintained.[1]

Without a comprehension of which functions the family has fulfilled in the past, the historian cannot make proper judgments concerning those functions which it is failing to perform today. It is clear that many of the responsibilities formerly met by the family are now passing by default to institutions, both governmental and private.[2] In an excess of nostalgia, those concerned with the family often attribute to it abilities and responsibilities which it never possessed. Society must come to terms with the changing nature of the family. Cooperation with change rather than rigid insistence on discarded patterns is essential.

The changing nature of the family dictates a flexible outlook on the part of governmental policy-makers. On no other subject is public opinion so inflamed as on the family. Many call for an instant return to the supposed family of the nineteenth century, in which, it is thought, all responsibilities were met by the family itself. In an excess of pessimism concerning the present state of the family, others call for instant experimentation with new forms of nurturing. Neither group should sway policy-makers. Recent historical research has cast grave doubts on many common and current generalizations on families and their roles. Historical perspective on the family can guide policy-makers. Institutions both public and private must be established to meet those responsibilities which the changing family is unwilling or unable to sustain. To preserve essentials, it is necessary to understand what the essentials are. Studies of the family should help policy-makers to recognize these essentials and to discard the peripheral. Those involved in family legislation should be able to look to scholars for encouragement in making courageous and judicious decisions and in carrying these out with confidence.

Besides historical perspective, two techniques of studying the family deserve particular attention. The study of family photographs offers unique access to the details of past family life. Photographs allow the viewer to enter people's houses, observe the choices and arrangements of furniture, notice which objects were chosen by the family to be part of the photo, and view how the family posed themselves before the camera. As the Smithsonian colloquium made clear, the development of a vocabulary to describe and understand visual images is a necessity. A start has been made; much more must follow. New methodologies need to be developed that advance the primitive state of the art of understanding images and penetrating their meanings. Photographs are ubiquitous in our society, framed on tables, in albums, even in boxes in attics. The sheer number of photographs has probably devalued them. Both formal pictures and snapshots should be studied. Posed photographs show the family as it would like to be shown; snapshots can reveal the family in its most off-guard moments. A number of snapshots taken at various times can give a sense of change over time in the life of a family; efforts should be made to comprehend this often underrated form of photography.

Another area which promises great returns in family studies is the recording of oral history. In the memories of family members can be found the values by which families lived and incidents in the past of both the family and of individuals. Oral history can uncover family details even photography cannot reach. Researchers at the Smithsonian Folklife Program found that photographs today have a tendency to record only the happier incidents of life; in verbal reminiscences the deeper notes are sometimes sounded. Yet photographs can also be the catalyst which encourages people to relate stories of great depth and sorrow. A blending of photographs and oral history can be enormously valuable, in that emotions can be tapped, then fused with photographs to provide family histories of great richness and variety. Most important, the values by which families live can be discovered through oral history; values which cannot be found in any raw statistics or record. For example, abortions, a burning issue of the 1970s, will not be recorded in any family document or photograph or government statistic. Families do not usually record illegal events. But abortions which took place in the 1920s or 1930s might be revealed in reminiscences obtainable only through oral interviews. With a firmer grasp on the number and demographic details of abortions in the past, the present situation might become clearer. Indeed, without historical perspective, some or all of the prevailing views of abortions may be seriously in error.

Ideally, a complete family history would include visual, oral, quantitative and documentary sources. Such a blending is certainly not beyond the competence of a family wishing to delve deeply into its background. What is needed is a new sensitivity to the presence of untapped resources available to both family members and historians. Unlooked at photographs, elderly relatives never interviewed, unsearched records, and old documents carelessly thrown away have all too often impeded efforts to create a family history. Scholars too must learn to use the full range of sources available to them. No longer can one specialized field be accepted as "family history," and other specialties must be integrated into the larger field. Family historians of the future will be those scholars who can best combine data from many types of sources to create a larger picture. Like the family it studies, the field is changing. The future direction will be towards more inclusive, not more specialized, family history.

The Smithsonian–American University Bicentennial Family

History Project (devised by my co-editor Allan J. Lichtman), although never carried out, proposed a four part project using many disciplines and sources. First, a widely distributed self-administered questionnaire; second, a carefully designed survey of a cross-section of the population, to be carried out by a trained interviewer, to elicit a wide range of information on family backgrounds; third, oral histories from a representative sample of individuals selected from phase two; fourth, an intensive family study by scholars, spending considerable time with perhaps fifty or seventy-five families of varying ethnic and class backgrounds. These scholars would have interviewed as many family members as possible, engaging at the same time in document retrieval and analysis. All information would have been, as far as possible, computerized and statistically analyzed, and thus would have been both qualitative and quantitative. Such phenomena as social and geographic mobility, changing mores, and life-styles could have been studied more closely than ever before. The information would have been relevant to the concerns of historians, sociologists, anthropologists, and other humanists and social scientists. Unfortunately, the proper funding for such a large operation was not forthcoming, but the planning of it demonstrates, in a most practical way, how family history can use many types of sources and weave from them the richest possible tapestry of history.

The continued integration of the social sciences and family history should yield high dividends in the future. Records can lead historians astray, and explanations may be fashioned without due consideration of appropriate models of behavior. The social sciences can enrich the bare bones of the historical records, pointing out where continuities of attitude existed, where breaks occurred, and where balances were struck. Important facets of family behavior that might completely escape the historian will be emphasized and enlarged upon by the social scientist. The critical faculties of social science are also enormously valuable to any historian working with the family. In his essay "Continuity Across Generations: The Adams Family Myth," David F. Musto uses the insights of psychiatry to illuminate the generational continuity of the Adams family. Anthropology is employed by Jacquelyne Johnson Jackson and Bertram Emmanuel Walls, in "Aging Patterns in Black Families," to illuminate the aging patterns of blacks in the American South. Francis L. K. Hsu suggests, in his article "Roots of the American Family: From Noah to Now," the use of cross-cultural literature to increase Americans' sensitivity to the desirability of family relationships found in cultures other than their own. The essays in this book are prime evidence of interdisciplinary contributions to family studies. Finally, the social scientist can sometimes restate and redefine a problem in such a way that the solution becomes more evident. Without the social sciences, present-day policy-makers would be at a loss to turn historical insights into policies, and thereby help present-day families to cope with today's problems.

In his commentary at the Symposium, Bernard Bailyn argued that we have not effectively integrated the analysis of latent and manifest events. Moreover, he warned that concepts used by social scientists "come out of our own society" and are "limited in significant ways by our world." These ideas thus "relate principally to our circumstances" and cannot be uncritically applied "to altogether different situations in different eras." The problem, Bailyn concluded, can be overcome only by "retaining open minds that are sensitive to variations that do not fit current notions and retain the capacity for surprise while assimilating as questions the conclusions of modern science."

Bailyn has thus suggested a crucial problem of great depth and broad implications. Looked at in its widest perspective, it affects the entire field of family studies. Not only are social scientists restricted by the era in which they live, they are also restricted by the fact that their lives have been shaped by their families of nurture and they live (except in a very few cases) within their families of procreation. This fact limits the capability of social scientists fully to grasp the structures underlying the institution. It is difficult, if not impossible, to observe with detachment a group of which one is irrevocably and continuously a member. Devra G. Kleiman's conclusions about the human family contain ideas of great subtlety. Perhaps her experience in dealing with relationships within animal families has given her the distance necessary to draw new and unusually perceptive conclusions concerning relationships within human families.

Ultimately, it must be admitted that there is a limit to the imagination of the social scientist and a limit to the distance that can be achieved between the institution under scrutiny (the family) and its investigators. Admitting this should in no way deter attempts to comprehend as fully as possible families of the present and families of past times. Social scientists and historians should stand ready to admit their limitations and, as Bailyn suggests, to keep open minds and "retain the capacity for surprise."

Cooperation between history and social science is mutually beneficial. History has, in several cases, shown that conclusions reached by social scientists were erroneous. Evidence lately uncovered by historians shows that, contrary to the Moynihan Report, slavery did not destroy the commitment of blacks to stable family life. Daniel P. Moynihan relied on backward projections from sociological theory to conclude that slavery had undermined the black family, creating a "tangle of pathology" that had persisted into the twentieth century. Research by scholars such as John Blassingame, Herbert Gutman, Robert W. Fogel, and Stanley Engerman, who actually studied black families in the nineteenth century, suggests that blacks maintained a commitment to family life during slavery and that most black families were united and stable during the period following emancipation. Studies of colonial America show that the encroachment of government on people's lives is not a modern phenomenon. Historians have shown that divorce rates began to climb in the last decade of the nineteenth century, not in the "permissive" twentieth century. In all these cases the social scientist and the historian, as is essential, worked together.

Finally, if family studies are to yield real dividends for this generation as well as for historical understanding, then the family must be defined in its broadest sense. A family cannot be restricted to a mother, father, and children. Historical studies indicate that at one time boarders and lodgers were considered part of and influenced the families in which they lived. Even the so-called extended family may be too narrowly defined. Families may consist of flexible kin groups, not necessarily residing in the same house, and often sharing the roles typically ascribed to mothers and fathers. Aunts, uncles, grandparents, and cousins can play other and more primary roles. The constriction of the family into what is today regarded as socially desirable may distort what ought to be a free and fluid structure. The attempt to practice "social engineering" through family studies should be firmly resisted. Just as Margaret Mead showed an entire generation that growing up in Samoa was as appropriate for Samoans as American bringing up was for Americans, so we today must not circumscribe the families of the future by prescribing "allowed" family structures. We should keep as open minds as possible, closing no doors, prohibiting nothing. Accurate descriptions of families of the past and present should help us to choose our own future. Only in this way can family structures respond to future needs and provide for their members a satisfactory and sane family life.

Notes

1. Theodore Lidz, *The Family and Human Adaption* (New York, International University Press, Inc., 1963), p. 37.

2. This is not a new development. Modern America is merely continuing a process begun in the early nineteenth century. See David J. Rothman, *The Discovery of the Asylum: Social Order and Disorder in the New Republic* (Boston: Little Brown and Co., 1971).

Selected Bibliography

We have selected accessible works that introduce general readers to studies of the family and to the reconstruction of personal family history.

Agee, James, and Evans, Walker. *Let Us Now Praise Famous Men*. Boston: Houghton Mifflin, 1960.

American Genealogical Research Institute Staff. *How to Trace Your Family Tree*. Garden City, New York: Doubleday, 1975.

Aries, Philippe. *Centuries of Childhood: A Social History of Family Life*. New York: Vintage, 1962.

Bane, Mary Jo. *Here to Stay: American Families in the Twentieth Century*. New York: Basic Books, 1976.

Baum, Willa K. *Oral History for the Local Historical Society*. 2nd. ed. Nashville, Tenn.: American Association for State and Local History, 1971.

Bernard, Jessie. *The Future of Marriage*. New York: Bantam, 1973.

Blassingame, John W. *The Slave Community: Plantation Life in the Antebellum South*. New York: Oxford, 1972.

Blockson, Charles L., with Ron Fry. *Black Genealogy*. Englewood Cliffs, N. J.: Prentice-Hall, 1977.

Boatright, Mody, et al., eds. *The Family Saga and Other Phases of American Folklore*. Urbana, Ill.: University of Illinois Press, 1958.

Chafe, William H. *The American Woman: Her Changing Social, Economic, and Political Roles, 1920–1970*. New York: Oxford, 1972.

Colket, Meredith B., Jr. *Guide to Genealogical Records in the National Archives*. Washington, D. C.: Government Printing Office, 1964. To be supplanted by Bill R. Linder and James D. Walker, *Guide to Genealogical Records in the National Archives*. forthcoming.

Cooper, Wyatt. *Families: A Memoir and a Celebration*. New York: Harper and Row, 1975.

Cott, Nancy F. *The Bonds of Womanhood: "Woman's Sphere" in New England, 1780–1835*. New Haven, Conn.: Yale University Press, 1977.

Daedalus. Spring 1977. *The Family*.

Demos, John. *A Little Commonwealth: Family Life in Plymouth Colony*. New York: Oxford, 1970.

Demos, John, and Boocock, Serane S., eds. *Turning Points: Historical and Sociological Essays on the Family*. Chicago: University of Chicago Press, 1978.

Dexter, Lewis Anthony. *Elite and Specialized Interviewing*. Evanston, Ill.: Northwestern University Press, 1970.

Doane, Gilbert H. *Searching for Your Ancestors: The How and Why of Genealogy*. 4th ed. Minneapolis: University of Minnesota Press, 1973.

Elder, Glen H., Jr. *Children of the Great Depression: Social Change in Life Experience*. Chicago: University of Chicago Press, 1974.

Felt, Thomas E. *Researching, Writing, and Publishing Local History*. Nashville, Tenn.: American Association for State and Local History, 1976.

Filene, Peter G. *Him, Her, Self: Sex Roles in Modern America*. New York: Mentor, 1974.

Fischer, David Hackett. *Growing Old in America*. New York: Oxford, 1977.

Flaherty, David H. *Privacy in Colonial New England,* 1630–1776. Charlottesville, Va.: University of Virginia Press, 1972.

Fogel, Robert W., and Engerman, Stanley L. *Time on the Cross*. 2 vols. Boston: Little Brown, 1974.

Fried, Morton, ed. *Centennial Papers on Ancient Society by Lewis Henry Morgan*. in preparation.

Genovese, Eugene V. *Roll Jordan, Roll: The World the Slaves Made*. New York: Pantheon, 1974.

Goode, William J. *World Revolution and Family Patterns*. New York: Free Press, 1970.

Gordon, Michael, ed. *The American Family in Social-Historical Perspective.* 2nd ed. New York: St. Martin's, 1978.

———. *The American Family: Past, Present, and Future.* New York: Random House, 1978.

Graves, Ken, and Payne, Mitchell. *American Snapshots.* Oakland, Cal.: Scrimshaw, 1977.

Green, Jonathan, ed. *The Snapshot.* Millerton, N. Y.: Aperture, 1974.

Greenwood, Val D. *The Researcher's Guide to American Genealogy.* Baltimore: Genealogical Publishing Co., 1973.

Grele, Ronald J. *Envelopes of Sound: Six Practitioners Discuss the Method, Theory, and Practice of Oral History and Oral Testimony.* Chicago: Precedent, 1975.

Greven, Philip J., Jr. *Four Generations: Population, Land and Family in Colonial Andover, Massachusetts.* Ithaca, N. Y.: Cornell University Press, 1970.

Gutman, Herbert G. *The Black Family in Slavery and Freedom, 1750–1925.* New York: Pantheon, 1976.

Hareven, Tamara K., ed. *Family and Kin in Urban Communities, 1700–1930.* New York: Watts, 1977.

Heiss, Jerold. *The Case of the Black Family: A Sociological Inquiry.* New York: Columbia University Press, 1975.

Hsu, Francis L. K., ed. *Kinship and Community.* Chicago: Aldine, 1971.

Katz, Michael B. *The People of Hamilton, Canada West: Family and Class in a Mid-Nineteenth Century City.* Cambridge, Mass.: Harvard University Press, 1975.

Keniston, Kenneth, and the Carnegie Council on Children. *All Our Children: The American Family Under Pressure.* New York: Harcourt Brace Jovanovich, 1977.

Kett, Joseph F. *Rites of Passage: Adolescence in America, 1790 to the Present.* New York: Basic Books, 1977.

Kohl, Seena B. *Working Together: Women and Family in Southwestern Saskatchewan. Toronto:* Holt, Rinehart and Winston of Canada, 1976.

Kramer, Sydelle, and Masur, Jenny. *Jewish Grandmothers.* Boston: Beacon, 1975.

Lamb, Michael E. ed. *The Role of the Father in Child Development.* New York: Wiley, 1975.

Lasch, Christopher. *Haven in a Heartless World: The Family Beseiged.* New York: Basic Books, 1977.

Laslett, Peter. *The World We Have Lost.* 2nd ed. New York: Scribner's, 1974.

Leichter, Hope J., ed. *The Family as Educator.* New York: Teacher's College Press, 1975.

Lesy, Michael. *Wisconsin Death Trip.* New York: Pantheon, 1973.

Lichtman, Allan J. *Your Family History: How to Use Oral History, Personal Family Archives, and Public Documents to Discover Your Heritage.* New York: Vintage, 1978.

———., and French, Valerie. *Historians and the Living Past: The Theory and Practice of Historical Study.* Arlington Heights, Ill.: AHM, 1978.

Lidz, Theodore. *The Family and Human Adaptation.* New York: International Universities Press, 1963.

Lynch, Kevin. *What Time is this Place?* Cambridge, Mass.: MIT Press, 1976.

Montell, William C. *The Saga of Coe Ridge: A Study in Oral History.* Knoxville, Tenn.: University of Tennessee Press, 1970.

Morgan, Edmund S. *The Puritan Family.* Boston: Boston Public Library, 1944.

Moss, William W. *Oral History Program Manual.* New York: Praeger, 1974.

Noren, Catherine Hanf. *The Camera of My Family.* New York: Alfred A. Knopf, 1976.

Rabb, Theodore K. and Rotberg, Robert I., eds. *The Family in History: Interdisciplinary Essays*. New York: Harper & Row, 1971.

Rosenberg, Charles, ed. *The Family in History*. Philadelphia: University of Pennsylvania Press, 1975.

Rossi, Alice S., Kagan, Jerome, Haraven, Tamara K. *The Family*. New York: W. W. Norton & Company, Inc., 1978.

Rottenberg, Dan. *Finding Our Fathers: A Guidebook to Jewish Genealogy*. New York: Random House, 1977.

Russo, David J. *Families and Communities: A New View of American History*. Nashville: American Association for State and Local History, 1974.

Schneider, David M. *American Kinship: A Cultural Account*. Englewood Cliffs, N. J.: Prentice-Hall, 1968.

———., and Smith, Raymond T. *Class Differences in American Kinship*. Ann Arbor, Michigan: University of Michigan Press, 1978.

Shackelford, Laurel, and Weinberg, Bill. *Our Appalachia*. New York: Hill and Wang, 1977.

Shorter, Edward. *The Making of the Modern Family*. New York: Basic Books, 1975.

Shumway, Gary L., and Hartley, William G. *An Oral History Primer*. Salt Lake City: Deseret, 1974.

Simpson, Jeffrey. *The American Family: A History in Photographs*. New York: Viking, 1976.

Slater, Philip. *Footholds: Understanding the Shifting Sexual and Family Tensions in Our Culture*. New York: Dutton, 1977.

Sontag, Susan. *On Photography*. New York: Farrar, Strauss and Giroux, 1977.

Stack, Carol B. *All Our Kin*. New York: Harper & Row, 1974.

Stannard, David E., ed. *Death in America*. Philadelphia: University of Pennsylvania Press, 1975.

Stewart, T. Dale. *The People of America*. New York: Scribner's, 1973.

Stone, Lawrence. *The Family, Sex, and Marriage in England, 1500–1800*. New York: Harper & Row, 1977.

Thernstrom, Stephan. *Poverty and Progress: Social Mobility in a Nineteenth Century City*. Cambridge, Mass.: Harvard University Press, 1964.

Vansina, Jan. *Oral Tradition: A Study in Historical Methodology*. London: Routledge and Kegan Paul, 1965.

Vaughan, Victor C., III., and Brazelton, T. Berry, eds. *The Family: Can It Be Saved?* Chicago: Year Book Medical Publishers, 1976.

Watts, Jim, and Davis, Allen F. *Generations: Your Family in Modern American History*. 2nd ed. New York: Alfred A. Knopf, 1978.

Weitzman, David. *Underfoot: An Everyday Guide to Exploring the American Past*. New York: Scribner's, 1976.

Welling, William. *Collectors' Guide to Nineteenth-Century Photographs*. New York: Collier Books, 1976.

Westin, Jeane Eddy. *Finding Your Roots: How Every American Can Trace His Ancestors—At Home and Abroad*. Los Angeles: J. P. Tarcher, 1977.

Westoff, Charles F., and Ryder, Norman B. *The Contraceptive Revolution*. Princeton, N. J.: Princeton University Press, 1977.

Wilson, Edward O. *Sociobiology: The New Synthesis*. Cambridge, Mass.: Harvard University Press, 1975.

Winch, Robert F. *The Modern Family*. 3rd ed. New York: Holt, Rinehart and Winston, 1971.

Wright, Norman E. *Building an American Pedigree*. Provo, Utah: Brigham Young University Press, 1974.

Zeitlin, Steven, et al., eds. *Family Folklore*. Washington, D. C.: Smithsonian Institution, 1976.

Index